The secret history of clubs: particularly the Kit-Cat, Beef-Stake, Vertuosos, Quacks, Knights of the Golden-Fleece, Florists, Beaus, &c. with their original: ...

Edward Ward

ECCO
PRINT EDITIONS

ECCO

Eighteenth Century
Collections Online
Print Editions

Gale ECCO Print Editions

Relive history with *Eighteenth Century Collections Online*, now available in print for the independent historian and collector. This series includes the most significant English-language and foreign-language works printed in Great Britain during the eighteenth century, and is organized in seven different subject areas including literature and language; medicine, science, and technology; and religion and philosophy. The collection also includes thousands of important works from the Americas.

The eighteenth century has been called "The Age of Enlightenment." It was a period of rapid advance in print culture and publishing, in world exploration, and in the rapid growth of science and technology – all of which had a profound impact on the political and cultural landscape. At the end of the century the American Revolution, French Revolution and Industrial Revolution, perhaps three of the most significant events in modern history, set in motion developments that eventually dominated world political, economic, and social life.

In a groundbreaking effort, Gale initiated a revolution of its own: digitization of epic proportions to preserve these invaluable works in the largest online archive of its kind. Contributions from major world libraries constitute over 175,000 original printed works. Scanned images of the actual pages, rather than transcriptions, recreate the works *as they first appeared.*

Now for the first time, these high-quality digital scans of original works are available via print-on-demand, making them readily accessible to libraries, students, independent scholars, and readers of all ages.

For our initial release we have created seven robust collections to form one the world's most comprehensive catalogs of 18th century works.

Initial Gale ECCO Print Editions collections include:

History and Geography
Rich in titles on English life and social history, this collection spans the world as it was known to eighteenth-century historians and explorers. Titles include a wealth of travel accounts and diaries, histories of nations from throughout the world, and maps and charts of a world that was still being discovered. Students of the War of American Independence will find fascinating accounts from the British side of conflict.

Social Science

Delve into what it was like to live during the eighteenth century by reading the first-hand accounts of everyday people, including city dwellers and farmers, businessmen and bankers, artisans and merchants, artists and their patrons, politicians and their constituents. Original texts make the American, French, and Industrial revolutions vividly contemporary.

Medicine, Science and Technology

Medical theory and practice of the 1700s developed rapidly, as is evidenced by the extensive collection, which includes descriptions of diseases, their conditions, and treatments. Books on science and technology, agriculture, military technology, natural philosophy, even cookbooks, are all contained here.

Literature and Language

Western literary study flows out of eighteenth-century works by Alexander Pope, Daniel Defoe, Henry Fielding, Frances Burney, Denis Diderot, Johann Gottfried Herder, Johann Wolfgang von Goethe, and others. Experience the birth of the modern novel, or compare the development of language using dictionaries and grammar discourses.

Religion and Philosophy

The Age of Enlightenment profoundly enriched religious and philosophical understanding and continues to influence present-day thinking. Works collected here include masterpieces by David Hume, Immanuel Kant, and Jean-Jacques Rousseau, as well as religious sermons and moral debates on the issues of the day, such as the slave trade. The Age of Reason saw conflict between Protestantism and Catholicism transformed into one between faith and logic -- a debate that continues in the twenty-first century.

Law and Reference

This collection reveals the history of English common law and Empire law in a vastly changing world of British expansion. Dominating the legal field is the *Commentaries of the Law of England* by Sir William Blackstone, which first appeared in 1765. Reference works such as almanacs and catalogues continue to educate us by revealing the day-to-day workings of society.

Fine Arts

The eighteenth-century fascination with Greek and Roman antiquity followed the systematic excavation of the ruins at Pompeii and Herculaneum in southern Italy; and after 1750 a neoclassical style dominated all artistic fields. The titles here trace developments in mostly English-language works on painting, sculpture, architecture, music, theater, and other disciplines. Instructional works on musical instruments, catalogs of art objects, comic operas, and more are also included.

bibliolife
old books. new life.

The BiblioLife Network

This project was made possible in part by the BiblioLife Network (BLN), a project aimed at addressing some of the huge challenges facing book preservationists around the world. The BLN includes libraries, library networks, archives, subject matter experts, online communities and library service providers. We believe every book ever published should be available as a high-quality print reproduction; printed on-demand anywhere in the world. This insures the ongoing accessibility of the content and helps generate sustainable revenue for the libraries and organizations that work to preserve these important materials.

The following book is in the "public domain" and represents an authentic reproduction of the text as printed by the original publisher. While we have attempted to accurately maintain the integrity of the original work, there are sometimes problems with the original work or the micro-film from which the books were digitized. This can result in minor errors in reproduction. Possible imperfections include missing and blurred pages, poor pictures, markings and other reproduction issues beyond our control. Because this work is culturally important, we have made it available as part of our commitment to protecting, preserving, and promoting the world's literature.

GUIDE TO FOLD-OUTS MAPS and OVERSIZED IMAGES

The book you are reading was digitized from microfilm captured over the past thirty to forty years. Years after the creation of the original microfilm, the book was converted to digital files and made available in an online database.

In an online database, page images do not need to conform to the size restrictions found in a printed book. When converting these images back into a printed bound book, the page sizes are standardized in ways that maintain the detail of the original. For large images, such as fold-out maps, the original page image is split into two or more pages

Guidelines used to determine how to split the page image follows:

• Some images are split vertically; large images require vertical and horizontal splits.
• For horizontal splits, the content is split left to right.
• For vertical splits, the content is split from top to bottom.
• For both vertical and horizontal splits, the image is processed from top left to bottom right.

THE

Secret History

OF

CLUBS:

PARTICULARLY THE

Kit=Cat,		Knights of the
Beef=Stake,	} } {	Golden-Fleece,
Uertuolos,		Floriſts,
Quacks,		Beaus, &c.

WITH THEIR

ORIGINAL:

AND THE

CHARACTERS

OF THE

Moſt Noted Members thereof.

Poeta qui pavide cantat, rariſſime placet.

LONDON
Printed, and Sold by the Bookſellers, 1709.

THE
Epiſtle Dedicatory.

To that Luciferous and Sublime Lunatick, the Emperor of the Moon; Governour of the Tides; Corrector of
Female Conſtitutions; Cornuted Me-
tropolitan of all revolving Cities; and
principal Director of thoſe Churches
moſt ſubject to Mutation.

Lofty Sir,

SInce thoſe who enjoy the
Fat of our Neather-World,
are grown ſo Lean Spirited
as to love their Gold too
well to be tickl'd out of it
with a few extravagant
Complements, or Hyper-
bolical Adulations, I thought I might as well
take this Opportunity of expreſſing my Gratitude to your illuſtrious Highneſs, for the won-

A 2   derful

derful Favours I have oft receiv'd, at late Hours, from the refulgent Horns of your revolving Throne: For, many a ſtubborn Adverſary, who has been miſchievouſly poſted at the Corner of a Street, have I happily eſcap'd thro' the pleaſing Benefit of your lucid Rays, which often give me a fore-ſight of thoſe Dangers that I cannot but confeſs I ſhould be too apt to ſtumble upon, if totally depriv'd of your benigne Influence. Many a dirty Aquaduct have I ſtraddl'd over, by the Means of your Aſſiſtance, which, in all Probability, would have exacted Homage upon my Hands and Knees, had not the kind Interpoſition of your diffuſive Splendor conducted me with Safety over the purling Naſtineſs, which has been running full Speed into the ſoft Embraces of ſome Neighbouring Common-Shore, as a drunken Leacher does into the ſinful Arms of ſome more filthy Strumpet.

Let others, who bleſs themſelves with high Conceits of their own Merit, ſing aloud the Vertues of their generous Patrons, and boaſt the kind Reception, and the liberal
Donations,

Donations, that their Works and themselves never fail to meet with, from those who are ambitious of Rivaling *Mecænas* in his bountiful Character. As to my Part, I am always jealous of the Wisdom and Integrity of such great Personages, who are fond of being beholden to other Mens Flatteries for a publick Reputation, which, in my Opinion, is always built upon the surest Foundation, when it happens to be enjoy'd uncontended for, and gradually acquir'd by habitual Vertue, without Purchase-Money paid to those who have but a slender Title themselves, to what they sell to others.

The best Way to make a right Judgment of the Justice and Bounty of a great Man, is, not to look into the Books of his Flatterers, but those of his Creditors; and the more Crosses we behold in the latter, the greater Honour we shall find in the Lord; the more Hospitality in his House; and the better Decorum in his Family. Also, the best Testimonies that a rich and powerful Man can give the World of his Abilities, is an Honourable Discharge of those great Employ-

ments

ments he undertakes for the Publick, and to be Bold and Forward under all Immergencies, more for the Sake of his Country's Good, and a Deſire of making manifeſt his own Fortitude and Integrity, than for the large Rewards which attend ſuch Services; that he may diſſeminate Vertue by his own great Example, and encourage others, under all National Difficulties, to take up the like Reſolutions.

What ſignifies a great Man's Bounty to the cringing Author of a fulſome Dedication, if he proves a bad Pay-Maſter to the Tradeſmen that he Deals with; or his expenſive keeping a Theatrical Miſtreſs, if he be ſtingy and ingrateful to his poor Friends and Relations; or his Liberality at *Pontac's*, if penurious to his own Servant's? In ſhort, ſuch a Man's Character, at beſt, is but like the Party-colour'd Robes of a Serjeant at Law, that look as if one Side was patch'd up by the Plaintiff, and the other by the Defendant. So that if ſuch a Patron would but impartially examine what Sort of Dreſs his Reputation wears, he

would

he would be apt to find, tho' one Side is varnish'd o'er by the Artifice of *Poets*, and the Praise of *Sicophants*, that the other is degraded with long unpaid Bills, uncharitable Neglects, and unrewarded Services.

Therefore, as I cannot put Confidence enough in my own Merits to impose my Performances upon such a worthy Person as (if ever I have any) I shall chuse for my Patron, so I think it a little beneath me to flatter a Knave, or a Fool, or to wear out my best Pomps in dancing Attendance after such Quality, who have Nothing to be proud of but their ill-got Estates; and have the Vanity to think, that Power, without Justice, and Riches, without Honesty, ought to be highly complemented, and extravagantly well spoken of, tho' some who possess both, know in their own Consciences, that to call 'em either Just, Generous, or Valiant, would be as great an Absurdity, as to drink a Bumper to an honest *Cavilier*, in Pious Memory of Old *Noll* and *Bradshaw*, or to Swear that *Oats* and *Bedlow* were as substantial Witnesses to the *Popish-Plot*,

as

as are to be found to the Popiſh Faith, in all *Fox*'s Book of Martyrs.

Therefore, upon theſe Conſiderations, and ſome others in reſerve, I have humbly preſumed to addreſs the following Hiſtory to your imperial Inconſtancy, well conſidering, that tho' you always go arm'd with a Buſh at your Back, yet I bleſs my Stars that they have plac'd me out of of the Reach of your longeſt Faggot-Bat: And as I expect Nothing but your Moonſhine to reward my Labours, in Caſe they are honour'd with your Highneſs's Approbation, ſo I hope I ſhall have Nothing but a dark Night to puniſh me, when I need a light one, in caſe I have diſoblig'd you.

I am ſenſible your Lucidity may very much wonder why I chuſe you for a Patron, ſince we have Abundance of Quality under the Lunary Influence of your Silver Rays, who are my nearer Neighbours, but to tell you the Truth of the Matter, having read in the Works of a late Celebrated Poet, *viz.*

Great

Great Wits to Madness nearly are Ally'd,
And thin Partitions do their Bounds divide;

I concluded from thence, that there could be no great Difference between a Poet and a Lunatick; and consequently imagin'd, that a few splendid Akers in your Watry Dominions might do an Author as much Service as the Windy Promises of a great Man, or a Plentiful Estate in that remote Country, call'd, *The Mountain of Parnassus,* where Poets generally jointure their Wives, and make Settlements for their Children.

Besides, as I have principally treated of the Madness of Mankind in the following Sheets so I thought the Lunacies of this World a proper Subject to entertain your Highness, that you might discover thereby, what a wonderful Influence your glittering Pomp has upon all sublunary Mortals; for tho' we cannot but allow that you have some Spots in your lucid Dominions, which are palpable Dissenters from your establish'd Brightness, yet we, who are beneath you, cannot but admire your

Lustre,

Luſtre, notwithſtanding your Inconſtancy, ſince we know you to be a Favourer of Revolution Principles; for which Virtue, as heretofore by the *Perſians*, you are now ador'd by Thouſands, who ought to have the Precedency of

Your

Unchangeable

Humble Servant.

THE

THE
PREFACE.

S Sheriffs wear their Chains, and Lord-Mayors their Formalities, to draw Respect from the Publick, and the better to protect their Worships from Vulgar Insolence, so a Book that is but big enough for the costly Dress of a Calves-Skin Doublet, ought never to appear without Dedication and Preface, for fear the World should Laugh at it for receding from the fashion. Besides, most Authors are of Opinion, That such Frontispieces are the Ornaments of a Book, that often recommend it to the modish Reader, as a Tempting Dress does the hiden Premises of a Home-spun Dowdy to a Beaus Embraces. Therefore I presently resolved, like other Gentlemen of my Rank and Faculty, to tiffle up my Off-spring with as much Gaity, as if it was design'd only for the Company of such Persons who admire Books as they do Women, for the Newness of their Faces.

I

The Preface.

I dare not tell you in the Preface what a lushious Entertainment I have provided you in the Book, for fear a Bill of Fare should happen to pall your Appetites. I use a Proem as some People do long Graces before Meat, only to suspend your Eating for a little time, after a decent Manner, that you may fall too with the greater eagerness, when your humble Servant,' at the end of the Preface, instead of Amen, *has given you License to proceed.*

Nor shall I sneakingly beg your Favour, or anticipate your Judgment by a selfish Commendation of my own Performances, because extolling the intrinsick worth of what you must buy before you try, makes a Preface so like a Quack's Bill, that I abhor the thoughts of it. Besides, as an Author must stand and fall by the Judgment of his Readers, he ought, in modesty, to Post-pone his own fond Sentiments till he hears their Censures, for should he say he's Witty, and the World think him Dull, he'll have a difficult Matter to bring over the Majority to be of his Opinion.

I shall neither alledge the hurry of other Business, or the insufficiency of Time, as an Appology for my Blunders, tho', perhaps, I have as

much

The Preface.

much reason to use a Travellers License, instead of a Poet's, to extenuate my Faults as other Authors that do, yet I am so far from perswading any body to think I have more Wit than I have, or tha I am more infallible than I am, that I think my self oblig'd to inform the Reader, that nothing can provoke me to shew my self a fond Father of any thing that's my own, besides my Children.

Some of the Sons of Parnassus may think it but a Complement due to their extraordinary Merits, to have their Works Read within their own hearing, and Commended before their Faces: As for my part, if any Body should Treat me with so course an Entertainment, I should presently wonder what Sins I had Committed, that Providence should enjoin me so severe a Pennance, for I can compare it to nothing, but, that Necessity having forc'd me to Dung another Man's Ground, and the Owner, because he's pleas'd with the freedom I have taken, should thrust my Nose into my own Puddings. Civet we know is grateful to many Persons Nostrils, yet the Cat that yields it has always the Modesty to turn her Head from her own Excrement.

Tagging

The Preface.

Tagging of Verse, and Writing of Books, are become as sharp Trades, in this keen Age, as Making of Knives and Sisars; and if the former, as well as the latter, are not well Ground to a smart Edge, they may lie upon the Book-seller's Stall till they are bought up by the Band-Box-Maker; yet, if they happen to be so sharp as to scratch a Courtier on the Forehead; cut an Alderman for the Simples, or to scarrify a Knave that is but Rich and Powerful, there is presently a worse Roaring with 'em, than there is with a foolish Child that has hook'd his Fingers into a Clasp'd-Knife, and the poor Author who had Whetted his Wits to get a Penny, threatned with nothing less than that Reverend Machine, which us'd, heretofore, to be the Property of Saints, till Invaded by the Sinners.

Therefore I shall not acquaint you here with the Liberties I have taken in the Book, but, refer you to the first Chapter, which will presently introduce you to the whole Design of

Your

Humble Servant.

THE

THE
HISTORY
OF
CLUBS, &c.

CHAP. I.
Of CLUBS in General.

THO' the Promotion of Trade, and the Benefits that arise from Humane Conversation, are the specious Pretences that every Tippling-Club, or Society, are apt to assign as a reasonable Plea for their Unprofitable Meetings; yet most Considerate Men, who have ever been Engag'd in such sort of Compotations, have found by Experience, that the general End thereof, is a Promiscuous Encouragement of Vice, Faction, and Folly,

B   at

at the unneceſſary Expence of that Time and
Money which might be better imploy'd in
their own Buſineſs, or ſpent with much more
Comfort in their ſeveral Families.

For notwithſtanding their formal Orders,
exemplify'd at large by ſome Scrivener's Apprentice, and Oſtentatiouſly hung up in Lacquer'd Frames, as the Laws of the Society;
the ridiculous Chaplets that Crown the empty
Noddles of their officious Stewards, and A-
dorn their Temples like Fiddlers in a Muſick-
Booth; their honorary White-Wands, which,
like a Church-Wardens Pew, they wear as
Badges of their fantaſtical Authority; con-
temptible Ceremonies, which heretofore have
been frequently ſupported in all ſuch ſort of
Bacchanalian Communities, preſuming thereby
to Govern one another with ſuch a ſolemn
Decorum, as might preſerve Peace, Unity,
and Sobriety; and puniſh all Immorality and
Prophaneſs, by *Pecuniary* Amercements, that
they might have the more to be Drunk with
at their next Quarterly Feſtival: Yet, in ſpite
of all the care that ſuch ſort of Cabals could
ever take for the Prevention of Looſe Talk,
Miſchievous Cavels, and Inordinate Tippling,
the principal Felicities that ever were enjoy'd
by the giddy Members and Promoters of ſuch
Suck-Bottle Aſſemblies, have been inebrious
Health-Drinking, and impertinent Tittle Tattle,
much rather becoming a ſet of Ally-Goſſips, or
a gang of Swill-Belly'd Wine-Porters, than a
formal

formal Body of such reputable Members, who are bound by their Stations which Providence, has plac'd them in, to have a greater regard to a Sober Life, a Regular Deportment, and the Wellfare of their Families, which can never be truly observ'd by any Man, who imprudently engages in such sort of Meetings, and is as much intent upon his Club-Night, .as a *Wood-street* Sergeant upon a Sheriffs Feast.

Besides, how Ridiculous is it for such mix'd Societies to have their set meetings at Taverns and Ale-Houses, in hopes, by the efficacy of a few insignificant Orders, to preserve themselves within the bounds of Discretion and Sobriety, when the only way to keep our Head-strong Appetites in due Subjection, is to avoid those Occasions that may tempt us to give a Loose to our inordinate Desires; for certainly, no number of Prudent Men would Constitute a Meeting at a Publick *Bawdy-House,* and there propose, by a Table of Laws against Fornication and Adultery, to fortify weak Nature against the temptations of the Petticoat, and be able to limit themselves to a reserv'd Modesty, thro' the fear of forfeiting, perhaps, a Six-Penny Trifle, a Punishment not adequate to those sinful Pleasures they are liable to be tempted to. Therefore, is it not equally senseless for a Body of Men to hold their Nightly Congressions in either a Tavern or an Ale-House? Places that Fatten, and grow Rich by the Vicious Habits of Unwary Mortals; and there vainly hope,

where

where their Vertue is undermin'd with whole
Cellars full of Temptations, to keep themfelves fecure from the Bewitching Prevalency
of the inebrious Grape, or from a more bane-
ful excefs of thofe Dropfical Juices extracted
by Adulterating Brewers from our grofferMalt,
efpecially when fuch Tippling Societies have
nothing to Awe them in the height of their
Jollity from a perfuit of Drunkennefs, and a
fhameful Lapfe into all the Follies that attend
it, but a few lame Laws of their own making,
which themfelves, at all times, have the power
to Difpence with : Nor have the Penalties of
their Orders, if duly executed, any other Tendency, than to lay up a Store, to Promote, at
another time, thofe very Vices which they
Amerce at prefent; fo that there is fo great an
Incoherency between the Penalties they inflict,
and the End they propofe by it, that it is impoffible a fober Decorum fhould ever be preferv'd in thofe Societies who eftablifh conftant
meetings in fuch Houfes, where the utmoft
Arts and Subtilties are daily practis'd to decoy
their Benefactors into a Ruinous Extravagance.
Therefore, a Man may as reafonably propofe to
fecure himfelf in Peace, by haunting a Bear-
Garden on the publick Days of their confus'd
Revels, as to wifely govern himfelf within the
bounds of Sobriety, by making himfelf a Member of a Tavern-Convention, or what is more
Scandalous, tho' lefs Expenfive, an Ale-Houfe
Club.

But

But, befides the Inconveniencies already mention'd, there are many hidden Snakes that often lurk in the dark recefses of fuch pernicious Afsemblies, only known to thofe leading Perfons who have been the promoters of them. It may be frequently Obferv'd, That in all fuch Societies, there are one, or more of the Principal Members, who, in refpect to their Riches, fome Offices that they hold, or for a knack of Prating, which they have happily acquir'd beyond the reft of the Company, are highly Reverenc'd by their meaner Afsociates, who having not arriv'd to equal Parts, or Fortune, are therefore too apt to liften to the former, as the very Oracles of Reafon, fo that when ever thofe Cocks of the Fraternity, who fet themfelves up to be Prolocutors of the Society, are unhappily difpos'd, thro' Pride, Ignorance, or Intereft, to efpoufe any Faction, either in Church or State, or diffufe any Heterodox Notion, tho' never fo repugnant to the Principles of Chriftianity, no fooner is the Fools Bolt fhot upon the Door of Underftanding, but the Character of the Perfon adds a Sanction to the Mifchief, and the wicked feeds of Sedition and Difsention are fpeedily Difseminated among the weaker Brethren, not only to the hurt of themfelves, but to the injury of the Publick; for it is by fuch Societies, that corrupt Statefmen, afsifted by their evil Agents, promote and advance their dark Intrigues and ambi-

tious

tious Defigns, which prove not only fatal to thofe purblind Votaries, who have no knowledge of the fecret Workings of Great Men, but often precipitate a whole Nation into a deluge of Miferies.

Thus when the leading Members of fuch Clubs and Societies, prove Men of ill-Defign, or if not fo, either fond encouragers of their own Errors, or Miftakes, when once they find they have Reputation, Argument, or Cunning enough to impofe their own interefted Suggeftions, or partial Sentiments, or Reports, upon the reft of their Affociates, they never fail to ufe their utmoft endeavours to feduce them to have a Fair conceit of their Fouleft Undertakings, and to bring them to a good Opinion of what they Say or Do, tho' they know in their own Confciences, that neither their Talk, or their Practifes, have any other Authority than what they derive from a felfifh regard to fome by-end, in which they propofe their Defigns fhould terminate ; fo that fuch crafty Juglers are always the greateft promoters of Select Clubs and Meetings, that they may have the better opportunity of broaching fuch Matters as may be prelimenary to the Projects they have in hand, and draw in whole Societies at once, to be ignorant abetters of fome dangerous Molition, hammer'd out in the dark, to gratify the Revenge of fome difgufted Favourite, or to advance the underhand Defigns of an impatient fet of difcarded

Courtiers,

Courtiers, who could never prepare the Publick for their purpose, had they not Agents
abroad to work upon the Ignorance, and to
take-advantage of the blind Credulity of such
unguarded Societies, that always lie expos'd
to the subtile decoys of those crafty Under-
strappers, who cultivate the People, and make
them fit to nourish those evil Seeds that are to
be scatter'd among 'em: Nor do such busie
Agents ever want means to procure their admiſſion into any publick Company they have
a mind to Bias by their Treacherous Inſinua-
tions.

- By ſuch ſort of Artifices the Worſt of Men
are made popularly Good, and the Beſt often
Aſpers'd, and loaded with undeſerv'd Calum-
ny ; and where ever they come, only ſuch
Healths propos'd as may advance the Reputation of their deſigning Maſters, and all ſuch
Rejected, by way of Contempt, who, by their
Honeſt Policy, have in any wife obſtructed the
Ambition of the former, that, like the Buckets
of a Well, the one ſide may Sink the lower,
whilſt the other Riſes.

By theſe ſort of Stratagems, Firſt Publick
Societies, and next, whole Nations, are often
Miſled into dangerous Errors; and Tavern
Clubs have been frequently made the proper
Vehicle, in which our Politick Empericks
have convey'd their Poiſon into the Heart of
the Kingdom. Nor, indeed, have there been
any Plots, or Conſpiracies in any Reign, but

what

what have been firſt Hatch'd, and then Nouriſh'd in theſe ſort of Societies, to the ruin
and deſtruction of many unwary Fathers of
poor innocent Families; Men that have been
drawn in, without fore-ſight of the Danger,
to follow ſuch Bell-weathers, who have been
the firſt Broachers of the Helliſh Machina-
tions, and afterwards the Betrayers of their
own wicked Projects, that themſelves might
eſcape the Nooſe, by Sacrificing others to the
untimely Halter; and this has been the Fatallity that has often attended ſuch Societies,
who have firſt began as Clubs, and afterwards,
by the Artifice of ſome ill Brethren, have
been corrupted into Factions.

But to Treat in particular of ſuch ſort of
Cabals who have heretofore Fomented, or
thoſe who at preſent make it their principal
buſineſs to Widen, with freſh Wedges, our National Diviſions, it could not be done Juſtly,
without Reviving, at an ill time of day, thoſe
ridiculous Promotions, tumultuous Emulati-
ons, ſpit-fire Huzzas, and noiſey Miſcarriages,
on all Sides, that ought forever hereafter to lie
Bury'd in Oblivion, unleſs the violent Procee-
dings of one inveterate Party ſhould provoke
another to the like Recrimination. However,
let all Sides deport themſelves as they think fit;
and their Politick Clubs and Societies perſue
the Dictates of their petulant Humours with
what warmth they pleaſe, I ſhall have nothing
to ſay to any of 'em in this Treatiſe, any further

ther than what I have already hinted, that e-
very modeft Reader might have a necessary
caution, in a few words, againft such dangerous Meetings, which have been the Bane of
many a Well-meaning, but Imprudent Man;
for when ever the Foxes come among the
Geese, they seldom quit the Flock till they
have made a Slaughter; and where ever the
latter hold their conftant Affemblies, the former, in Difguife, will creep into their company, and play either the part of State Spies, or
Factious Seducers, to the injury of the Innocent.

My Defign in hand is forreign from every
thing that can give offence to either Party, or
Perfon: But as all Ages have been made Merry by the fantaftical Whimfies, and ridiculous
Affectations of such humourfome Societies, as
have made themfelves a Town-Talk by their
fingular Follies, inebrious Extravagancies, comical Projections, vitious Encouragements, and
uncommon Practices, I am perfwaded to believe,
it can be thought no breach of Morality, or
Good Manners, to expofe the Vanity of thofe
Whimfical Clubs, who have been proud to Diftinguifh themfelues by such amufing Deno-
minations, that the moft morofe *Cynick* would
be fcarce able to hear their Titles without
burfting into Laughter: Nor have the frantick Cuftoms, jocular Diverfions, and prepofterous Government of such fuddle-cap Affemblies, been lefs Remarkable than their feveral
Diftinctions.

Diſtinctions. Therefore, all that I ſhall pro-
miſe is, *A Merry History of the divers Clubs,
and Societies, both Famous and Infamous, that
for Sixty Years, and upwards, have been publickly Noted about* London, *for advancing and
encouraging all thoſe Vices, Immorallities, Follies, and Indecencies, that they ought to be a-
ſham'd of: The ſame being Imbelliſh'd with a-
bundance of pleaſant Stories, Jeſts, Poems, and
comical Tranſactions, pertinent thereto, that the
World may ſee herein, the old Proverb vereſ'd,
viz.* That Birds of a feather flock together.

CHAP.

CHAP. II.
Of the VERTUOSO's Club.

THIS Eminent Club was at firft
Eftablifh'd by fome of the Principal Members of the *Royal Society*, and held every *Thurfday*,
at a certain Tavern in *Cornhill*,
where the Vintner that kept it,
has, according to his Merit, made a Fortunate
Step from his Bar to his Coach, and has furren-
der'd his Houfe to fo diligent a Son, whofe prudent Management, winning Deportment, and
indefatigable Induftry, have made him a fingular
Example to the whole Fraternity, and will,
undoubtedly, be attended with the like Prof-
perity, that has fo juftly Rewarded the Pains
and Vigilence of his Generous Father. The
chief Defign of the aforementioned Club, was
to propagate New Whims, advance Mechanick Excercifes, and to promote Ufelefs, as
well as Ufeful Experiments. In order to carry
on this commendable Undertaking; any Frantick Artift, Chimical Operator, or Whimfical
Projector, that had but a Crotchet in their
Heads, or but Dream'd themfelves into fome
                                    ftrange

ſtrange fanciful Diſcovery, might be kindly admitted, as welcome Brethren, into this Teeming Society, where each Member was reſpected, not according to his Quality, but the Searches he had made into the Miſteries of Nature, and the Novelties, tho' Trifles, that were owing to his Invention: So that a Mad-Man, who had Beggar'd himſelf by his Bellows and his Furnaces, in a vain purſuit of the Philoſophers-Stone; or the crazy Phyſician, who had waſted his Patrimony, by endeavouring to recover that Infallible Noſtrum, *Sal Graminis,* from the Duſt and Aſhes of a burnt Hay-cock, were as much Reverenc'd here, as thoſe Mechanick Quality, who, to ſhew themſelves *Vertuoſos,* would ſit Turning of Ivory above in their Garrets, whilſt their Ladies below ſtairs, by the help of their He-Couſins, were providing Horns for their Families.

No ſooner were the patch'd Aſſembly met together on their Club-Night, but every Man, in hopes to advance his Reputation, would be ſo wonderful buſie about one Experiment or other, that the very Elements could not reſt for 'em: And the whole Company divide themſelves into ſo many ſeveral Cabals, that they ſat like Train-Band-Men at a Captains Treat, where there are Four, or Six, appointed to a Bottle. Some, by thoſe Hermetical Bellows, call'd an *Æolipile,* would be trying, with an empty Bottle, whether Nature would admit of a Vacuum. Others, like buſie Chandlers,

dlers, would be handling their Scales to nicely
difcover the Difference in the weight betwixt Wine and Water. A Third fort of Phy-
lofophers, would be Condenfing the Smoak of
their Tobacco into Oyl upon their Pipes, and
then affert the fame, in fpite of her nine Lives,
to be rank Poifon to a Cat. A Fifth Cabal,
perhaps, would be a Knot of Mathematicians,
who would fit fo long Wrangling about fqua-
ring the Circle, till, with Drinking and Rattle-
ing, they were ready to let fall a naufeous Perpendicular from their Mouths to the Chamber-Pot. Another little Party would be deep-
ly engag'd in a Learned Difpute about Tranfmutation of Metals, and contend fo warmly
about turning Lead into Gold, till the Bar had
a juft Claim to all the Silver in their Pockets,
whilft the reft, whofe Wifdom lay chiefly in
their Riches, fat liftening to edify by the noifie
Confufion.

So have I heard, when wealthy Dons
Defcend among Apollo's Sons,
The Riming Crew turn pert Repeaters
Of Panegyricks, Songs, and Satyrs;
And make themfelves Diverting Affes,
To pleafure Fools o'th' upper Claffis,
Who only recompence their Wit,
With fome poor parfimonious Treat:

And

And for their merry Puns and Strains,
Reward their Guts, instead of Brains.
Who therefore would exhaust his Store
Among the Rich? to still be Poor,
And barter Wit, which few possess,
For that which is in value less?

By the working Brains of this notable Society, many wonderful Discoveries have been
made, to the Amusement of the Publick; and
as many whimsical Undertakings advanc'd,
that have languish'd on this side their intended Issue, as ever were Projected among the
Straw in *Moorfields*, ever since the Palace of
Bethlehem was first built for the kind entertainment of those very Orphans which the
City Chamber had Distracted; so that they
Wisely took care, to be provided of Guests,
before they rais'd their Hospital.

Among the many Maggots that had the
Honour to crawl out of the fertile Noddles
of these fanciful Vertuosos, the Invention of
the *Barometer* has, in part, a title to the Clubs
Paternity, for they had the Reputation of
the first Lucky Thought, tho' Mr. *Tompion*, the
Watchmaker, brought the Project to perfection, so as to make it Useful. But Mr. *Patrick*,
in the *Old-Baily*, who, for several Years, has
been the principal maker of that Instrument,
has pluck'd the Feather out of all their Caps,
by

by giving the *Barometer*, of late, very great Improvements.

> *The Clumsy Mason the Foundation lays,*
> *But he that Crowns the Work deserves the Praise:*
> *Hopkins and Sternhold did much Fame acquire,*
> *Till Tate and Brady Tun'd the Heavenly Lyre:*
> *Dryden and Shadwell held the Bays for Years,*
> *But both resign the Crown when Garth appears,*
> *The Greatest Heroe must his Helmet vail,*
> *When one more Mighty turns the ticklish Scale:*
> *The Glitt'ring Stars are by the Moon out shone,*
> *And she submits her Glory to the Sun;*
> *Nor would his Lustre dazzle Humane Eyes,*
> *Should o'er his Head a greater Light arise.*

But besides this notable Invention of the Weather-Glass, by which our Gentlemen and Ladies of the middle Quality are infallibly told when it's a right Season to put on their Best Cloths, and when they ought not to venture an Intrigue in the Fields without their Cloaks and Umbrella's, they have been famous promoters of many merry Conceits, that at once deserve both Laughter and Admiration, as in particular: The conveying *Hamstead* Air into the City of *London* by Subterranean Pipes, as they do the *New-River* Water, for the benefit of all Sickly and Consumptive Families. The New Art of Navigation, containing infallible

Rules

Rules, how to make a Ship Sail in the very Teeth of the Wind: Alfo how to turn Sea Brine into frefh Water, and make it as Wholefome for the Body, and as pleafant to the Palate as Brandy, Punch, or *French* Claret. The way to bring Fowls to be cheaper than Butchers-Meat, by making Mutton-Cuftards with Sheeps-Trotters for my Lord Mayor's Table, in order to prevent the confumption of Eggs, which muft confequently promote the encreafe of Poultery. The Art of Good Hufbandry: Shewing how a Man may Brew without Water, Bake without Fire, and Live, like a Prince, upon three Halfe Pence a Day, and as often as he Dines have fix Difhes to his Table. The Nuptial Calendar, exactly Calculated for the Meridian of *London*, wherein a Marry'd Man may look at any time, and fee how often he has been made a Cuckold: To which is added, a very ufeful Table, by which he may Difcover, Who, How, Where, and When, and all the other particulars of his Wife's Backflidings. The Vifible Circulation of the Gudgeons-Blood, by the help of a Microfcope and a Wax-Candle, from whence a Young Anatomift may draw a Thoufand falfe Conclufions, and become a Bubble to *Spectacle-John*, for fhewing him the Experiment. The ready way to melt Pewter without Sea-cole, Charcole, Wood, Turf, old Rags, or Cinders, by kindling a vehement Fire, with two Liquids, upon Plate, Difh, Spoon, or Porringer: Originally

Invented

Invented for the cleanly Broiling of Dry'd-Sprats, and Red-Herrings for the *Royal-Society.* The New Art of Cookery, by that excellent Contrivance of a portable Kitchen, call'd, by fome, *a Digefter,* and by others, *a Dog-ftarver,* by the ufe of which, a Man may Stew a Leg of Beef, at a Half-Penny charge, till the Flefh is difolv'd into Strong-Broth, and the Bones become as foft as Butter'd Apple-Pye. An irrepeatable number of thefe kind of Curiofities have been the famous products of their exuberant Noddles, and the applaufe of fuch Gentlemen who are as Whimfical as themfelves, the accuftomary Rewards they have obtain'd by their Labours.

So have I feen an Antiquary,
A Bag of Rufty Trinkets carry:
Old Canker'd Coins, defac'd by Time,
With fcarce one Letter round the Rim:
Stamp'd with a Something like a Head,
With Eyes defac'd, and Nofe decay'd,
Suppos'd the Phiz of fome old Hero,
Aguftus, Julius, Otho, Nero,
Or of fome ftrange forgotten Prince,
That plaid the Tyrant Ages fince;
Yet when he fhews his mouldy Baubles,
On Tavern, or on Ale-Houfe Tables,

C   *Among*

Among old-fashion'd Fools, who, like
Himself, are pleas'd with things Antique:
The Knot of Coxcombs all agree
To praise the Dross, as well as he;
So joining in Opinion, place
High value on the rusty Face.

Thus Vertuoso's *make a pother,*
About their Whims, to please each other;
And wond'rous Maggots will advance-ye,
That have no Being but in Fancy.

This Club of Vertuoso's, upon a full Night, when some eminent Maggot-munger, for the satisfaction of the Society, had appointed to Demonstrate the force of Air, by some Hermetical Pot-gun, To shew the difference of the Gravity between the Smoak of Tobacco and that of Colts-foot and Bittany, or to try some other such-like Experiment, were always compos'd of such an odd mixture of Mankind, That, like a Society of Ringers at a Quarterly Feast, here sat a nice Beau next to a dirty Blacksmith; there a purblind Philosopher next to a talkative Spectacle-maker; yonder a half-witted Whim of Quality, next to a ragged Mathematician; on the other side, a consumtive Astronomer next to a water-gruel Physician; above them, a transmutator of Mettals,
next

next to a Philosopher-Stone-Hunter, at the
lower-end, a prating Engineer, next to a
clumsie-Fisted Mason; at the upper-end of all,
perhaps, an atheistical Chymist, next to a
whimsie-headed Lecturer; and these the Learned of the Wise-akers wedg'd here and there
with quaint Artificers, and noisy Opperators,
in all Faculties; some bending beneath the load
of Years and indefatigable Labour, some as
thin-Jaw'd and heavy-Ey'd, with abstemious
Living and nocturnal Studdy, as if, like *Pha-
roah*'s Lean-Kine, they were design'd by Heaven, to warn the World of a Famine; others
looking as Wild, and deporting themselves as
Frenzically, as if the disapointment of their
Projects had made them subject to a Lunacy.
When they were thus met, happy was the
Man that could find out a New Star in the
Firmament; discover a wry step in the Suns
progress; assign new Reasons for the spots of
the Moon, or add one stick to the bundle of
Faggots which have been so long burthensome
to the Back of her old Companion; or, indeed,
impart any crooked Secret to the learn'd Society, that might puzzle their Brains, and disturb their Rest for a Month afterwards, in
consulting upon their Pillows how to Strai-
ghten the Project, that it might appear Upright in the Eye of Reason, and the knotty
Difficulty be so rectify'd, as to bring Honour
to Themselves, and Advantage to the Publick.
But besides the Spirit of Invention, that, by

the

the help of good Claret, ſo Inſpir'd the Society, the whole Company were ſo infected with an itch of Curioſity, that if a Man funk'd a Pipe, and could not give a Reaſon for the Blewneſs of the Smoak, he that aſk'd the queſtion would think him an unworthy Member of ſo Philo-ſophical a Club, who did themſelves the Ho-nour to conceit they were the Wiſeſt Body in the Kingdom. In ſhort, they have been plagu'd and peſter'd with ſo many Banters and Lam-poons, as if the Muſes were fearful they ſhould invade *Parnaſſus*, and make their Poetical King-dom ſubject to the ſtrict Government of Philo-ſophers.

Apollo's *Sons are Poets Born,*
    Tho' finiſh'd in the Schools,
And love their Wit ſhould ſhew their Scorn,
    To thoſe who deem 'em Fools.

Philoſophers think Poets Mad,
    And Poetry but Froth,
In fruitleſs gingle finely Clad,
    To pleaſe and tickle Youth.

But Poets know Philoſophers
    More empty Fables feign,
Since Nature, whilſt the World is hers,
    Still makes their Searches vain.

For

For tho' they're Grave and Wise in Dress,
 And boast their Studies past,
Yet, Sceptick like, they must confess,
 They nothing know at last.

Then why may'nt Poets, like the rest,
 Help carry on the Cheat,
Since all the World is but a Jest,
 And Knowledge but Conceit?

When our Affembly of Vertuoso's were in the Zenith of their Glory, and the Town was Amus'd Weekly with fome new Experiment, or wonderful Difcovery, which the Philofophical Conjurers pretended to have made by their deep infpection into the Secrets of Nature, an unlucky Gentleman, who had Travel'd into *Ægypt,* where the Inhabitants, by eating much Manna, and other Purgative Diets, were forc'd, when they went to Bed, to wear Plugs in their Fundaments, to keep their Laxative Bum-fiddles from Difhonouring their Sheets; which unfavory Stopples, as foon as up in a Morning, it was their cuftom to difcharge in their neighbouring Ditches, or in fuch-like conveniencies, and to empty their Veffels of thofe troublefome Grounds which had been very uneafie under their clofe Imprifonment, and all Night long been ftruggling

C 3

for

for a vent. The Gentleman being accuftom'd
for the benefit of the Air, to walk the Fields
in the Morning, and feeing a great number of
thefe Fundament-Plugs lie along in the Ditches,
had the whimfical Curiofity to pick up fome
of the cleaneft, which the Rain had wafh'd,
and the Sun dry'd, and putting 'em in a Bag,
brought them over to *England*; and refiding
in *London*, happen'd to hear of the Fame of
our Vertuofo's Club, and how welcome any
foreign Novelty was to the inquifitive Wife-
akers. Upon which, by the affiftance of a
Friend, he got admittance into the Society,
taking along with him his *Ægyptian* Cargo of
ftinking Suppofitories, reporting to their Wif-
doms, That the fame was a Drugg of fuch
fingular Efficacy, that the Natives where it
grew, by Vertve thereof, would ftop any fort
of Flux, or Loofenefs, in a minute; and that
he therefore fubmitted it to the Judgment of
fo Learned a Society, in hopes, by their fkill
in all Phyfical Products, they might make it
ufeful to their own Country. With that they
were handed about to the moft Judicious of the
Members, every one nibling at the fharp-end
that had lain ftewing in the Dregs, fome nod-
ding their Heads, as if they had found by the
Tafte, what Analogy it had with fome other
Species that was noted for its Vertue. Others
fpitting out what they had chew'd and mumbl'd, for fear the Secret fhould produce fome
poyfonous effect. One declaring, it muft be a

great

great Dryer, because of the Spiciness of its Taste. Another, That it was certainly a powerful Antiscorbutick, because so full of Saline Particles. A Third, That he believ'd it was Antivenereal, because its biting Taste had some affinity with Guaicum. A Fourth, Asserting it a great Narcotique, for that it had numb'd his Tongue, by conveying it to his Palate. Thus the Jest went round, till every Member of the Club, who had the least skill in Physick, had most gravely deliver'd his Judgmatical Opinion. At last a pert Physician, who was crowded among the rest, was so curious as to ask the Gentleman, How the Natives us'd to take it? To which the Traveller answer'd, always in at the Fundament, over-Night, and shot it out again the next Morning; and that those very Pledgets he had handed to the Board, for ought he knew, had been fifty times apply'd to the same uses. With that one began to Spit, another Keck, a third Spew, a fourth, in a Passion, crying, Z——s, *Sir, I hope they did not wear them in their Arses!* As sure, reply'd the Gentleman, *as you have had them in your Mouths.* Upon which, the merry Traveller having gather'd up his Plugs and return'd them to his Sachel, was, by the enrag'd Members, Expel'd, or rather, Spew'd out of the Company, for the odious Indignity he had put upon the Society.

Many such sort of Jests, by the Ridiculers of Inginuity, us'd to be put upon this grave
Assembly

Aſſembly of Philoſophizing Vertuoſo's, till, at length, quite tir'd with the Affronts of the Town, and their own Unprofitable Labours, they dwindl'd from an Eminent Club of Experimental Philoſophers, into a little Cinical Cabal of half-pint Moraliſts, who now meet every Night, at the ſame Tavern, over their five-penny Nipperkins, and ſet themſelves up for nice Regulators of their natural Appetites, refuſing all Healths, eaeh taking off his Thimble-full according to the liberty of his own Conſcience, paying, juſt to a Farthing, what himſelf calls for; and ſtarting at a Minute, that they may have one Leg in their Beds exactly as *Bow-Bell* proclaims the Hour of Nine.

Thus the grave Searchers into Nature,
So ſkill'd in Earth, Air, Fire, and Water,
That no ſtrange Earthquake could ariſe,
Or pointed Lightning gild the Skies ;
No Hurrican its force expand,
Or Inundation drown the Land,
But they could give good Reaſon why,
The Winds or Waters roſe ſo high.
Yet theſe more Wiſe, when o'er the Bottle,
Than 'Cartes, Lock, or Ariſtotle.
Could not ſecure their Reputation,
Againſt that Tyrant Defamation,

But

But dwindled from a Club, ſo Noted
For many Arts they had promoted,
Into a quaint penurious Set,
Who Drink by Rule, and Eat by Weight.

 So ancient Rome, *who once was Fam'd,*
For all the Arts that could be nam'd,
Is now become a Den of Monks,
Fat Fryers, and Religious Punks ;
Which ſhews that no Community,
Publick or Private, long can be,
From fatal Revolution free.

CHAP,

CHAP. III.

Of the Knights of the Order of the GOLDEN-FLEECE.

THIS Rattle-Brain'd Society of Mechanick Worthies, were most Solemnly Establish'd, several Years since, by the Whimsical Contrivance of a Merry Company of Tipling Citizens, and Jocular Change-Brokers, that they might meet every Night, and wash away their Consciences with salubrious Claret, that the mental Reservations, and falacious Assurances, the one had us'd in their Shops; and the deceitful Wheedles, and stock-jobbing Honesty, by which the other had out-witted their Merchants, might be no impediment to their Nights Rest, but that they might Sleep without Repentance, and Rise the next Day with a strong propensity to the same Practice; so Sin on, *de Die in Diem*, till they came to be Aldermen. Tho' they had consented to Form themselves into a

Regular

Regular Society, yet they fcorn'd, like a Bread-and-Cheefe-Club, held by Handicrafts in an Ale-Houfe, to have their Orders hung up in a Gilt-Frame, like a Quacks-Bill in a Phyfical Coffee-Houfe; or to be under the formal Government of a brace of addl'd-headed Stewards, but agree'd among themfelves, That every new Member fhould pay Eighteen Pence, as an initating Fee, and be Nick-Nam'd, by two God-Fathers chofen out of the Society, who, as he fat in his Chair, were to bid him Rife up *Sir Timothy Turdpie*, or by any fuch-like Title that fhould come into their Noddles; and by this Ceremony, Dub him a Brother, and a Knight of the moft noble Order of the *Golden-Fleece.*

No fooner had the new Worthy thus pafs'd his Adoption, and receiv'd his Honour, but the Regefter was call'd for with abundance of formality, and his Title enter'd in great order, that he might take his Place at the Board, and fo become a new Laughing-ftock, for his Name-fake, to the reft of the Fraternity, who were all Dignify'd with as whimfical Diftinctions as the wit of their God-Fathers could invent, and make applicable to the Follies of their God-Sons. Therefore, as the Titles fo confer'd, were generally adapted to the Merits of the Worthies who had the honour to bear 'em, I have thought it not amifs to Amufe the Reader with a copy of their Regifter, that, in a great meafure, he may be able to judge of the

excellent

excellent Qualifications of the Worshipful Knights of the famous Golden Order, whose Names, at least, will be as good an Entertainment as the *Dramatæ Personæ* of a whimsical Farce.

A List of the Knights of the Noble Order of the *F L E E C E*.

Sr. *Jeremy Sausebox,*
Sr. *Timothy Addlepate,*
Sr. *Rumbus Rattle,*
Sr. *Humphry Clodpate,*
Sr. *Goliah Fightall,*
Sr. *Boozy Prateall,*
Sr. *Crazy Careful,*
Sr. *Noisie Blunder,*
Sr. *Sipall Paylittle,*
Sr. *Bumper Reelhome,*
Sr. *Maudlin Smocklove,*
Sr. *Courtly Flatcap,*
Sr. *Cavil Moody,*
Sr. *Querpo Prim,*
Sr. *Thunder Plugtail,*
Sr. *Drowsie Whifall,*
Sr. *Talkative Dolittle,*
Sr. *Samuel Sousrown,*
Sr. *Goodly Godly,*
Sr. *Bumkin Guzzle,*
Sr. *Dapper Pert,*

Sr. *Peter Squabble,*
Sr. *Puny Milksop,*
Sr. *Skinny Fretwell,*
Sr. *Positive Start,*
Sr. *Swigbelly Situp,*
Sr. *Whimsie Careless,*
Sr. *Looby Grunt,*
Sr. *Trumpeter Tellall,*
Sr. *Crocky Grimlook,*
Sr. *Ninny Sneer,*
Sr. *Thwackem Bluff,*
Sr. *Babie Dandle,*
Sr. *Nicholas Ninny,*
Sr. *Gregory Growler,*
Sr. *Snapum Catchpenny,*
Sr. *Pauper Readywit,*
Sr. *Damnum Surly,*
Sr. *Peter Puzzle,*
Sr. *Samuel Snapall,*
Sr. *Barnaby Busie,*
Sr. *Costly Squeamish.*

When

When their Golden Worſhips, thus notably Diſtinguiſhed, were met in a Body at their general Rendevous, and had ſaluted one another by their *Kent-ſtreet* Titles, then their brittle Fuſees were charg'd with Sot-weed, and every one began to puff a ſalutory Whiff, to warm the ambient Air, and beget a drowthy ardour in the Guts of the Fraternity, that ſuch ſort of Healths might be freely circulated, as were moſt agreeable to the Dubb'd Society, having little other buſineſs to excerciſe the Faculties of their worſhipful Members, beſides Drinking plentifully; Smoaking inceſſantly; telling Stories lamely; talking Politicks wildly; diſputing Principles warmly; and, at laſt, to dwindle into luſhious Bawdy, which every one took his turn to expreſs moſt feelingly.

So Buxom Goſſips, when they meet,
To give themſelves a private Treat;
And at ſome Paſtry-Cooks Regale,
With Pidgeon-Pies, and Bottl'd-Ale,
At firſt, put on their Modeſt Airs,
Like Nuns juſt ſtepping to their Pray'rs;
But, when the Glaſs has flown about,
Crown'd with a Dram, or mix'd with Stout,
Then Pious Dame, with Bawdy Jeſt,
Revives the Genius of the reſt;
Who caſting off their ſtarch'd Diſguiſe,
Shew by their Tongues, as well as Eyes,

That

That the fame vicious dregs of Nature,
Still lurk in e'ery Humane Creature;
Only they're ftifl'd here and there,
By Intereft, or Religious Fear:
But when good Liquor interpofes,
God Bacchus *is to hard for* Mofes.

This fantaſtical Order of Dubb'd Fuddle-caps, were no fooner Eſtabliſh'd, but they en-creas'd as faſt as a *Moorfields* Rabble upon an *Eaſter* Holiday; for the great Ambition that abundance of City-Rattles had to the Honour of Knighthood, tho' fo whimſically confer'd, that the ceremony of their Inſtallment, and their ridiculous Titles, made 'em a publick Laughing-Stock to their whole acquaintance; yet fancying, like Farmers when a Bird has ſhit upon their Heads, That there was fome thing Prophettical in the ſham Dignity, they crowded in apace to be Dubb'd Coxcombs of the worſhipful Society, in hopes the counter-feit Diſtinction, by the power of Sympathy, might, at one time or other, bring them to be blown upon by the Breath of Honour, as many a Country Clod-Pate, who has been call'd Alderman in his Apprenticeſhip, has luckily, hereafter, aroſe in good earneſt to the Golden-Chain, as if the Preſages of his Friends had been the Riſe of the Looby, as the Predictions of Aſtrologers are often the very cauſe that
the

the fucceeding event happens to anfwer their Prophefies.

Thus Fools, who Credit Planet-gazers,
And think the Knaves wife Albumazars,
Conform their Lives to what they tell 'em,
And then believe the Stars compel 'em.

For many Years fucceffively, this Noble Order of the *Equiti Aurati,* continu'd their Society at the *Golden-Fleece* in *Cornhil,* till Sir *Jeremy Saufebox,* one of their principal Knights, and chief Leader, and Controller of the *Rattlebrain'd Community,* ftepping a little befides his Senfes, for a deplorable Accident that had happen'd in his Family, took leave of his Brotherhood, as he had of his Wits, and laid his Honour in the Duft, where Diftinctions ceafe, and all Men are reduc'd to the fame peaceable Level which they had long enjoy'd before their firft Creation. And then the dull Fraternity, thro' want of a merry *Zany* to excercife their Lungs with a little feafonable Laughter, and unhappily neglecting to be Shav'd and Blooded, fell into fuch a fit of the Melancholly Dumps, that feveral of the Order were in great danger of a Straw-Bed and a Dark-Room, if they had not neglected their Nocturnal Revels, and forfaken frenfical Claret, for fober Watergruel; and worfe Company, for the penitential Converfation of their own
Families:

Families: So that upon thefe Misfortunes, the Knights put a ftop to their Collar-Days; laid afide their Inftallment; proclaim'd a ceffation of Bumpers for fome time, till thofe who were Sick had recover'd their Health, and others their Senfes; and then, the better to prevent the debafement of their Honour, by its growing too common, they adjourn'd their Society from the *Fleece* in *Cornhill*, to the *Three-Tuns* in *Southwark*, that they might be more retir'd from the Bows and Compliments of the *London* Apprentices, who us'd to Salute the noble Knights by their Titles, as they pas'd too and fro about their common Occafions. Befides, They have a further Conveniency by their diftant removal; for fhould any of 'em be in danger of having their Honour invaded by any importunate Creditor, a light pair of Heeles will foon carry 'em into a neighbouring Sanctuary, where no Impatient Dun, or Catchpole Raparee, dare either tug them by the Sleeve, or take them by the Collar.

In Faithlefs Times, when Crowds Mifcarry,
'Tis good for Wife Men to be wary.
The tim'rous Hare, that's oft perfu'd,
Delights to harbour near a Wood.
Then who can blame the Knights for chufing,
So fit a Place for Rendevoufing?

To

To ſhew what a great regard they have for one anothers Converſation, tho' moſt of them live at a remote diſtance, yet the Geeſe, like Foxes that Prey far from home, Waddle every afternoon o'er the Corn-plaguing Pebbles of *London-Bridge*, to the *Tom-Turds-Arms*, in *Southwark* which ought, for their pains, to be the Banner of their Order, with this Motto, *viz.*

Let Honour ſtill be due to Jaſon's *Knights,*
Tho' Tom-Turds-Arms *the* Golden-Fleece
[*beſhites.*

Under this circumſtance their eminent Society remains at preſent, ſtill maintaining all their ancient Formalities that may promote Cachinnation, only their Penal-Laws of Forfeiture are quite laid aſide, becauſe they prov'd an Oppreſſion to thoſe poor Knights, whoſe Eſtates have been impair'd by Wagering and Stock-Jobbing. The accuſtomary Salutation, when any of the Society happen to meet by accident, tho' in the publick Street, is, *What Title, Brother?* Sir *Timothy Addlepate,* crys the worſhipful Member, or what ever Diſtinction he has the honour to bear, who preſently returns the like Compliment, of, *What Title, Brother?* Sir *Jeremy Sauceboe,* perhaps, replies the other. Z----s, ſays a merry Gentleman, who, at a time of their Greeting, happen'd to be paſſing by, *Tom Worſhips accoſt*

D   *one*

one another as if you were Knights and Aldermen of the City. Another time, an arch Drawer at the *Three-Tuns*, having Affronted some of the Noble Order by a surly answer, insomuch that a cholerick Knight, very full of resentment, told the Drawer, in a passion, he was a saucy Sir *Jackanapes*. *Indeed, Gentlemen*, replies the Youth, *I am highly Oblig'd to you, for you Honour me as much as if I was one of your Society.* Abundance of such sort of Rubs they meet with from their Acquaintance; yet, with a chearful Resolution, they still continue their Farce, and maintain their Fooleries, and value the Scoffs of the World no more, than a Nest of Guzzling Minters do the Reproaches of their Creditors, but are as proud of their sham-Honour, as a Stage-Heroe is of his tawdry Buskins; and glory as much in their imaginary Titles, as a company of old Soldiers do in their Scars and Scratches.

'Tis strange! that Men with Reason Blest,
Should make themselves a common jest;
And meet to Stigmatize each other,
That e'ery Fooll may have his Brother.
What Mortal, that has Sense or Thought,
Would strip Jack Adams of his Coat?
Or who would be by Friends Decoy'd,
To wear a Badge he would avoid?

And fondly to the World Proclaim
His Weaknefs, by fome Apifh Name.
For who can bear a Man Saluted,
By th' Title of Sir Crazy Hothead?
And not conceive the filly Afs,
Deferves the Name he does embrace;
And that 'tis well adapted to him,
That others may the better know him.
He therefore that is proud to take
A Foolifh Name, for Folly's Sake,
Shews plainly by his Indifcretion,
He well deferves the Appellation.

Thus, as the punifh'd Child, in Courfe
Muft Kifs the Rod, to pleafe the Nurfe,
So the Dubb'd Afs, t' oblige his Mates,
Oft hugs in jeft, the Name he hates.

CHAP.

CHAP. IV.

Of the NO-NOSE Club.

Merry Gentleman who had often hazarded his own Bolt-split, by Steering a Vitious Course among the Rocks of *Venus*, having obferv'd in his walks thro' our *Englifh Sodom*, that abundance of both Sexes had Sacrificed their Nofes to the God *Priapus*, and had un-luckily fallen into the *Æthiopian* Fafhion of Flat-Faces, pleas'd himfelf with an opinion, it muft prove a comical fight for fo many maim'd Leachers; fnuffling old Stallions; young un-fortunate Whoremafters; poor fcarify'd Bawds; and falivated Whetftones, to fhew their fcan-dalous Vizards in one Nofe-lefs Society: To accomplifh which, he made it his bufinefs, for fome time, to ftrole about the Town, on pur-pofe to pick acquaintance with all fuch ftigma-tiz'd Strumpets and Fornicators, as he thought might be propei Members of the Snuffling

Com-

Community, pretending fome thing or other that carry'd a face of Intereft to all that he talk'd with, appointing every one apart to meet him at the *Dog Tavern* in *Drury-Lane*, upon a certain Day, a little before Dinner-time, that they might Eat a bit together, and he would then acquaint them with the Secret. Being a well-bred Gentleman, and a Perfon that behav'd himfelf, to all he fpoke to, with an unfufpected Gravity; when the Day appointed came, every one was curious to know the upfhot of the matter. The Gentleman, againft the time, having order'd a very plentiful Dinner, acquainted the Vintner, who were like to be his Guefts, that he might not be furpris'd at fo ill-favour'd an appearance, but pay them that Refpect, when they came to afk for him, that might encourage them to tarry. When the Morning came, no fooner was the hand of *Covent-Garden* Dial upon the ftroak of the Hour prefix'd; but the No-Nofe Company began to drop in apace, like Scald-Heads and Cripples to a Mumper's Feaft, afking for Mr. *Crumpton,* which was the feign'd Name the Gentleman had taken upon him, fucceeding one another fo thick, with jarring Voices, like the brazen Strings of a crack'd Dulcimore, that the Drawer could fcarce fhew one up Stairs before he had another to conduct; the anfwer at the Bar being, to all that enquir'd, That Mr. *Crumpton* had been there, and defir'd every one that afk'd for him would walk

up

up Stairs, and he would wait upon 'em prefently. As the Number encreas'd, the Surprife grew the greater among all that were prefent, who ftar'd at one another with fuch unaccuftom'd Bafhfulnefs, and confus'd Odnefs, as if every Sinner beheld their own Iniquities in the Faces of their Companions. However, feeing the Cloth laid in extraord'nary order, every one was curious, when once enter'd, to attend the fequel: At length a fnorting old Fellow, whofe Nofe was utterly fwallow'd up by his Cheeks, as if his Head had been troubl'd with an Earthquake, having a little more Impudence than the reft of the Snuffletonians, *Egad*, fays he, *if by chance we fhould fall together by the Ears, how long might we all fight before we fhould have bloody Nofes?* *Ads-flefh*, fays another, *now you talk of Nofes, I have been looking this half hour to find one in the Company.* God be prais'd, fays a Third, *tho' we have no Nofes we have e'ery one a Mouth, and that, by fpreading of the Table, feems at prefent, to be the moft ufeful Member.* A meer Trick, I dare engage, fays a Bridge-fallen Lady, *that is put upon us by fome whimfual Gentleman, that loves to make a Jeft of other Peoples Misfortunes.* Let him Jeft and be Damn'd, cries a Dub-Snouted Bully, *if he comes but among us, and Treats us handfomely.* If he does not, fays he, *I'll pull him by the Nofe till he wifhes himfelf without one, like the reft of the Company.* Pray, Gentlemen, and Ladies. cries an old drowthy Captain of *White-friers,*

friers, who had forsaken the Pleasures of
Whoring for those of Drinking, *don't let us sit
and Choak at the Fountain-Head*; and with
that they knock'd for the Drawer, and ask'd
him, *If they might not call for Wine without the
danger of being stop'd for the Reckoning:* Who
answer'd, *yes, for what they pleas'd, only the
Gentleman desir'd it might be the forfeiture of a
Quart, if any one should presume to put their
Nose in the Glass.* The Proposal was so modest, that 'twas presently agreed to, so all sorts
of Wines were immediately brought them, to
Whet before Dinner, and sharpen their Wits,
that the Snoutless Society might be the better
Company for the Master of the Feast. No
sooner had two or three Glasses a piece gone
round the Company, and put the Mercury on
float which lay lurking in their Weather-Glas-
ses, but growing a little familiar, there was
such a Snuffling among 'em, that had a Herd
of Swine been snorting o'er their Wash, and
an *Irish*-Harper playing St. *Patrick's* Jigg in the
midst of 'em, it could not, for certain, have punish'd the Ear with a more ungrateful Jargon.

Fall'n Palats now, and Bridge-less Noses,
Eat up by Crude Mercurial Doses,
And Tongues impair'd by Salivations,
Or half devour'd by Ulcerations,
After each other, Drank their Glasses
And never Keck'd, or made wry-Faces,

As

As if they all knew very well,
Which way their yielding Nofes fell;
Had therefore each the fame Protection,
Againft Venereal Infection;
And valu'd not what Pockey Venom,
Could tinge the Glafs that pafs'd between 'em:
But Nofelefs Sir, and Snuffing Madam,
Since all had been alike at Hadem,
Took care, 'tis true, to Drink all up,
But thought it fcorn to rinfe the Cup.
So Night-Men, who with Tubbs and Pails,
Carry off the drippings of our Tails,
With Hands unwafh'd, in fultry Weather,
Will Sweat, Eat, Drink, and Stink together.

The Dinner being now ready, the Mafter of
the Feaft, conducted by the Vintner, walk'd
up Stairs to Compliment his Flat-Nos'd Guefts
with a hearty Welcome, and to return them
Thanks that they had done him the Honour
to remember their Words, and, according to
his wifhes, to Grace the Entertainment he had
provided for them, with fo large an Appearance
of both Sexes. Upon which, a Brandy-Fac'd
Bully, whofe Carbuncle Cheeks, between Pox
and *Poculum,* look'd as Blood-Red as a frefh
Stake cut off from a Buttock of Bull-Beef,
prefuming to be wifer than the reft of the
Company,

Company, undertook to be Spokes-man, and return'd the following answer.

"Sir, I understand, by the unfortunate
"Sportsmen and Ladies present, That you
"were equally importunate with every one
"of us, to meet you here about extraor-
"dinary Business that should prove to our
"Advantage, in hopes of which, you may
"*plainly* see, in every ones Face, that we
"came in such haste, to give our Personal at-
"tendance, that we left our Noses behind us.
"Therefore, Sir, tho' we appear before you
"without our proper Ornaments, and have
"steer'd our selves hither without our Bolt-
"sprits, yet we must *flatly* tell you, That we
"expect to be Respected, since Soldiers full of
"Scars, and old Abby Monuments, defac'd by
"Antiquity, are always most Venerable.
"Therefore, if you any way Affront us, we
"shall toss up our Snouts, and, perhaps, bring
"yours upon a *level* with the rest of the Com-
"pany's; or if you have any design to draw us
"into Expence, you will find your self de-
"ceiv'd, for we are not Persons to be *led by the*
"*Nose* into such an Inconveniency. We there-
"fore hope, that you mean us well; and if so,
"then by your own single *Roman*, you may
"lead us any whither: For tho' our selves
"have no Bucklers to guard our War-like
"Faces, yet, like Persons who have no Money,
"we love to follow those that have.

By

By way of Reply to this notable Speech, the Gentleman told them, That tho' his meager Jaws were unhappily difgrac'd with fuch an Eliphants Trunk, yet his Father, and his Grandfather made nothing of theirs, but kifs'd them away before they came to be Thirty, yet Liv'd fo long afterwards, that they follow'd their Nofes out of this World into the next at Forty Years diftance; Therefore, he had fo great a refpect for all Perfons under the fame circumftance, that he was only covetous of fuch an opportunity as they had given him, to convince them of the Friendfhip he had for all Flat-Faces; and tho' it fo happen'd, that his unneceffary Griftle was ftill ftanding, yet he had run fair hazards of making his Countenance *even* with them; and therefore beg'd Pardon, That he fhould thruft his Nofe into fuch a Nofelefs-Society, being truly fenfible, That nothing was more Ridiculous in publick Company, than for a Gentleman to be Singular.

> One *Nofe*, among fuch *Nofelefs Gueft*,
> *Was only fit to be a Jeft*;
> *And look'd, with its affiring Bridge*,
> *But like a Houfe with lofty Ridge*.
> *Built by fome whimfical old Fop*,
> *Amidft a Street that's Flat at Top*.
>
>   *A Wife Man hem'd about with Fools*,
> *Muft bear the Blockheads Ridicules*:

The

The Modest Dame, with Whores surrounded,
Must be by Impudence Confounded:
The Female Saint in Querpo Hood,
Will bait the Lass with high Commode.
Why then should not one mighty Nose,
With patience bear the Scoffs of those
Who hate to see a Nose appear,
Because themselves have none to wear,
Since he is always made the Jest,
That is the most unlike the rest?

The Dinner being now brought to the Table, and the Scare-Crows seated according to their Seniority, as soon as their Food was Sanctify'd with a short Grace, they all fell to Grinding and Snuffling, for want of clear Passages, like fat Aldermen at my Lord Mayor's Feast, who, when tir'd with their Journey from *London* to *Westminster,* commonly Eat their Custard between Sleeping and Waking. Among the rest of the Entertainment, there happen'd to be a couple of fat Pigs, which the Cook, to make a Jest, had merrily sent up with both their Snouts cut off: The Gentleman being offended to see the Pigs Heads so strangely mangl'd, sent for the Cook up Stairs to know the reason of it, who Answer'd, *He had cut off their Snouts to put the Pigs in the Fashion; for that he thought it not fit for two such Swinish Crea-*
tures,

tures to run their unmannerly Nofes into fuch good Company that had but one amongft them. A Pox take you, Reply'd an old Snuffler, *for the Son of a Dripping-Pan! The fewer Nofes there are in the Company, the more there ought to be in the Feaft, for the Ladies know, That Flat Things always love long Snouts.*

As foon as they had Eaten off the Edge of their Appetites, being all highly pleas'd with their plentiful Entertainment, the Founder's Health was difh'd about in a Eumper, till they all grew as Frolickfome as fo many Jugs and Bumkins at a Country Houfe-Warming ; and then they began to Jeft, and be as Merry with one anothers Iniquities, as if their Sins were their Pride, and their Sufferings their Glory, every one being as free of their paft Vices and Intrigues, as Goffips o'er their Ale, are of their Hufbands Infirmities, that the fingle-Nos'd Gentleman was fo Delighted with his Guefts, that he gave them his Company moft part of the Day, and fat like *Don John* among his gaftly Affembly of defac'd Monuments, juft ftarted from their Pedeftals to take a Dinner with the Libertine. Thus, in Eating, Drinking, and Jefting, they pafs'd away their Time, till the Wine and the Mercury, by their united Forces, made them totter about the Room, like Drunken Boors at a *Dutch* Wedding: And then the Founder of the Feaft paid the Reck'ning Generoufly, bid them heartily Welcome, and Invited them

that

that Day Month, to such another Entertainment, which kind Hospitallity he several times repeated, and call'd the Society by the Name of *The No-Nose Club*: But the bountiful Promoter, within less than a Year, happening, in spight of his Nose, to Die in a Salivation, the Flat-Fac'd Community were unhappily Dissolv'd: The last of their Meeting, at the request of the Deceas'd, being to Solemnize his Funeral, where every one had a Ring, in *Pia Memoria* of their Generous Benefactor, whose Remains were Honour'd with the following Elegy.

Mourn all ye No-Nos'd Bullies of the Age,
Whose batter'd Snouts the Worlds decay presage,
And shew, whilst Living, how the fairest Face,
Adorn'd by Nature with each Charming Grace,
Tho' a Chaste stranger to the joys of Love,
Must Rot when Underground, like yours Above;
And that fair Bridge, which in such form does
[*grow,*
Beneath whose Gristly Arch such Juices flow,
When Dead, like your fallen Noses, e'er you die,
Must tumble, and in Flat Disorder lie.

Mourn e'ery Punk, whose ruin'd Front Pro-
[*claims*
How much sh'as suffer'd, by Venereal Flames;

Who

Who, by her Dents and Scars, deters the Young
From Loves bewitching Sports, for which they
[*Long.*

Weep all who dare, without a Mask, disclose
A sinking Bridge, or Face without a Nose.
Let Grief alone your Salivation prove,
Till flowing Eyes your Malady remove,
And quite discharge the Pocky dregs of Love.

Mourn for the loss of such a gen'rous Friend,
Whose Lofty Nose no Humble Snout Disdain'd,
But tho' of Roman Height, would stoop so Low,
As to Sooth those who ne'er a Nose could show.
So a Kind Beautious Dutches, once Admir'd
By all that saw her, and by all Desir'd,
To shew the Gen'rous Humour of her Grace,
Maintain'd a Player with a Pan-cake-Face,
As if she had a strong desire to Kiss
The Monkey, till her Nose was Flat as his.
Who then can Crumpton, *for his Fancy, Blame,*
Since Birth, *and* Honour, *once persu'd the same?*

O Weep! And Flux out your Lamenting Eyes,
Till flowing Grief each hidden Ulcer Dries;

And

And your Contagious Tears Corrode your Cheeks,
As Merc'ry does their Mouths who spit three
[*Weeks:*
For sure no Noseless Club could ever find,
One single Nose so Bountiful and Kind.
But now, alass! He's sunk into the Deep,
Where neither Kings, or Slaves, a Nose can keep,
But where Proud Beauties, Strutting Beaus, and
[*all,*
Must soon into the Noseless Fashion fall.
Thither your Friend, in Complaisance, is gone,
To have his Nose, like yours, reduc'd to none;
For Worms to Beauty do as Fatal prove
Below, as Pox and Physick do Above.

CHAP.

CHAP. V.

Of the FARTING Club.

OF all the fantastical Clubs that ever took Pains to make themselves Stink in the Nostrils of the Publick, sure no ridiculous Community ever came up to this windy Society, which was certainly Establish'd by a parcel of empty Sparks, about Thirty Years since, at a Publick-House in *Cripple-Gate* Parish, where they us'd to meet once a Week to poison the Neighbouring Air with their unsavory *Crepitations*, and were so vain in their Ambition to out Fart one another, that they us'd to Diet themselves against their Club-Nights, with Cabbage, Onions, and Pease-porridge, that every one's Bum-fiddle might be the better qualify'd to sound forth its Emulation. The Stewards, who were chosen once a Quarter, being the *Auricular* Judges of all Fundamental Disputes that should

should arise between the Buttocks of the odoriferous Assembly. The Liquors that they
drank, in order to Tune their Arses, were new
Ale and Juniper Water, till every one was
swell'd like a blown Bag-Pipe, and then they
began to Thunder out whole Volleys, like a
Regiment of Trainbands in a vigorous Attack
upon *Bunhill-Fields* Dunghill, till the Room
they sat in Stunk ten times stronger than a
Tom-Turd's Lay-Stall: Yet, in their windy
Eruptions, they had so nice a regard to Lapet-
Cleanliness, that an old Alms-Woman had a
better Pension from the Club, than she had
from the Parish, to give her constant attendance in the next Room, and if any Member
was suspected of a Brewers Miscarriage, he
was presently sent in to be examin'd by the
Matron, who, after searching his Breeches, and
narrowly inspecting the hind-Lappet of his
Shirt thro' her crack'd Spectacles, made her
Report accordingly; if unsoil'd, then a spank
on the Bum was given to the Looby, as a token
of his Cleanliness; but if the nasty Bird had
befoul'd his Nest, then, *Beshit upon honour,*
was her return to the Board, and the Laxative
Offender was Amerc'd for his Default. When
ever any Health was begun in the Society, it
was always honour'd with the Windy Compliment of a Gun from the Stern, and drank
with as much Formality, as Commanders push
about the Royal Health on board their wooden
Citadels, every Member's affection to the Per-

E   son

son nam'd, being meafur'd by the ftrength and loudnefs of the Stinking Report with which he crown'd his Bumper. Thus who ever wanted a Fart for a Great Man's Health, was enjoin'd the Pennance of a Brimmer extraordinary; alfo look'd upon by the whole Company, as an Unmannerly Fellow. They were all profitable Cuftomers to the Grey-Pea-Woman, who us'd to double her quantity upon the Club-Night, for the benefit of the Society, and attend 'em as conftantly, as the Dame with her Firmity, does the *Hofpital-Gate* every *Smithfield* Market, each charging his Guts with the Fartative Pills, by fhoveling down whole Handfuls, that what went in like Bullets, might come out like Gun-Powder. Tho' their weekly Meeting was held in Honour to the Rump, yet every Club-Night they drank the King's health, and then there was fuch Trumping about, to fignalize their Loyalty, that the Victualer was forc'd to burn Rofemary in his Kitchen, for fear the expanfion of the naufeous Fumes fhould Poifon his other Cuftomers: So that tho' the Society was begun, and carry'd on, for fome time, with abundance of Secrefie, yet they were foon Smelt out, infomuch that the found of their Bumfiddles reach'd the Ears of the Neighbourhood, where, in an Alley adjacent, there happen'd to dwell an arch Fellow, who, by long Study and Experience, had acquir'd an admirable perfection in the New Art of Farting, by claping his

his right Hand under his left Arm-pit, where
he would gather Wind, and discharge it so
surprisingly, that he would give you a Lady's
Fart, a Brewer's Fart, a Bumkin's Fart, an Old
Woman's Slur, or a Maden Fizzle, &c. so very
Tunable and Natural, that they should entertain the Ears, without offending the Nostrils,
and provoke Laughter, by the Sound, without
the punishment of a Stink: And this windy
Operator having heard of the Fame of this expert Consort of Wind-Musick, made interest
to be admitted into the Trumpetting-Society,
that he might manifest his Excellence among
the Cracking Performers, still concealing to
himself the Mistery he was Master of, that
what he did by Art, might pass for the works
of Nature; and tho' it was his daily practice
to offer his Farts at Taverns, as Fidlers at a
Fair do their Scrapes and Sonnets, yet he did
not care they should know his Calling, for fear
they should except against so Mercenary a
Factor as should make Farts a Commodity. No
sooner had they receiv'd him into their Foist-
ing Assembly, and, according to custom, wel-
com'd their new Brother with a thundering
Peal of Buttock Ordinance, but, in respect to
the Company, he Faces them with his Arse, and
returns their Compliment with such a succession
of Trumps, that he gave them more diversity
of Sounds in one cleanly Volley, than their
whole Consort of Fundaments were able to
imitate; upon which, he was as kindly em-

brac'd,

brac'd, with all the marks of Favour, as if they took him to be a God of the Winds, and his Arſe to be a Miracle, allowing him at once to be an abſolute Maſter of the Science of *Ventoſity,* and reſpected him as much as a School of young Fencers do the Gladiator that teaches 'em: Every Crepitant Member ſtraining his Backſide to come up to the Excellency of their worthy Example, till the old Woman was forc'd to run home for freſh Diſhclouts, to wipe away the dregs of their over-fruitful endeavours, till at laſt ſome of the Members, thro' their penetrating Judgment, diſcovering the Falacy, and finding the croaking Harmony they ſo much admir'd to be perform'd by Art inſtead of Nature, in a mighty paſſion, they Stunk him out of the Society, for an Emperick and a Counterfeit, tho', upon humble Submiſſion, they afterwards admitted him into a ſervile Poſt, and allow'd him Six Pence a Night to be Muſician in Ordinary to their Farting Club.

Since he who by deceitful Arts,
With Arms inſtead of Arſe lets Farts,
Shall be Diſpis'd, becauſe his Fun,
Can't fairly call the Sound its own.
Then what muſt he deſerve who Steals
His Wit, and treads on others Heels?
Whoſe buſie Tongue makes publick uſe
Of what his Brains could ne'er produce.

This

Thus the Stinking Society continu'd their
Farting Confort for fome Years, with abundance of Decorum, till they had brought their
Arfes, by the help of their Mufician, into fuch
excellent Tune, that they could command
their Fundaments, with as much Dexterity as
the beft of the City Waits can a Double
Curtill; infomuch, that when any of the
Members were fo merrily difpos'd, as to entertain the reft with a Song or Madrigal, the
whole Choir of Bumfiddles ftruck into the
Chorous, in fuch admirable Order, that a
Stranger might have thought the whole Society had fed upon *Scotch* Bagpipes, and that
the Drones had ftuck in their Arfes, not that I
can fay they made a Sweet Harmony, becaufe
the Breath of their Inftruments came from
fuch Rotten Lungs, that every now and then
would follow the Sound, in fpite of all
Retention. In thefe fort of Windy Recreations,
they us'd to pafs away their Club-Evenings,
till at length they grew fo Famous thro' the
whole Parifh, that Neighbours and Paffengers
us'd to ftop under the Window, and lend an
Ear to their Arfes, as if their Farts had been
as Mufical as a noife of Trumpets; and the
very Boys and Girls, in imitation of their
Harmony, went Trumping with their Mouths
along the Streets to School, till their Mafters
were forc'd to whip 'em till they Stunk, to
make 'em leave off Farting. No fooner were
they thus arriv'd to the Zenith of their Glo-

ry, infomuch that their Repute began to reach
the Ears, if not the Noftrils of the Publick,
but fome of the leading Members of the Crack-
fart Community, by extravagantly Eating of
Cabbage-Porridge, to put their Inftruments in
Tune, flung themfelves, fome into the Cholick,
and others into a Diarrhæa, that feveral of the
beft Performers went Farting out of the
World, and left nothing to Pofterity, but
an odious Stink behind them, it being pofitively afferted, by the Phyficians that attended
them, That the Windy Diets they had Eaten
to Excefs, had begot a Hurricane in their Guts,
which had blown the whole Frame of Nature
off the Hinges, and for want of a free Difcharge thro' the *Inteftinum Rectum*, had extended the *Lactes* into perfect Organ-Pipes, made
Bellows of their Lungs, and puff'd up the
Veffels into fuch *Turgent Veficules*, that had
quite Stagnated the *Diaftole Motion* upon the
Arteries, and confequently ftop'd the Pulfation
of the Heart, to the Death of the Patients; and
tho' the Wind found vent juft upon their Ex-
piration, yet Nature was then too far fpent to
be Reliev'd thereby. This Opinion of the confult of Phyficians, taking Wind among the fur-
viving Society, who had attended feveral of
their Brethren to the Grave, to Honour their
defunct Members, with a Volley of Farts, as
the Military Heroes difcharge a Round of Muf-
quets, at the noble Interment of a Brother Soldier, and finding fome reafons to fufpect that
the

the fame Food would bring 'em to the fame End, they had the wit to diffolve their Club, change their Cabbage-Diet into Subftantial Beef, and fo tie up their Fundaments by degrees, from their accuftomary Crepitation.

We Read that Tubal Cain *firft found,*
In Cockle-Shels, fweet Muficks Sound;
And that the Rural Nymphs and Swains,
Tun'd Reeds and Oat-Straws, on their Plains:
But fure no Mortal Flefh and Blood,
E'er heard before, fince Noah's *Flood,*
Of Mufick fizzl'd from a Gut,
Extended to the Windy Scut.
Well may fo many Bards *Excreet*
The Dregs and Fefs of their Wit,
In Beaftly Songs, and Bawdy Verfes,
Since Men Play Tunes upon their Arfes,
E'en let fuch Heads and Tails Unite,
That one may Sing what th' others Write;
For fwelling Rhimes are often found,
Like naufeous Farts, meer empty Sound.

CHAP. VI.

Of the MAN-KILLING Club.

IN the happy Reign of King *CHARLES* the Second; when Peace and Plenty had made the Nation Rich, and the People Wanton, an agreeable Knot of Town Bullies, broken Life-guard Men, and old fcarify'd Prize-fighters, us'd to hold a Meeting at a blind Ale-Houfe on the back-fide of St. *Clement's*, where they honour'd their Affembly with the Heroick Title of, *The Man-killing Club* ; who, over Burnt-Brandy and *Yorkfhire* Stingo, us'd to boaft their Duels, Rancounters, Broken Noddles, Scuffles, Bum-Bailiff Skirmifhes, and Midnight Adventures, as if they thought it as much Bravery to hazard a Crack'd Crown with a Cannibal of the Law, as it was to Sally out of *Tangier* for Three Pence a Day, to kill *Moors* for their Arfe-Clouts. Out of this Bluftering Society, any angry Gentleman, for a fmall Gratuity, might have been furnifh'd

with

with a bloody Hand, and a ſtrong pair of Whiſ-
kers, who, at a minutes warning, would have
boldy undertaken any ſort of Villainy, tho' to
the hazard of a Halter, for nothing came amiſs
to the Ruffainly Bravadoes, that the Devil
could ſuggeſt, or his Agents perpetrate; yet if
any Body queſtion'd their Religion, or their
Loyalty, they were more in danger of looſing
their Noſes, than by an inveterate Pox; and a
ſubſequent Salivation.

Bullies, like Whores, tho' ne're ſo Wicked grown,
Are always Loyal to the Church and Crown;
The reaſons plain, becauſe alike they Dread
Hanging whilſt Living, Damning when they're
                                        [*Dead.*
Therefore in thoſe two Pow'rs they put their
                                        [*Troth,*
To be more ſafe, in time of need, 'twixt both.
So Bawds ſpeak well of Heav'n, thro' fear of Hell,
And cover Impious Lives, with Vertue's Veil.

The Reaſons why they aſſum'd ſuch a Scare-
Crow Name, as before mention'd, were, Firſt,
Becauſe they admitted of none but ſuch tho-
row-pac'd Deſperadoes, who had each kill'd his
Man. And, Secondly, That their Club might
be Terrible to the Sheriffs Mermidons, and
fighten them from attempting to put their
Parchment Dabs upon the Shoulders of the
                                        Society;

Society; for whatever they Scor'd, was always chalk'd up in a Dooms-Day Character, and all they cuuld Borrow, as good as a clear Purchafe. Tho' every Man among 'em fet up for a Gentleman, and would talk as much of Honour, as an old Whore does of Confcience, or a Court Pimp of Fidelity; yet not a Man had more Honefty in his Breaft, than a Plot-Evidence, or more Humanity in his Nature, than the *Ctzar* of *Mofco.* However they were fuch agreeable Company, for one another, that their rugged Features, full of Scars and Scratches, made 'em look like the rough-hewn Heads of half-finifh'd Statues, when the ftroaks of the Chiffel are left vifible in their Faces; or rather, like fo many rufty Bombardeers, taken out of our Bomb-Catches, to Project Fire-Works for our next Peace, That an indifferent Phifiognomift might as eafily have read their Deftinies in their Looks, as a Child can fee great O in the middle of his Horn-Book. Blood, Wounds, and Slaughter, were the common Toppicks of their bluftering Difcourfes, Drawing, their familiar Excercife, when Hot-Headed, but as for Hanging, 'twas as erkfome a fubject, as the talk of the Small-Pox is to fuch Perfons who have generally the misfortune to Die of the fame Diftemper, as if good Providence, by fome fecret Impulfe, gave Nature a fore-fight of her own Fatallity.

The

The Mariner is Aw'd the most
By Sands, in which at last he's lost.
Shovel, that Triumph'd o'er the Main,
Dreaded the Rock that prov'd his Bane.
Who, therefore, of the Wiser few
In Argument, can plainly shew,
Whether we've power, or not, to shun
Those Shelves, we fear to split upon?

A Gentleman of Fortune, whose chief dependance was on the curtesie of Harlots, and the folly and extravagancy of such Bubbles which the blind Gypsie should happen to fling in his way, having heard of the Fame of this Cut-Throat Society, and looking upon himself to be every way Quallify'd for such modest Conversation, he cocks up his Caster one Evening, claps his left Hand upon the pummil of his Sword, and putting on that Impudence that was necessary to Recommend him, adds the Title of Captain to his own Name, and pays a visit to the Club, humbly desiring the favour to be admitted as a Member. In Answer to his Request, one of the Bear-Garden Elders of the Hectorian Assembly, told him, *So worthy a Gentleman should be very welcome, provided he was Quallify'd according to the Laws of their Society.* So desiring him to sit down, they proceeded to Examine him, and ask'd him, *Whether he had Kill'd his Man?*

without

without which instance of his Bravery, they could not possibly Admit him. The new Candidate being a Gentleman of more Honour than to impose a falsaty upon the Company at first sight, told them the truth of the matter, most modestly Replying, *That he could not alledge he had kill'd a Whole Man, but that an honest brave Fellow, and himself together, had kill'd a Man between 'em.* To which his Examiner reply'd, *That he then had but title to one half of the Honour, and therefore could not be Enter'd without breach of Orders.* Z——s, says a generous Bully, on the other-side the Table, *it's pity so worthy a Gentleman should be put out of Countenance: Ye all know I have kill'd my Man fairly, single hand, and Captain* Pinkum *and I kill'd another between us; and rather than the Gentleman shall be baulk'd, I'll lend him half a Man, and then he may pass Muster, without any exception.* Which kind offer was thankfully accepted, also allow'd on by the Company, and so the Gentleman, paying his Initiation Fee, in a Porringer of Burnt Brandy, was accordingly Admitted, upon a promise, That he would satisfy the Debt he had contracted in the Club, as soon as ever he was able. Under this strict Discipline the Petticoat Champions continu'd their Society for several Years, till the Bailiffs catching some, and the Gallows the rest; so that for want of a fresh supply, to keep up the Reputation of so singular a Society, the came Club dwindl'd, first into Scandal, and next, to Nothing.

No

No Ancient Sodom, *or* Gomorra,
From whence the Prieſts ſuch Stories borrow,
Or Rome, *with all her Valiant Sons,*
Who dealt ſo much in Blood and Wounds,
And did ſo many Quarrels make,
As if they Fought for Fiting's ſake,
Could ever boaſt a Club of Ruffains,
Like our Man-Killing *Ragamuffins :*
Such Bluſt'ring, Swearing, Daring Knaves,
They ſlew their Men by Wholes and Ha'ves,
Propoſing little other Gains,
Than Goal and Halter for their pains,
The true Deſerts of all ſuch Fellows,
Who Hazard Life, to Win a Gallows,
When diſtant Armies want their Aid,
Where they may barter Blood for Bread ;
And riſe, by dint of Hurly-Burly,
To be as Great as Captain Surly.
But 'tis too true, that Bully Varlets,
Who Fight at Home, for Bawds and Harlots,
Prove Cowards, fearful to be Kill'd,
Where Bleeding Troops Manure the Field.
  So Cow'rdly Dunghill-Cocks defy
Their Rivals, when their Hens are nigh ;
But for more nobler Wars unfit ;
They fly the Battles of the Pit.

CHAP.

CHAP. VII.

Of the SURLY *Club.*

THIS Wrangling Society was chiefly Compos'd of Mafter Carmen, Lightermen, old *Billingsgate* Porters, and rufty Tun-Belly'd Badge Watermen, and Kept at a Mungril Tavern near *Billingsgate-Dock,* where City Dames us'd to Treat their Journey-men with Sneakers of Punch and new Oifters. The principal Ends that the Members propos'd, in thus convening themfelves together once a Week, were to exercife the Spirit of Contradiction; and to Teach and Perfect one another in the Art and Miftery of Foul-Language, that they might not want Impudence to abufe Paffengers upon the *Thames,* Gentlemen in the Street, lafh their Horfes for their own Faults, and curfe one another, heartily, when they happen'd to Meet, and Joftle at the corner of a Street. He that could put on a Countenance like a Boatfwain in hard-Weather, and Growl

and

and Snarl like a curft Maftiff over a Bullocks Liver, was a Member fit for the Thwarting Society; and the more indirect Anfwers, or furly impertinent Returns he could make to any Queftion, the more he was refpected for his contradictory Humour, and crofs-grain'd Abillities: For if any Grumbling Affociate was fo far corrupted with good Manners, as to make a civil Reply to any thing that was afk'd him, he was look'd upon to be an Effeminate Coxcomb, who had fuck'd in too much of his Mother's Milk; and for his affectation of Gentility, was turn'd out of the Company, for by the Orders of the Society, their whole Evenings Converfation was to confift of nothing but furly Interruptions, and crofs Purpofes. And when any new Candidate made a tender of his Service to the Noify Board, if the Refponfes that he gave upon his knotty Examination, were not as oppofit to their Queries, as the petulant Anfwers of a provok'd Wife, to the whimfical Interrogatories of a drunken Hufband, he was rejected, as unworthy of any Poft in the Contumacious Affembly.

Their way of drawing new Crabs into their Varges Club, was, the Members giving out among their guzzling Acquaintance, That the Society, at prefent, wanted a Stoker, to attend their Fire, a Skinker, to light Paper to ignify their Pipes; a Chalk-Accountant, to keep a Trencher-Regifter of the Club Reckoning, to prevent their Landlord's Double-Scoring at
the

the Bar, or the like: Every Office afcertain'd to be worth Twenty Pounds *per Annum,* the leaft Penny; and that any Man might be admitted that could but humour the Society, in a Surly Deportment, for that they were a true Proteftant Club, and hated all manner of Ceremony, as Popifh Superftition. By this means they us'd to decoy the ruggedft Fellows they could meet with, to offer their Service to the Board, fo that they have had feveral Candidates of a Night, to make intereft for the fame Vacancy, who were call'd in, one by one, and thus Examin'd, by the Elders of the Community, *viz. Do you think your felf Quallify'd to ferve this Society, in the Poft of a Stoker?* If the Loobily Candidate happen'd to anfwer, *yes, Gentlemen. Get you gone, for a faucy, ignorant Block-head. What fool could recommend fuch an illiterate Coxcomb to this Honourable Board? No no, you may turn your Arfe upon us, we admit of no Lady's Lap-Dogs into our Service.* Thus they prefently difpatch'd all fuch, who were any ways Infected with Good Manners, and turn'd them a drift, as Whores do their Maids, for having too much Modefty. But if a Rough-hewn Coal-heaver, or any fuch like contentious Clodpate, who had been better Inftructed how to behave himfelf, came to offer his Service, and when they afk'd him, whether he was Quallify'd for the Place, if he had the Breeding to Anfwer, What a Pox was that to them; and that he would have the Office in

fpite

spite of their Teeth, then he was presently approv'd of, with abundance of applause, and admitted to his Post, *Nemine Contradicente:* And when thus let into the Secret, for the Credit of the Society, would Brag of the Profits of his new Imployment, tho' not worth two Pence, to carry on the Jest, and to draw other Surly Fools into the like Disappointment. By these sort of Stratagems they us'd to hedge in their Cuckows, till, at last, they grew so Numerous, and rais'd such a publick Stock, by their Forfeitures and Amercements, that they allow'd Pensions to all such Termagant Widows of their defunct Members, as were able, upon occasion, to Scold three Hours by the Clock without any Hessitation.

Since such wild brutish Herds we see,
Will have their Acts of Charity;
And, even Rogues, that dread the Gallows,
Have pity on their Starving Fellows,
'Tis strange that those, so far exceeding
In Riches, Grace, and better Breeding,
Should be so slack, amidst their Store,
In deeds of Mercy to the Poor.

By this Guzzle-Booby Society, the Bumping-Post at *Billingsgate* was first erected, to

harden

harden the Buttocks of their Members once a
Year, that they ſhould never bridle their abu-
ſive Tongues, thro' a cowardly fear of having
their Back-ſides kick'd for their Ill-Manners ;
but the laudable Cuſtom, of late Years, is ſo far
degenerated from its Original purpoſe, that now
the Block is only made a wooden Bug-bear in
the *Whitſon-Holidays*, to terrify Paſſengers out
of Full-Pots of Ale, and Quarterns of Brandy,
that the Clod-Skul'd Fraternity of Oyſter-Por-
ters, who claim the Benefit of this tremendous
Stump, may get Drunk therewith, and in their
quarrelſome Humours, knock one anothers
Block-Heads againſt the Bump-Tail Poſt, to
try which is hardeſt.

During the flouriſhing Proſperity of this ca-
velling Society, the Language of *Billingsgate*
was very much Improv'd : Nor had it ever been
Famous for ſo peculiar a Dialect, had not many
ſpit-Fire Agravations, bawdy Adages, provoking
Phraſes, quaint Oaths, and thundering Mouth-
Granadoes, been owing to the Invention of
theſe expert Maſters of all manner of Ill-Lan-
guage, who, like Paſſengers upon the Water,
very ſeldom met, but they made it their Diverſion to abuſe each other, that their Tongues
might be tip'd with Venom upon all occaſions,
like a Courtiers of the Law, whoſe principal
Qualification is to Bait and Blacken an Obnoxious Delinquent, at the Bar of Juſtice.

Therefore

Therefore, since Orators, who wear
Their proud Distinctions at the Bar,
Will Condescend to foul their Mouths,
With vile Reproaches, and Untruths,
To Blacken, and to Lessen such,
Who've said, perhaps, a Word too much,
Then well may such Unthinking Vermin,
As Porters, Watermen, and Carmen,
Asperse each other with their Tongues,
To exercise their baser Lungs.

CHAP.

CHAP. VIII.

Of the ATHEISTICAL Club.

THIS Unbelieving Society of Irreligious Profligates, Met, for several Years, at an eminent Tavern in *Westminster*, where, over the Bottle, they us'd to assert the Devil's Cause, against the Priest's Prerogative; and argue the wide World into so precarious a State, as if the whole Frame of Nature was but one Cake of Attoms, Moulded, by meer Accident, into the Form it bears, afterwards hard Bak'd in the spacious Oven of Immensity; and that the Heavens were no more than the Upper-crust, and Hell, the Bottom of the Loaf. Such sort of Ridiculous, as well as Impious Systems they us'd frequently to Advance, out of their Heathenish Maggots; and rather than give Credit to *Moses*'s Book of *Genesis*, they would fancy, That the first race of Mankind grew upon Trees, like *Solon* Geese,

Geeſe, or ſtarted up, like Muſhroons, thought-
leſs and forlorn, till, by length of Time, they
were improv'd from *Tomthumbs* into Men of
Stature, and ſo from ignorant Pigmies became
rational Creatures.

The audacious Members of this unchriſtian
Society were chiefly whimſical Phyſicians,
half-learn'd Gentlemen, crackbrain'd Phyloſo-
phers, and conceited Libertines, who having
over-charg'd their Brains, by Reading ill Authors, with more than their Judgments were
able to digeſt, unhappily retain'd the moſt pernicious Part, which they carefully improv'd to
render themſelves Singular by their Heterodox
Notions. Government was ſo Toſs'd and To-
loniz'd among 'em, as if the Venerable Oecono-
my was only fit to be made the Rabbles Foot-
ball; and the Hierarchy worry'd with ſuch
unmannerly Contempt, between Jeſt and Earneſt, as if they miſtook the Church to be a Mon-
ſter, and therefore reſolv'd themſelves into
Snarling Whelps to have the ſport of Baiting
Her. Religion they made their Buſineſs to
Banter into Prieſtcraft, as if every Man's Breaſt
ought to be his holy Tabernacle, himſelf the
Teacher, and his own partial Sentiments the
only Goſpel by which he was to Preach. If the
Name of Prieſt was but ſtarted amongſt them
to beſure they join'd full Cry after the ſacred
Function, till they had forc'd the holy Robe to
run the Gantlope thro' the Company, believing
themſelves to be infallibly in the Right, becauſe

their

their Club, more Impious than *Sodom*, was too wicked to have one Righteous Member in their whole Society to let them know the contrary.

So have I heard a Knot of Fellows,
O'er brimming Flaggons, in an Ale-Houſe,
Accuſe the Conduct of the State,
And rail at Men they're Taught to hate ;
But when their Talk has giv'n Offence
To Sitters by of better Senſe,
And once they're ſmartly taken up,
They Eat their Words and Drink their Cup ;
Bluſh that they nothing have to ſay ;
When thus Oppos'd, But riſing Pay,
And ſneak, like burnt-Tail Dogs, away.

By theſe dimſighted Conjurers, whoſe willful Ignorance would behold nothing beyond the reach and meaſure of their imperfect Senſes, many dangerous Principles were ſcatter'd thro' the Town, to the diſcouragement of Piety, the over-throw of Virtue, and the leſſening of Obedience to Superiour Powers, that all Men might ſet up to be their own Maſters, and caſt off the Yoak of lawful Authority, which they deem'd Tyranny, and degenerate into a State of Heatheniſh Brutality, which they accounted freedom ; that their Luſts and Paſſions might have a range unbounded, and themſelves

felves have the honour to be thought the
Wife Patriots, and the Generous Reftorers of
the People's Liberty, who have always been
obferv'd to be moft Wicked, and confequently
moft Miferable, when their Tedders have been
ftretch'd to an unreafonable length, and their
Offences countenanc'd by Connivance and Im-
punity. It is a pretty Comedy, that fuch a Society, who have not Gratitude enough to own Him
that Made them, fhould fet themfelves up for
State Directors, and Pious Inftructors of Morality, and Good Manners, when they never met,
but, in Contempt of Heaven, they did their
Grand Mafter, the Devil, more Kindnefs upon
Earth, than twice the Number of his Infernal
Emiffaries.

Among the reft of the Infidels, who had the
Honour to make up this Antichriftian Society,
there was a famous Phyfician, that, in fpite of
his Art, was forc'd, many Years fince, to try
the Grand Experiment, who was fo thoroughly confirm'd in the Mortality of the Soul, that
he would frequently fay, he had no more than
a Goofe, and therefore thought it not worth
looking after : But, fays a Modeft Gentleman,
in return to the Doctor, Had you but half the
Brains of a Goofe, you'd be of another Opinion.
However, the Phyfician was very Eminent in
his Profeffion, and accounted a Man of Wit,
and being Drinking one Night in his Atheiftical Society, a furprizing Storm happen'd to
arife of a fuddain, infomuch that the Flafhes

of

of Lightening, and violence of the Thunder, ftruck a vifible Terror upon feveral of the Company, and put a great Damp to their Prophane Merriment. The Storm increafing to an unufual extremity, a Gentleman in the Company, under a great aftonifhment, happen'd to thus exprefs himfelf: *Blefs us! What's the meaning that it Thunders fo exceffively? I'll tell you, Sir,* crys the Doctor, *the Gods Kans are Empty, and they are Clacking the Lids for more Nectar.* At fuch fort of Repartees he had a ready Wit, efpecially when the Jeft would admit of any Prophanefs, which unhappy Talent had infected the whole Society; that to banter Religion, ridicule the Priefthood, and to make a mock of what was Good and Holy, were their principal Diverfions.

A Knot of merry Gentlemen frequenting the fame Tavern, and hearing what a prophane Society us'd to conftantly meet in the next Room to them, they laid their Heads together to confult of Ways and Means, how to try the Refolutions of thefe daring Sons of Thunder, by fome furprifing Adventure, that might give a ftartling Shock to their Atheiftical Infidelity: The better to accomplifh their commendable Undertaking, they appointed a meeting at Pofture *Clark*'s Tavern, in order to engage him in their intended Project, who being fingularly Qualify'd for the Defign in hand, and being a Man forward enough in fuch fort of Unluckinefs, he prefently confented to give them his

Assistance. When they were thus agreed, a Night was appointed for the execution of their Frollick; accordingly, at the Time prefix'd, they met *Clark* at the Tavern, who brought under his Cloak a Bear's Skin, which he had long kept by him for such sort of Adventures. When they were in this readiness, having often heard the Vintner with the Club at the Devil, for bringing a Scandal upon his House, they thought it not improper to make him acquainted with their Jocular Contrivance, who was well enough pleas'd with their Whim in agitation, and promis'd to be aiding in all he could, and to give them Notice when it was most convenient for their Sham-Devil to make his Personal appearance. When they had thus far proceeded, and most of the Libertines, according to Custom, were met together in their Club-Room, they thought it high time for Old *Nick*'s Representative to shift off his Humane Apparel, and to lace himself into his Diabolical Jacket; which was no sooner done, but the Vintner inform'd them, that the Club were all very busie in ridiculing Religion, and making a jest of Damnation, saying, himself would step in and Snuff the Candles, that Satan might the better sneak in behind him, upon All-fours, and, unperceiv'd, put himself in a Corner till he found a seasonable Opportunity of performing what he intended. Accordingly they procceeded with very good effect, and the Devil possest himself of a convenient Post, without discove-

ry,

ry, where he lay Perdu for fome time, till at laft one of the Hot-headed Members amongft the reft of their Atheiftical Difcourfe, happen'd to fay, That he wonder'd the majority of Mankind could be fo filly as to believe there were any fuch Goblins, as Ghofts, or Apparitions, fince he was well fatisfy'd that the Devil himfelf, which the Priefts made fuch a Buftle about, was nothing more than a Poetical Fiction; Upon which Words, the foul Fiend in the Corner made a damnable Yawn, which occafion'd the whole Society, in a terrible furprife, to direct their Eyes towards the Place from whence the Noife was emitted, where they beheld the Bear playing fifty Monkey Tricks, as if he was as Mad as a March Hare. *Z——ds,* fays one, *there's the Devil indeed, come for fome of the Society.* *That's true,* crys the Bear in a tremendous Voice: *Is it fo?* crys a Fat Gentleman, *then take a Lean one,* and away he fcour'd down Stairs with the reft after him, as if the Devil drove them, leaving only a Scotch Gentleman behind them, who having more Courage than the reft, refolv'd to be further fatisfied; upon which the Bear advances, and raifing himfelf upright claps his two Fore-paws upon the upper-end of the Table; the *Scotchman* not caring to fit within his reach, began to Sidle to a greater diftance, upon which the Bear fills a Bumper of Claret, gives the *Scotchman* a Nod, and takes it off at a Gulph: *Marry, Sir Deel,* crys the *Scot, ye have a gude fwallow* to your. *Wem:* I always *Whet before I devour,* crys the Bear: With that the *Scotchman* Sidled a little farther, not yet satisfy'd whether the Devil was in Jest or in Earnest, at length recovering a little more Courage, very civilly cry'd, *Wol ye Smauk a Peep, Sir Deel? Will you be mine,* replies the Devil in the Hoarse Voice of a Boatswain? *Haud a little, Sir Deel,* crys the bonny *Scot, twaw Words to that Bargain;* upon which the Bear, who had an admirable Knack of Metamorphosing his Shapes, put himself, of a sudden, into a terrible Posture, as if he was just going to seize the *Scotchman* as a Prey; at the sight of which away ran *Sawny* Headlong down Stairs, as much frighted as the rest.

The Picture of ill-Luck, having thus dispers'd the Society, whip'd out two or three Card Matches, which he had brought for that Purpose, and lighting them at a Candle perfum'd the Room with his Infernal Breath, and so return'd to his Company to make themselves Merry with their comical Transaction. The frighted Society were all fled, for Refuge, into the Publick Kitchen, where, half bereft of their Senses, they stood staring at one another as if they were Gally'd. The Doctor not happening that Night to come so Early as was usual, lost his share of the Devil's Entertainment; but stepping in with another Gentleman, just as the Frisk was over, being told at the Bar what a sad Confusion the whole Society had

been

been put in by a ſtrange Apparition, was conducted into the Kitchen to the reſt of his Aſſociates, where he found them gazing in ſuch a frantick Conſternation, that he cry'd, *Z—ds, Gentlemen, has one poor Devil-frighted ye all out of your Wits? By my Saul, Doctor*, replies the *Scotch* Gentleman, *had your ſen been there, by Criſs and St.* Andrew, *I believe the faw Fiend wod have tain you with him a Pickback; for, by my Saul, if I had not ran for't, I had been but a Morſel with him.* Prithee, Frank, ſays the Doctor to the Gentleman that came in with him, *let you and I ſtep up and try if we can have a ſight of this terrible Hobgoblin.* The Gentleman agreeing, up Stairs they went, where finding a damnable ſtink of Sulphur, and ſeeing every thing in Diſorder, they did not care for ſtaying, but return'd preſently. *Did you ſee the Devil,* cries their frighted Companions? *Not I*, replies the Doctor, *but I believe he has been there, for he has left a damn'd ſtink of Fire and Brimſtone behind him.* So, all the whole Company being ſtrangely ſurpris'd, they juſt ſat long enough to recover their Senſes, and ſo diſſolv'd their Club, and never met afterwards; moſt of them conforming from that time to a Sober Chriſtian Life, believing that the Devil, by Divine Mercy, was really let looſe from his Infernal Chains on purpoſe to worry them out of thoſe Atheiſtical Mazes, in which they had been bewildred; ſo that what was intended for the Di-

verſion

verſion of the One Company, prov'd the Reformation of the Other.

Thus Libertines, to Vice reſign'd,
Avers'd to be by Laws confin'd,
Diſdaining Vertue's ſober Rules,
As only fit to Govern Fools,
When met together in a Body,
Each ſtrives to be the greateſt Noddy;
And to Excell his impious Brother,
In ſome new Wickedneſs or other;
Becauſe he fears to be their Jeſt,
If more a Coward than the reſt.

So ſilly Children met to Sport,
Will wade and trample thro' the Dirt,
And ſpite of Parents angry Threats,
Will follow their unlucky Mates;
Leſt counted Daſtards at their Play,
By thoſe who lead the Miry-Way.

Yet Atheiſts, tho', when o'er their Wine,
They Laugh and Scoff at things Divine,
And fear no puniſhment of Evil,
Becauſe they never ſaw the Devil,
Scarce one durſt tarry in a Room
That's dark, for fear the Feind ſhould come:
                                                    Or

Or croſs a Church-Yard in the Night,
Leſt met by ſome Infernal Sprite.
Which plainly ſhews they've not the Heart,
To ſtand by what they dare aſſert.

   So Cow'rdly Bullies boaſt and rattle,
As if they fear'd no bloody Battle ;
But ſkulk, like Daſtards, and are ſhy
Of Facing Dangers they defy,
Becauſe they find they are not nigh.

C H A P. IX.

Of the Club of UGLY-FACES.

Certain Uferer, Nam'd *Hatchet*, from whofe fingular Afpect is deriv'd that common Saying, fo oft apply'd to any homely Perfon, *viz.* That he is a Hatchet-Fac'd Fellow, being a Man who always lug'd about with him at leaft two pound of Nofe, befet as thick with magnificent Rubies as the Gills of a Turkey-Cock going to Battle in the height of his Jealoufy, infomuch that moft of his Phiz lay fkreen'd beneath the umbrage of the prolifick Member, whofe ftupendious Magnitude was fo very aftonifhing, that a Butchers arch Boy, with a Tray of Beef upon his Shoulder, meeting with his Nofefhip in *Newgate-ftreet*, made a full ftop juft before him, crying, *Pray, Sir, put by your Snout a little, that my Buttock of Beef, and your Fiery Nofe, may pafs by without joftling. A good Boy,* Replies *Hatchet*; and to humour the jeft, put his Trunk by accordingly. *Thank you, Mafter,* fays

the

the Lad, *for your Civility*; *but well may Stakes be Six-Pence a pound, since you wear as many upon your Nose as a Butcher can well cut off the Rump, or Ach-bone of a good Bullock.* Many such fort of Rubs his unmerciful Boltfprit us'd to meet with in the Street; for No-body could pass by such a Mountain of a Nose, without thinking, or saying something extraordinary upon so flaming a Subject. Thus finding himself a Jest among most People, who were not distinguishable by some Disproportion or other as remarkable as his own, it occasion'd him to be inclinable to such fort of Company, whose ill compos'd Countenances, in case they jefted with his Nose, might give him an equal opportunity of returning their Jokes, that he might make himself as merry with his Companion's Infirmites, as they could be in bantering the mighty Buckler of his hard-favour'd Frontispiece: Upon this account he had chosen in his Neighbourhood three or four scare-Crow Visages, that were scarce to be parallel'd in any Parish but his own; and these, in an Evening, when his Cloak and his Tallies were laid by, he commonly selected as his principal Associates, who admitting by degrees an additional Number of uncooth-look'd Mortals into their cloudy featur'd Company, at length grew so numerous, that they thought fit to refolve themselves into a regular Society, which was soon after ftigmatiz'd by one of their own unlucky Members, and call'd, *The Club of Ugly Faces*;

Faces; becaufe the majority of the Company, efpecially thofe who had been *Hatchet's* Cronies, were fcarce any of them handfome enough for a Painter to Draw a Devil by. To anfwer the Tallyman's fuperabounding Snout, a fecond had a Chin as long as a grave Patriarchal Beard, and in fhape like a Shoeing-Horn. A Third, disfigur'd with a Mouth like a Gallon-Pot, when both fides are fquees'd near clofe together. A Fourth, with a Nofe like the Pummel of an Andiron, and as full of Warts as the Beak of a Cropper Pidgeon. A Fifth, with Eyes like a Tumbler, one biger than the other. A Sixth, with a pair of Convex Cheeks, as if, like *Æolus,* the God of the Winds, he had ftop'd his Breath for a time, to be the better able to difcharge a Hurrican. A Seventh, with as many Wens and Warts upon his Forehead as there are Knots and Prickles upon an old *Thornback.* An Eighth, with a pair of fkinny Jaws that wrap'd over in Folds, like the top of an Old Boot, or the Hide of a *Rhinoceros.* A Ninth, with a Tufh ftrutting beyond his Lips, as if he had been begot by a *Man-Teger.* A Tenth, with a Hair-Lip, that had drawn his Mouth into as many corners as a Minc'd-Pye, made by the Huffify Wife of a formal Mathematician. The Eleventh, with a huge Lauderdale Head, as big, in Circumference, as the Golden Ball under St. *Paul's* Crofs, and a Face fo fiery, that the ruddy Front of the Orbicular Lump, which ftood fo Elevated upon his lofty

G   Shoulders

Shoulders, made it look like the flaming Urn
on the Top of the Monument. A Twelfth, with
a Countenance as if his Parents, when he was
Young, had clap'd his Chin upon an Anvil,
and gave him a Knock upon the Crown with
a Smith's Sledge, that had shorten'd his Phiz,
and struck all his Features out of their proper
places; with many other such Comical, Clow-
nish, Surly, Antick, Moody, Booby Faces, that
the Wooden Gravers, who cut the Prints for
the frightful Heads upon Stone-Bottles, and
the Carvers, who us'd to noch out preposterous
Cherubs upon Bafe-Viols, and stern Whiskers
upon Barbers Blocks, were often introduc'd upon their Club-Nights, by some Interest or other,
on purpose to oblige their fancy with new Originals, that each might Sell their Commodities, for the singularity of the Faces with which
they had adorn'd 'em.

Since British *Ladies skill'd in Features,*
Admire Dutch *Dogs for handsome Creatures:*
And Men oft leave their Beauteous Spouses,
For Nauseous Punks, and Dowdy Blowzes:
Why not Great Fiddles please our Maids,
For wearing strange prepost'rous Heads?
Or Barber's Block be priz'd for having
A Phiz to humour Fools while Shaving?
For awkward things affect the Eyes
The most, by giving new surprise,

That

That makes fo many handfome Laffes,
Chufe empty Beaus with Ugly Faces,
As fome do Apes for odd Grimaces.

Thus e'ery one wearing fomething as remarkable in his Countenance, as if Nature had defign'd them as fo many Foils to fet off the Beauty of her more perfect Work, They feldom diftinguifh'd one another by their Names; but generally faluted each other, when they Drank round, after the following manner, *viz. Here* Nofe *my Service to you; Thank you* Chin: *Here's to you* Blabber-lip; *Your Servant Mr.* Squint: *My Love to you Neighbour* Goggle; *I am yours Neighbour* Allmouth: *Here's tow'rds you Brother* Thinjaws; *I'll Pledge you Brother* Plump-cheeks. In this fort of Dialect they us'd to put about the Cup till they had made themfelves Merry; and then, like a parcel of Dowdy Strumpets Quarreling in an Alley, they would vie Beauty, and upbraid each other with their feveral Infirmities, thus Guzzle down Malt Dregs till every one had his Belly-full, and then reel'd Home to their Hatchet-fac'd Spoufes, and by mutual Drudgery, hammer out Ugly Faces for the next Generation.

Should true Proportion e'ery Mortal Grace,
And Simitry be feen in e'ery Face:
Beauty no longer would be thought Divine;
Nor would its Charms with half the Luftre fhine:

No Courtly Dame a killing Look could boaſt,
If once the Foils of Homelineſs were loſt.
The duſky Sky ſets off the ſilver Moon,
And Neighbouring Clouds add Bluſhes to the Sun:
So Ugly Faces make the Fair ſeem bright,
And give them pow'r to humane Love excite,
As Darkneſs makes the Perſians worſhip Light.
    Therefore 'tis fit the Blare, or Goggle Ey'd,
Should get his Likeneſs on his Shipton Bride;
And that the mighty Noſe, enrich'd with Wines
Which, like a glowing lump of Coral ſhines,
Should on ſome drunken Bride's Pimgenet Face,
For the next Age beget a Monſt'rous Race;
That Beauty, when with homely looks compar'd,
May be for ever honour'd with regard,
And when ſhe grants what Man with joy receives,
Be doubly bleſt for thoſe Delights ſhe gives.
    But ſhould one level run thro' humane Race,
And neither Sex could ſhew a homely Face,
Beauty would loſe it's Power, Love decline;
No diſtant Spark for Wife, or Miſtreſs pine,
Or make a difference 'twixt his own or mine.
    Therefore let Ugly Faces ſtill unite,
And Get their Likeneſs, not in Love, but Spite,
That e'ery Slave may have his homely Mate,
Whilſt Beauty crowns the Actions of the Great.

CHAP. X.

Of the SPLIT-FARTHING Club.

THIS Parſimonious Society of Canary-Bibing Citizens, held their Weekly Meeting at the Old Queen's-Head in *Biſhops-gate-ſtreet*, their thrifty Juncto being chiefly compos'd of ſuch penurious Miſers that ſeldom drank Wine, but on their Club Nights, and then it was to conſult how to improve their Riches, by the puniſhment of their Guts, and to become, in time, Lord Mayors and Aldermen, by pinching large Eſtates out of the Cubbards of their Families. The famous Sir *John Pickplumb*, of ever Curſed Memory; the eminent Doctor *Hook*, of *Gotham* Colledge; *Buggeranto Covert*, that Died in his own Dung, and left his Wealth to his Catamite, were the principal Members of this Money Loving Club; and ſeveral worthy Followers of their Generous Examples, now Living, were the reſt of the Society, who Enter'd themſelves purely to be inſtructed in the Arts of Phylargiry and good Huſbandry. The Dearneſs of Bread-

G 3   Corn;

Corn; the Extravagance of their Children; the Waste and Prodigality of their half-Starv'd Servants; the Profitable Buying in of Six-Shilling Beer, Stale-Bread, and Wheel-barrow Cheese, were the chief Toppicks of their Save-penny Discourses; and how to subsist a large Family at little Cost, and to Dine themselves lushiously for Two-pence half-penny a Head, were the most useful Projects that were advanc'd among 'em. Hot *Grey-Pees,* or Baked *Ox-Cheek,* were commonly their Supper Meats : Nor could any Hungry Member call for a Farthing-worth of the One, or a Penny-worth of the Other, till it was first put to the Vote, and carry'd, by the Majority, unless he would pay for it out of his own Pocket, and that was look'd upon by the rest, to be great Extravagance : For the Healthful Conformity to one Meal a Day, and that Eaten with abundance of Moderation, was a standing Rule among the Thinjaw'd Fraternity, and who ever exceeded that abstemious Precept, without assigning a substantial Reason for so doing, was condemn'd for his Voracity, and predicted to Die a Beggar, for so expensively humouring his unreasonable Appetite. If any Smoker among 'em left his Box behind him, and wanted to borrow a Pipe of Tobacco of a Brother, it would not be lent without a Note of his Hand, which was commonly Written round the Bowl of a broken Tobacco-Pipe, to prevent the waste of Paper, and always made payable, the next Club Night, with ten Corns
Interest.

Intereſt. One would be Querying which was the greateſt Charity, in a Death-Bed Penitent, to diſcharge Twenty poor Debtors out of *Lud-gate* Priſon; to leave five Hundred Pounds to the *Blue-Coat* Hoſpital; to build an Alms-Houſe for decay'd Widows, or a School for Indigent Orphans. A Second would be aſking the Opinion of the Company, which was the beſt place for a Charitable Foundation, *Bunhill-Fields* Layſtall, or *White-Chapple* Dunghill. A Third would be for erecting a New Work-Houſe, that the Poor might not fall into a habit of Lazineſs for want of hard Labour. A Fourth would be projecting a New Houſe of Correction, that Beggars might be Whipp'd out of their Rags and Lice, and forc'd to Card Wooll, and Knock Hemp, for Sheepſhead Porridge, and clean Linnen of a Groat a Yard. A Fifth would be laying down a Computation of the Charge to turn *Greſham* Colledge into a publick Nurſery, for the Pious Education of Fatherleſs Brats, and Poor Foundlings; tho' not a wretched Soul in the whole Company had Liberality enough to give Six-pence to relieve the Wants of a Neceſſitous Relation.

Thus talk as if they meant to be
Profuſe in works of Charity;
And that the Poor ſhould be Befriended,
By Pious Gifts they ne'er intended;

For

For if one Bag of droſſy Wealth,
Would bribe off Death, and purchaſe Health,
They'd rather hazard Life and Soul,
To keep poſſeſſion of the whole
To the laſt Hour, than give a part,
For th' needful help of Men of Art.

What Wretches, therefore, can comply
To give the Poor, what they deny
Themſelves, in ſuch Extremity?

Once a Quarter they had a Miſers Feaſt; but to ſave Charges they us'd to Beg their *Veniſon* of ſome Great Man; Cheat the Keeper of his Fees; make their Country Tenants ſend them Fowls and Bacon; and engage the Maſter of the Houſe to give them the Dreſſing, that they might Stuff their Guts at no other Expence than of Bread and Wine; and go Home afterwards without Curſing their Mouths for impoſing upon their Pockets. Backward Tenants, and high Taxes, were the greateſt of their Grievances; but good Security, and large Intereſt, were the beloved Quarries, that the Avaritious Hawks were always ready to fly at: Extravagancy they accounted the very Sin againſt the Holy Ghoſt, and nothing was approv'd a more commendable Vertue than exceſſive Covetouſneſs: A News-Paper Entertainment, and a Sober Diſh of Coffee, were
thought

thought a liberal Treat for a punctual Debtor, upon the payment of a fum, tho' with unreafonable Extortion: And, *How d'ye Coufin? I am glad to fee you*, was the utmoft Hofpitality that ever was found in their Houfes, by a poor Relation. One would highly commend the Frugality of the Man that built him a new Barn out of the fcrapings of his Cheefe. Another would applaud the Good-Husbandry of the Farmer, who never wore any other Clothes than what was made of the Wooll that he pick'd off the Hedges. A Third, would extol the Prudence of the Citizen, who kept a Load of Faggots in his Houfe, to warm his Servants in cold Weather, by handing them up-ftairs and down, between the Garret and the Cellar. One would be wrap'd up in an old Kerfy-Coat, made feven Years before, by fome old purblind Botcher, to prevent the terrible Surprife of Canvas, Stay-Tape, and Buckrum, thofe abominable Articles of a Taylor's Bill. Another, with a particolour'd Wig on, fifty times more fcandalous than a *Welch* Attorneys, which is commonly made of a difagrecable Mixture, of Goats-Beards, Cows-Tails, Horfes Manes, with a fmall addition of his Wives Hair, and, perhaps, his Daughters. A Third, with a patch'd Coat on, that had been firft made by fome of his Anceftors, and worn down to the third or fourth Generation, till Age had given it fuch a greafy Glofs, that a Loufe could not crawl up the polifh'd Camlet, without endangering

his

his Neck, for want of fure Footing. A Fourth, with his Noddle cover'd with an Old flaping *Oliverian* Cafter, that has coft him near as much in new Vamping, at two-pence a time, as would have Cap'd a Regiment, yet could not frame a Heart to part with fo much Money at once, as would buy a New one, for fear he fhould pine himfelf, afterwards, into a Fit of Sicknefs, or punifh his Inteftines with the Twifting of the Guts, by Starving his Body to fetch the Sum up again. A Fifth, diftinguifh'd as a Gentlemen by a little Rufty old Rapier, that might be gueft, by its Antiquity, to have been kept in the Family, as a badge of Honour, ever fince the time of *Robinhood,* or the blind Beg-gar of *Bethnal-Green.* A Sixth, with his fpin-dle Shanks in a pair of courfe Yarn Stockins, almoft Darn'd as much as the good Hufsif's Hofe in the Library at *Oxford,* which has not enough left of the firft Knitting, to fhew its Original Contexture. A Seventh, with a Pair of pink'd Shoes on, for the eafe of his Corns, that look'd as if they had been as often at the Coblers, as ever the Owner had been at Church, or Coffee-Houfe. Thus every one was fo fin-gular in fome or other of their Habiliments, that their covetous Difpofitions were as vifible in their Dreffes, as in their meagre Counte-nances, who made up fuch a Starv'd Society of poor Macerated Mortals, that had they all to have been open'd, it would certainly have puz-zled a good Anatomift to have found one Ounce

of

of Fat among the whole Carrionly Affembly : For all that their Lean Carcaffes were capable of performing, were juft to Live and Move, and the principal fatisfaction they enjoy'd in their Minds, were to be Rich and Covetous. For tho' once a Week they were fo far infpir'd with the Spirit of Generofity, as each to lavifh an Extravagant Six-pence in fuch a Bug-bear place, as a Spendthrift Tavern ; yet they fumbl'd out the trifle, with fuch a miferly Regret, as if they Curs'd their Guts for depriving their Pockets, tho' of fo niggardly an Allowance. If there happen'd to be an odd Penny in the Reckoning, above their ufual Club, for Grey-Pees, or any other extraordinary; rather than any four would lay down their Farthings, and let the reft go Scot-free, a Farthing a Head was Collected round the Company, and the over-plus laid out in Writing-Paper, which Doctor *Hook*, the Mathematician, moft equally divided by Scale and Compafs, among the whole Society, that to keep the Ballance of Equity in a true Poife, every one might have a Slip according to his proportion ; for which exact method in the Diftribution of Juftice, they were Honour'd with the Title of *The Split-Farthing Club.*

Tho' Money is the root of Evil,
And leads fo many to the Devil,
Who do what's Infamous to get it,
And rend whole Kingdoms to come at it ;

Yet

Yet when by Fortune they have gain'd,
More Wealth than they know how to spend,
'Tis strange they still should Rob the Spittle,
To heap up what they use so little:
But yet we see that cursed Itch,
Of growing so profusely Rich,
Infects the most of Humane Race,
And makes the greater number Base:
The Lord, the Trader, and the Peasant,
Are all Corrupted with a spice on't:
The very Priests, that rail at Gold,
And those that lend for double fold,
Cannot forbear to hug the Darling,
But Hoard it with its Brother Sterling,
Persue, Improve it, and Adore it,
Nay, even Preach against it for it.

So the pert Damsel, fair of Feature,
To cover her Intrigues the better,
Will rail at Strumpets, when she knows
That she herself is one of those.

Therefore, since all are Money Lovers,
From Heroes down to Smithfield *Drovers;*
And most turn Knaves, when once they see,
A gainful Opportunity,

Why

Why should the Miser be so blam'd,
And for his large Extortion Damn'd,
Since all Men who have rais'd their Fortune,
By subtile Frauds behind the Curtain,
When once they're Rich, they grow Morose,
Proud, Cruel, Base, and Covetous?

So Statesmen that surround a Throne,
When once too Rich and Wealthy grown,
The greater Pow'r they still possess,
The more they Injure and Oppress:
Which plainly shews, that all Men wou'd
Be haughty Tyrants if they cou'd.

CHAP.

CHAP. XI.

Of the Club of Broken SHOPKEEPERS.

THIS Unfortunate Society is now held at the Sign of *Tumble-down-Dick*, a famous Boofing-Ken, within the dirty Confines of that Pious Sanctuary, call'd, *The Mint*, where Knaves, Sots, and Fools, as well as such unhappy Bankrupts who deferve Pity, find a fafe Retirement from the Revenge and Malice of their unmerciful Creditors, and whether many fly (like Fifh, out of the Frying-Pan into the Fire) from leffer Troubles into greater Miferies, and are foon taught to lavifh away their fmall Remains in fmoaky Holes, and lewd Company, till many, who are fkill'd in Bufinefs, and have liv'd Comfortably, and might ftill be Happy, would they take right Meafures whilft they have fomething in their power, are deluded into a ruinous Extravagance, that renders them, in a little time, fit only to nibble upon a Brown-George in fome foreign Garrifon, and, for a Groat a Day, to ftand the fhock of Cannon-Ball and Mufket-Bullet.

When

When the Guzzling Society aforemention'd,
are met in a Body, at their smoaky Rendes-
vouz, their chief Business is to wash away all
sense of their present Misfortunes; to damn
their Creditors, drink confusion to Bailiffs; and
to excuse their own Misconduct, by charging
their Ruin upon the extravagancy of their
Wives; the infidelity of their Servants; the
injustice of their Relations, or the hardships
put upon 'em by the Fraudulent Contrivances
of those they have Dealt with; but not a word
of their own Negligence; of their expensive
Pleasures; of their Tavern Revels; or their
profuse keeping both Whores and Horses;
Their Gaming, Racing, Sotting, High-Living,
Spending and Lending; these are all bury'd in
Oblivion, or craftily conceal'd from their Brethren in Affliction, that they may move one
another to a mutual Compassion, by the fictitious Severities which they pretend to have
met with, from such Persons whom they have
justly Provok'd, by their own Follies and Kna-
veries, to become their Enemies.

So Wanton Wives that prove unjust,
To satiate their unbridled Lust,
Find always something to excuse
The shameful Liberties they use,
And on their Spouses Failings charge,
The reasons why they Love at large:

Thus

Thus do their Husbands double Wrong,
Not only with the Tail, but Tongue;
And to extenuate their Shame,
Make those they Injure bear the Blame.

Among this promiscuous Assembly of Broken
Extravagants, one Slovenly Sot should sit puffing at the Board, in his Woollen Night-Cap,
so disguis'd with Dirt, and his Hands and Face
so grim'd with Naftinefs, that he look'd like
the Cook of a *New-Caftle* Collier, just step't on
Shore to enter an Action against the Master for
his Wages. A Second, in his Slip-shoes, and
Ungarter'd Stockins, like a Journeyman Taylor jump'd off the Shop-board for a Half-penny Roll and a Pint of Two-penny Stichback.
A Third, with a Carrotty Wig matted into
Elf-Locks, like the Mane of a Grafs-Horfe,
ridden by the Night-Mare, and all to fave the
trouble of combing the entangl'd Scare-Crow
once in a Week, thro' his averfion to Clean-
linefs, or, that for feven Years, he had made
the fweaty Mop do him the fervice of a Night-
cap. A Fourth, with his own Natural Rats-
Tails hanging by the fides of his Cheeks, twifted into greafy Ropes, that divided about his
Ears, like a Tag'd Knot upon a Footman's fhoul-
dier. A Fifth, with a Belly like a Church-
Warden of St. *Giles*'s Parifh, and a pair of pou-
ting Cheeks, puff'd up with fwallowing full
Winchefters

Winchesters at a Draught, till they were grown as unfizable as the fwanking Buttocks of a *Wapping* Hoftefs. A Sixth, without a Neckcloth, to fhew the unbutton'd Collar of a dirty Shirt, that was as Black and as Sweaty, as if the Beaft that wore it had taken an Oath of Abjuration againft Sope and Water. A Seventh, with Blood-fhot Eyes, and a Sottifh Countenance, whofe fodden Face look'd as if his Head had been ftew'd in hot Ale, or coddl'd in burnt Brandy. An Eighth, fcuer'd up in an old Freez Coat, whofe Buttons had flip'd fhell by long Thumbing, and his Noddle cover'd with a nòch'd Hat, like a Butchers Slaughter-Man's running Poft to the *Bear-Garden*. A Ninth, with a Vulturian Phiz, like a *Newgate* Solicitor's, adorn'd with powder'd Carrots, that look'd as if they were part of the Hangman's Fees the foregoing Seffions, much Honour'd by the reft, for his pretended knowledge in Law Quirks and Quiddities. A Tenth, who had Grace enough to work for his Living, and to keep his Family from the Parifh, with his Hands and Face as white as a Plaifterers, being juft ftep'd to a game at All-Fours from his pafting of Band-Boxes. Thus mix'd together, they us'd to fit over their Cards and their Liquor, Drinking, Rattling, and Swearing, like a crew of Buccaneers between Decks Gaming in Fair-Weather.

When ever a frefh Bankrupt, with the remains of his Stock, happens, by the Wheel of

H   ill

ill Fortune, to be tofs'd into their Territories, he is as heartily welcome into the Avery of Cormorants, as a brawny Caft-away *Dutch* Skipper, that fwims a fhoar upon a Wrack, is to a hungry crew of *Florida* Canibals; for e-very Old Stander, as long as their New Bro-ther can command a Groat, will ftick as clofe to him as a Horfe-Leach, till they have fuck'd him into a Level with their own Circumftan-ces; and by that time he'll have learnt to be as Sharp as themfelves, when his Five Shillings in the Pound is reduc'd to lefs than a Penny in the Hundred. When they were thus met, as foon as their crazy Noddles were a little warm'd by the narcottick Fumes of nafty Sot-Weed, ftinking Malt-Spirits, and large Drop-fical Go-downs of Mild and Stale, a broken Victualler would begin to rave againft the Rogue his Brewer, for Cheating him in bad Drink, and worfe Meafure. A Crack'd Coffee-Man would be curfing his Lafcivious Wife, and fwearing that fhe Ruin'd him by Treating her Sparks with *Nectar and Ambrocia, Ufque-baugh,* and Dr. *Stephens*'s Water. A half-witted Vintner, who was a good Servant, but a bad Mafter, would be damning his Wine-Merchant, for firft putting him into a Houfe, where he had bury'd all that he had fav'd in the time of his Service, and then for throwing him out of it to Lett it to another for a better Advantage. A Lady's Taylor would be railing againft his Mercer, and confounding of Qua-

lity,

lity, the firſt for Seizing all with an Execution,
and the latter, for their low Curſies, large Pro-
miſes, good Words, but bad Payments. A
Leaden-Hall Butcher would be Bitching his
Wife, for not only opening her Placket, but
her Pocket-Apron to his rogue of a Journeyman, and expenſively Treating the young
ſtrong-Back'd Raſcal at the *Ship-Tavern*, whilſt
himſelf was Entering his Puppy at the *Bear-
Garden*. A broken Goldſmith would be ſpit-
ting his Venom at *Mercers-Chappel*, and ſwear-
ing, That the Bank was a worſe Grievance than
the multitude of Lawyers, or a Standing Army.
A giddy young Draper would be railing at the
Play-Houſe; ſpeaking bitter words againſt
Maſk'd Ladies; and, biting his Thumb-Nails,
would ſit damning the Dice as bad as a young
Whore does the Society of Reformation. A
rattle-Headed Baker, no more Mealy-Mouth'd
than the reſt of the Society, to ſhew the Cruſ-
tineſs of his Temper, would throw out whole
Batches of hard-bak'd Words againſt my Lord
Mayor's Officers, for taking away Light-Bread,
and carrying it home to their own Houſes, inſtead of ſending it to *Ludgate* Priſon, or the
Counters. A decay'd Merchant would be
muttering at the Fury of the raging Seas, and
tempeſtuous Winds; and damning the *Cuſtom-
Houſe* Officers, as a Pack of Rogues, for ſeizing
Run Goods, that would otherwiſe have come
in the Nick of Time to a rare Market. An
avaritious Brewer, who had undone himſelf by

H 2　　　　　Concealments,

Concealments, would affirm, that the Officers
belonging to the *Excise* were as bad Rogues as
Informing Conftables; that the Commiffioners
were worfe Tyrants than the *French* King;
and that the whole Office was a more intollerable Grievance than the *Spanifh* Inquifition.
An unfortunate Bookfeller, who had unhappily been Crufh'd between bad Plays, and worfe
Sermons, would, with great Warmth, fit venting
his Spleen againft Modern Authors, and flinging out as many Invectives againft *Harry Hills*,
and the reft of the Pyrates, as if they had given him caufe to think 'em worfe Rogues
than thofe that were hang'd laft Seffions. A
Litigious Tallyman, undone by trufting of
Whores, implying Bailifts, and feeing Attorneys, would fit raving fo profufely againft the
Law and the Lawyers, as if he thought *Weft-
minfter-Hall* a more fatal Lottery than the
Royal-Oak. Others, more merry under the
Hand of Affliction, would be making a Jeft of
their feveral Misfortunes, as if, like *Diogenes,*
they had learn'd to defpife all that was truly
Comfortable, and to place the Happinefs of hu-
mane Life in Rags, Poverty, and Naftinefs.
Thus would they fit, fome Raving, fome
Muttering, fome Laughing, and others Gaming, till very Drunk and Drowfy, and then
they would reel Home to their dirty Rooms,
fheetlefs Beds, and fpaul'd Garrets, to feed the
Fleas, as well as worfe Vermin, till the next
Morning, without Scratching: But as foon as
they

they Awake they are ferreted up from their Flock Beds of little Eafe, that thofe who have Money may return to the Ale-Houfe for warm Purl, and thofe that have none, either Spunge upon the reft, or undergo the Pennance of a Day's Work to provide againft to Morrow.

Who would not rather chufe to ferve
His Country, than to Live and Starve,
Confin'd to fuch an odious Place,
Where Nothing profpers but Difgrace ?
If Dirt, and Want of Liberty,
Bad Liquor, and worfe Company,
A forry, bafe, unactive Life,
The Taunts of each proud Tapfter's Wife,
Damn'd ftinking Air, and miry Streets,
Bugs, loufy Rags, and nafty Sheets,
Are Comforts that can eafe the Weight
Of thofe that prove Unfortunate,
Then well might Debtors fly the Teafe
Of Bus'nefs, to enjoy their Eafe :
And fond of fuch a happy Place,
There fot and dream away their Days ;
But fince they're fure to meet the Curfe
Of making their Misfortunes worfe,
By fpending firft their fmall Remains,
Then Starving thro' Neglect of Pains,

H 3 *Till*

Till by an idle Habit made
Unfit for Labour, or for Trade,
Defigning, Treacherous, and Unjuft,
Too Knavifh for the World to truft ;
Fit only to frequent an Ale-Houfe,
Or do Things worthy of a Gallows ;
By Foes defpis'd, by Friends forfaken,
In dread of b'ing furpriz'd and taken,
That a clofe ftarving Goal may be
The End of all their Mifery.
Who then, that is not quite bereft
Of Senfe, and to his Follies left,
When once he finds Himfelf decline,
Would not his whole Remains refign
To thofe to whom he Owes the fame,
And fo preferve an Honeft fame,
Much rather than by Night to carry,
His Goods to fuch a Sanctuary,
And there o'er Ale in Clouds of Smoak,
Blown from their Pipes of Oronoke,
Sot away idly what they ought
To pay, and not conceal a Groat ?
But thofe who once have run aftray,
Still chufe fome ftrange Unlucky Way,
That leads them on to their Undoing,
As if predeftin'd to their Ruin.

C H A P.

CHAP. XII.

Of the MAN-HUNTERS *Club.*

PARCEL of wild young Rakes, whofe principal Education had been in *Chancery-Lane*, among thofe vertuous Accademies the fober Offices of the Law and Equity, frequenting a Tavern near the *Tennifcourt* Play-Houfe, on the back of *Lincolns-Inn-Fields*, at length fettl'd a Club there, that they might, every Evening, project new Extravagancies to Exercife the ungovernable Fury of their uncultivated Youth. Among the reft of their wild Maggots, and whimfical Contrivances, that they put in Practice, to entertain the Brutality of unpolifh'd Nature, they had form'd a New fort of Paftime, which was Hunting of Men over *Lincolns-Inn-Fields*, that they fhould happen to meet croffing at Ten or Eleven a Clock at Night, fo that about thofe Hours Two or Three couple of the Hair-brain'd Puppies us'd frequently to be commanded out by the Chair-Man, (to which

H 4

Hon-

Honourable Poſt the firſt Comer was Intitul'd)
who were to Beat about for Game, and to report, upon their Return, what Sport they had
met with, for the Diverſion of the Company.
When the Miſchievous Fools had thus ſhaken
off their Humanity, and taken upon 'em the Bea-
ſtial imitation of Hounds, Wolves, and Tygers,
they would lie Perdu upon the Graſs in one
of the Borders of the Fields, till they heard
ſome ſingle Perſon Treading along the Path-
way, then up they would all Start with their
Swords drawn, and running furiouſly towards
him, would cry, aloud, *That's he: Bloody-*
Wounds, that's he: Upon which, away would
run the Perſon, whether Gentle or Simple, as
if the Devil drove him, with the Pack of two
Leg'd Whelps making ſuch a Noiſe at his Heels,
that the Perſecuted Mortal, to eſcape the Fury
of his Followers, would ſpur on Nature, with his
Fear, to ſuch a violent ſpeed, that, with over-
ſtraining, the poor hunted Run-away, eſpecially
if a Coward, generally drop'd ſomething in his
Breeches that made him Stink as ſtrong as either *Fox* or *Pole-Cat.* Thus they ſcour'd him
along like a Buck in a Paddy-Courſe, till he
had taken Sanctuary in ſome of the adjacent
Streets, where he would run commonly into an
Ale-Houſe, half Dead with Fear, to recover
Breath, and to mundify his Breeches, and there
amuſe them with ſuch a terrible Story, as if
he had not only run, but fought the Gantlope
thro' a Regiment of Ruffians, and bravely Defended

fended himself, by his Hands, as well as Heels, from a Gang of Rogues, or a Drunken Company of Madmen. If they happen'd to bolt upon a sturdy Gentleman, that would rather chuse to Die in the Bed of Honour, than to owe his Safety to a nimble pair of Heels, the Cowards would shear off; cry they were all mistaken; that it was not he: But who ever ran for it, they pursu'd as close as if they were fully resolv'd both upon Robbery and Murder, that their *Game* being terrify'd with dreadful Apprehensions, would scour o'er the Field like an Insolvent Debtor before a Herd of Bailiffs, or a New Marry'd Seamen from a Gang of Pressmasters. And when the Rakehelly Hunters had thus delighted themselves with the mad Recreation of three or four such Chases, then tir'd with their Sport, they would return to the Club, and Entertain their Associates with the Particulars of their Pastime.

How *Wild is Youth? How Wicked and Pro-*
    [*phane,*
When Savage Nature only Governs Man?
And Unreform'd by Education, Steers
The two Leg'd Monster, in his Greener Years,
How Base to others? To 'imself Unjust;
Mad in his Cups, and Daring in his Lust;
Bold, Stubborn, Haughty, Insolent and Pert,
Slighting to Age, and Scoffing to Desert:

Wife

Wife in Opinion, Handfome in Conceit;
Rafh in his Judgment, Foolifh in his Wit;
Void of all Care, and Deftitute of Grace,
Vain in his Air, Fantaftick in his Drefs.
In Talk Contentious, when Provok'd a Bear,
Fickle in Love, a Tyrant to the Fair.
Hot in Perfuit of all his fond Defires,
Makes vig'rous Onfets, tho' he quickly Tires:
Efteems no Merit, but the Worth that dwells
In fome Fencers Hands, or Dancers Heels:
In Night Adventures does his Courage fhew,
And fticks at nothing that a Rake can do:
Kicks Whores, breaks Windows, Bullies where
                              [*he may*,
Revels all Night, and Dozes half the Day:
Glories in all his Madnefs, to his Shame,
Till Age, Pox, Want, or Wedlock, makes him Tame.

So the young fiery Colt, not Broke in Time,
Continues Headftrong, till he's paft his Prime:
A Thoufand wanton jadifh Tricks will play,
Start from the Track, and Plow the Miry Way,
Rend his ftrong Harnefs, from his Traces fly,
And with exalted Heels the Whip defy:
No Load behind his ftrenuous Shoulders take,
No Rider bear, or Saddle on his Back:

But

But Young and Pamper'd will the Thong despise,
And on' his hinder Feet in Triumph rise;
Till Poverty and Age his Vigour waste,
Stiffen his Limbs, and Tame the Vitious Beast:
Yet still, by fits and starts, he'll Jadish be,
Tho' Patient grown thro' meer Necessity.

So headstrong Man, that Rakes away his Youth,
Undisciplin'd in Vertue and in Truth,
Tho' Age Reforms him, yet he still retains,
Some tincture of his Lusts, whilst Life remains.

When this Juvenile Society of mad Libertines had, by Vertue of the Bottle, given a further Spur to their wicked Dispositions, which were before unbridl'd: Then a fulsome Repetition of all their bawdy Obsceneties, lushious Intrigues, drunken Rencounters, and amorous Adventures, were their principal Diversions, that they might vie Wickedness with one another, and vallue themselves the more upon those monstrous Inhumanities, which were infamously Scandalous, as if the Rakes had a Notion that their Reputations ought to be measur'd by the daringness of their Sins, and the number of their Vices. One would pluck out an Alphabetical Pocket-Book, where he had Register'd the Names of all the Loose Ladies that ever had oblig'd him, since his first
knowledge

knowledge of the pleafing difference between a Womans Honour and a Cart-Wheel, having fairly enter'd his whole Catalogue of Punks from Madam *Althea* down to Oyfter *Moll*; which was chiefly Read that the Company might make their merry Obfervation, how the A's and the M's were more flourifhing Letters than all the reft of the Alphabet. Another would be plucking out a *Tortoife* Shell Patch-Box, full of divers colour'd Reliques, that had been faithfully collected from the fublunary Banks of the feveral deep Water-Courfes, wherein he had been Dabbling; pretending to difcover the fundry Difpofitions of his many Miftreffes, by the different Crookednefs of each irregular Fangle he had Clandeftinely taken from their Cornigerous Premifes. A Third would be boafting how many Fans, Mafks, Rings, Pendants, and Necklaces, he had brought off as Trophies of the many Victories he had Valliantly obtain'd over his Punks and Paramours, and how he us'd to Rifle his old Caft-offs of their Sinful Ornaments, to fet up a new Face that better deferv'd them, and as foon as tir'd would ferve her the fame Sauce to add frefh Charms to her next Succeffor. A Fourth would be vaunting of his Drunken Conquefts; how many Bottles he had guzzled at a Sitting, and what inebrious Victims he had knock'd down with Bumpers into their own Spew. A Fifth would be magnifying his own ready Wit, in Oftentatioufly telling how he had Banter'd a Parfon

out

out of all his Divinity; a Stanch Puritan out of his Primitive Holiness; and prattl'd a pritty young Quaker out of her starch'd Virginity. A Sixth would be rattling of his Claps and his Doctors, and declare himself Father of as many Bastards as ever *Solomon* had Concubines, notwithstanding he had taken as many of *Saffold's* Pills as would have furnish'd a Mountebank for a Journey to *Portsmouth,* upon the arrival of the Fleet, when Salt-Beef, and Salt-Bitches had made one half of the Seamen Sick of the Pox, and the other of the Scurvey. Thus every one would endeavour to be as wickedly Diverting as his Tutor, Old Nick, and his own apt Genious would give him leave, till they were Drunk, and Mad enough to Strole from the Tavern into the Streets at Midnight, and then Hey-boys for scowring the Watch, battering their Lanthorns, knocking up their Whores, breaking Bawdy-House Windows, or any other Mischief that happen'd in their way, if it was but agreeable to that whimsical Rudeness which the Wine and the Devil had mutually infus'd into their crazy Noddles.

After this frantick manner they carry'd on their Revels for some Time, till some of the Hunters, meeting with their Match, happen'd to be kill'd in the Chase. Others drivling away their Lives into close Stools and spitting Pots; and the Army and the Navy robbing the Gallows of the rest. So that the

Club

Club broke firſt, and the Tavern ſoon afterwards; and thus the Town got purg'd of ſo infamous a Crew, who were only fit Inhabitants
for ſuch a frantick Nation where Piety is held a
Crime; Swearing an Accompliſhment; and
Drunkenneſs a Virtue; and where the Men
are all Mad, and the Women common Strumpets.

'Tis ſtrange a Chriſtian Country, where
The Laws ſo good and wholſome are,
Where Learning has for Ages flouriſh'd,
And e'ery uſeful Art been nouriſh'd;
Where Virtue, Piety, and Grace,
Are rooted deep, and ſpring apace;
Where true Religion does confound,
And ſtrike bold Atheiſm to the Ground;
Where Juſtice, Honeſty, and Money,
O'erflow like Canaan's *Milk and Honey,*
That ſuch a Land ſhould ſhew a Race
Of Libertines ſo Lewd and Baſe,
'Tis wonderful; but yet we know,
That Tares among the Corn will grow:
Nor can the beſt of Soils be freed
From yielding here and there a Weed:
The cleaneſt Garden ne'er was found
Without ſome Vermin in the Ground:

Where

Where the most noble Fruits are planted,
The Trees will be by Maggots haunted;
So in that Country, Town or Place,
That happens to abound in Grace,
Old Nick will raise his wicked Plants,
To vex and scandalize the Saints.

Therefore, altho' we find a Brood
Of Wicked Sons among the Good,
E'en let's suspend our Admiration,
Till Heav'n has Prun'd our pious Nation.

CHAP.

CHAP. XIII.

Of the YORKSHIRE Club.

THIS Acute Society of Northern Tikes was held at one of their Countrymen's Houses in the Rounds in *Smithfield* upon every Market Day, that, by confulting one another, they might be the better able to exercife their Cunning in this Southern Air, and maintain that Character they have Juftly deferv'd from the Credulous Bubbles of this half-witted City, whofe unpolifh'd Cocknies play the Knave fo foolifhly, as if they had never travel'd farther North than *Barnet,* or St. *Albanes.* The moft flourifhing Members among the Razor mettled Blades of this Catch-Penny Society, were Needle-pointed Innkeepers; Nick and Froth Victuallers; honeft Horfe Courfers, and pious *Yorkfhire* Attorneys; the reft good harmlefs Mafter Hoftlers, who us'd to meafure their Oats with the Bottom of of the Peck upwards, and Two or three innocent Farriers, who had

worm'd

worm'd their Maſters out of their Shops, and
themſelves into their Buſineſs.   When they
were met together in their Room next the
Market, all Ground as ſharp as the Knives and
Siſars in a Cutler's Shop, Horſe-Fleſh, for certain, was the firſt Subject that was ſtarted in the
Company ; and blind Eyes, Spavins, Founders,
and Malanders, the never failing Concomitants
that were interwoven with their Diſcourſes.
One, perhaps, had an old Batter'd Jade ſtuff'd
up with hot Grains and Maſhes, curry'd up to
Cheat ſome *London* Shop-keeper that wants an
Out-ſide Beaſt to carry his Wife in Triumph
to *Dulledge-Wells* or *Epſom*, that his Horns
may be new tip'd againſt the next Winter.
Another furniſhes the Market with an old
Crippl'd Hunter, in Order to Cozen ſome Merchant's prodigal Apprentice, that he may have
the Honour to halt after my Lord Mayor's
Hounds upon the uneaſy Back of his Two or
Three Leg'd Galloper, or Titup down to
Hackney-Marſh to loſe his Money like a Fool at
a Crimp-Horſe match.   A Third, it may be,
has a Boy-Rider upon a dimſighted Pony, a
little higher than a Bear-Dog, hoping that her
eaſy Amble may tempt ſome young Citizen to
buy the pretty Creature for the uſe of his
Miſtreſs, that he may carry ſome little Crack
out of *Exchange-Alley* to ſee *Windſor-Caſtle*,
without Galling the Premiſes, that ſhe need
not be ſhy of imparting her Favours, for fear
the Pain ſhould be greater than the Pleaſure.

I   A

A Fourth, with a poor Shoulder flip'd, or broken winded Hack, juft fet upon his Legs, for the Market Day, by a little Northern Horfe-Doctorfhip, that fome Cockney Ale-Houfe-Keeper, who lets out dull Jades for fifteen pence a Side, may be Cozen'd out of three or four Pounds of his Brewers Money. A Fifth, with a blundering fat Gelding, between a Coach and a Saddle, with a Dutch Dock, and Buttocks near as ftrong as an Elephant's, in Order to cheat fome of her Majefty's new Captains, by felling him into the Service. A Sixth, perhaps, with an odd pacing Coach-Horfe, of a Sorrel Colour, fit for the little Grave Chariot of any Phyfician that can match him; or for a Rope Dancer to ride upon after a Travelling Mountebank. A Seventh, with a Finikin Pad, under the Size of fourteen Hands, as merry as a young Midwife, yet as gentle as an old Cuckold, fit for any Court Leacher to prefent to a kept Miftrefs. Thus every one turns Jockey in fome Meafure or other; and feldom fail, upon their Club Day, to have their Scrubs, Jades, and Hobbies, fcowring round the Market; and when the Rider brings a Chap, tho' the batter'd Beaft has as many Faults as a rigid Fanatick is able to find in the Church Liturgy, and is fcarce fo found as an over-ridden Strumpet, yet the friendly Society are fo ready to fwear one for another, that they'll warrant a lame Horfe to have as found Limbs as ever ran upon *New-Market Heath*; and a
blind

blind Jade to have as goood Eyes as Sir *William Read,* the Oculift. When they difcover at the Window, where they fit upon the Watch, any likely Bubble hankering about any of their Tits, then down fteps a Member, and, to raife the Price, takes a wonderful liking to the fame Beaft, bids more than he is worth before the others Face, on purpofe to fpur on the Chap, and to make him the more fond of being confoundedly cheated, for as certain as he deals with a *Yorkfhire* Jockey, if he wants Judgment, and puts his Confidence in the Honefty of the Tike, he need not doubt of having fufficient Caufe to curfe his Bargain, and to blame himfelf for a Fool as much as the other for a Knave.

When the Bufinefs of the Day is pretty well over, and every cunning Member has top'd his Jade upon fome Bubble or other; and thofe who wanted, have furnifh'd their Stables, by Tricking and Swopping, with better Horfe-Flefh than what they've parted with, then the *Yorkfhire* Stingo is pufh'd Brifkly about, and every one, o'er his Cups, begins to merrily Expatiate upon the *Windgales* and Infirmities of the feveral dull Animals they have fo luckily difpos'd of, and feem equally pleas'd that they had brought their Horfes inftead of their Hogs to fo good a Market, till at length, the Liquor getting into their Noddles makes them change their Difcourfe, and then, like Whores at a Buttock Ball, they begin to vie honefty one with another, as if they thought it a Scandal to their Country to have a Knave amongſt them; now, the Healths of my Lord *Sharp* of *Hallifax,* Sir *Thomas Notable* of *Auldborough,* and the worthy Eſquire *Quickwit,* of *Skipton* upon *Craven,* and the reſt of the honeſt Gentlemen in all the Ridings in *Yorkſhire,* are bowl'd about the Company, till their tan'd Faces begin to look of a ruſty red, like their *Martlemas* Hung-Beef, or their worſe *Bacon:* Then they begin to rattle and fall foul upon one anothers Pedigrees, and, after a bantering Manner, to upbraid their own Brethren with their Pack-Horſe Journies, and Pennileſs long Walks out of a ſharp Air into a thriving Climate. *Marry,* crys one to his next Brother, *you have Thriven well, to riſe from Liquoring Carriers dirty Boots, to be the proud Landlord of the beſt Inn in* Smithfield. *Marry, that's nought,* replies the angry Hoſt, *I did not rob my Father of his Bridle, my Uncle of his Boots, and my Brother of his Spurs, and then ſteal a Horſe from my next Neighbour, to bring me to* London, *there ſell him for Money to buy a clean Shirt, a new Frock, and a Stable Broom to ſweep an Inn Yard for fat Scraps and the Bottoms of Muggs, till you got in to be the Hoſtler, and from thence rais'd your ſelf, by ſtealing of Oats, till you were able to lay down the Dung-Fork and Curry-Comb and to make your ſelf Maſter of a topping Victualing-Houſe.* By the Maſs, crys, a fat Attorney to a Weather-beaten Horſe-Courſer, *Times are well amended with you, ſince your Mother us'd to send you to Mr.* Frampton's *Stables to pick the Oats out of the Horse-Dung to make Oatmeal-Puddings for your Father against he came Home from Sheep-Stealing. Marry hang you,* replies the Jockey, *How many Times has your Mother sent you, when a little snivling Bastard, to pick the Wooll off other Peoples Hedges for your Sister to knit Nightcaps of for the old Cuckold your Father?* Thus, when in their Cups, they sit bantering one another, between Jest and Earnest, till, with much Talk, and much Liquor, their Tongues and their Legs, but not their Cunning, begin to fail 'em; then away reels a Horse-Courser in his Iron-Grey Coat and flapping Hat, with his long Switch, disguis'd on purpose like a Country Put, the better to play his Knaves Tricks the more unsuspected upon the Market-Day; after him an Attorney in his Weather-beaten Wig, with his Tun-Belly hoop'd round with a Horseman's Belt, for fear the Weight of his Guts should break the Wastband of his Breeches, after him a fustian Frock'd Ale-House-keeper, with a freckl'd Face like a *Scotch* Pedlar, very Prim about the Noddle, with his best Hat upon his flaxen Bob, but his Coat a little discredited behind with the Mark of his Apron-Strings, which leave a Seam in his Back as if he had been cut in two and afterwards stitch'd together again; next him an Inn-keeper in his Plate-button'd Sute, with his Trumpeters Cheeks, and *Flemish* Buttocks, giving Preceden-

I 3   *(y*

cy to the Victualler, becauſe Church-Warden
of his Pariſh; next him a luſty Maſter Hoſtler
in his Fur Cap, his own lank Hair, and a
white Apron, to which an Hoſtler, tho' he
frequently wears one, has but little Title, except he deſigns it for a Muckender to wipe the
driveling Noſtrils of his Glander'd Horſes;
after theſe a ſweaty Crew of Tag Rag and Bob-
Tail, who, as yet, have not had the lucky Opportunity of Feathering their Neſts, and are
therefore forc'd, upon all Occaſions, to Lye and
Swear for the reſt of their Countrymen, till
they can better their Fortunes, and do the
ſame for themſelves to their own peculiar Advantage. Thus when their Bellies are full, they
all blunder down Stairs, from the rich proſ-
perous Knave, to the poor clouted Underſtrap-
per, and without Side the Groundſel mutually
take Leave of one another, and ſo ſtagger Home
to their Inns, Bars, and Stables, to exerciſe
their Cunning till their next merry Meeting.

Thus ſome from Cart, and ſome from Plough,
And ſome from Living God knows how,
Wrap'd up in ſhrinking Cloth to hide,
And keep their Knavery warm beſide,
With brawny Buttocks, cas'd with Leather,
And Latchets Ty'd with Thongs together,
Fly from their Northern hungry Air,
To quit Oat-Bread *for better Fare.*

As

As Rooks *forsake the barren Ground,*
For Fields where standing Corn is found,
Or from the Hills their Wings expand,
To Tresspass on the new Sown Land,
So Northern Tikes, to shew their Wit,
Their Native Ægypt gladly quit,
For happy Canaan*'s Milk and Honey,*
Or what's as good; that is our Money,

Some on exalted Runlets Ride
To Town, as Bacchus *does, astride,*
And sit a Story high, at least,
Above the Carrier's groaning Beast;
So those who leave their Dearest Friends,
To Cross the Main for noble Ends,
Mounted on Quarter Deck they stand,
In Triumph quit their Native Land.

Some Tikes on Gennets make their Way,
Borrow'd, by Night, from Grass or Hay;
And when in London, *where unknown,*
One Brute sells t'other as his own;
And thus each Riders Horse or Mare,
The Charges of the Journey bear;
So Men, tho' press'd to leave the Nation,
Are forc'd to pay their Transportation;

And

And Ladies, when their Beaus beſtride 'em,
Are glad to oft Treat thoſe that Ride 'em.

 Others forſake their North Abodes,
To beat on Foot the Duſty Roads,
And, in their Journey, take the Pains
To pick up ſtragling Cocks and Hens :
But if their feather'd Friends deceive 'em,
Then humbly begging muſt relieve 'em,
Till tir'd, and then th' addreſs ſome Hoſt
To Grant an under Hoſtler's Poſt,
Where, if not hinder'd by Diſaſters,
They riſe Gradatim *till they're Maſters :*
So cunning Courtiers oft ſupplant
Others by Fraud, whoſe Power they want,
Then, Haughty grown, they Lord it o'er
Thoſe Perſons they Obey'd before.

C H A P.

CHAP. XIV.

Of the MOCK-HEROES Club.

THIS Heroick Society of fantaſtical Bravadoes was held at a
Nipperkin Ale-Houſe in *Bald-
win*'s Gardens, and compos'd
chiefly of Attorney's Clerks,
and young Shop-keepers, whoſe
Juvenile Prodigality, ſuffering their Whimſical
Fancies to Soar above their Stations, had infected them with an Itch of being thought brave
Fellows, tho' an Angry old Woman, arm'd with
her Diſtaff, would have been able to have Cud-
gel'd the whole bluſtering Fraternity. To
make themſelves more ridiculous, their Evening Congreſs was kept in a publick Room, at
a ſelect Table, which was carefully reſerv'd by
their *Scotch* Landlord for the valliant Members
of this Heroick Club. Every young Rattle, upon
his firſt Admiſſion, being honour'd by the reſt
with the ſwelling Name of ſome Victorious
Cæſar,

Cæsar, or Great General; every one being oblig'd, under a certain Forfeiture, to falute each other by their feveral Appellations which they had thus prou'dly affum'd to fhew their ridiculous Vanity; and becaufe none fhould have the Honour to attend them but Knight Errants, Champions, and Men fingular for their Fortitude. The Mafter of the Houfe they Dub'd *Don Quixot*, and the Efquire, his Tapfter, they Nick-nam'd *Sancho Pancho*; fo that when the Sham-Heroes were met over their diminitive Pewterkins of Treacly Hogwafh, their very manner of calling to their valliant Attendance provok'd Laughter among all the Sitters-by, who were Independant of their Company: And when they Complemented one another in Kiffing the Edges of their Half-pint Tankards, and prefenting their humble Services to their Heroick Brethren. Each prodigal Member faluted his Brother General with fuch fingular formality, that they were a perfect Farce to the feveral Companies that fat at other Tables to obferve the motions of thefe Mock-Bravadoes. One would Face about to his Left Hand Neighbour, with his Right-Hand charg'd with a brimming Tankard, crying, *Moft Noble* Scipio, *the Love and Friendfhip of a Soldier to you. The Thanks of a Brother to my Valliant Friend* Hannibal, *whom I cannot but vallue, tho' I had the Honour to Conquer. Moft Victorious* Alexander, *my Service to you,* crys another, *Thank you, my moft generous Adverfary,* Darius, *whom I love, tho' I have Beaten,* replies the
Grecian

Grecian Heroe. *My Respect's to you, brave* Cæsar, crys his *Roman* Opposite, *remembering the Battle of* Pharsalia. *Thank you Noble* Pompey, replies the proud Conqueror, *I think I gave you enough in spite of all your Conduct.* Pyrrhus, *here's to you, crys his* Roman *Adversary, remembring the Cabbage. I was Cooking in my Tent, when you sent an Ass Laden with Gold to tempt me to betray my Army; and afterwards, like a poor Spirited Prince, sent your Phisician to Poyson me; but I was too cunning to be catch'd in spite of all your Stratagems. Thank you, honest* Fabricius, replies the *Grecian* General, *I confess you did Maul me that Bout: But I think you were ne'er the Wiser for refusing your share of the Spoils, when your Family was so Needy, that your Daughters Portions were forc'd to be paid out of the publick Treasure. No matter for that, crys the Crusty Heroe, I had more Honour by that Action than ever was won at* Blenheim. Thus they us'd to salute each other, and Confabulate as formerly; as if they had been so many Buskin'd Heroes belonging to the Play-House met together over their Ale, to rehearse a Tragedy, in order to be perfect against the succeeding Night, whilst the Sitters by, between their Blushes and their Laughter, were ready to let fly their Laxitive Ale at the lower-end, to hear the Folly and Vanity of the proud affected Worthies, whose unfledg'd Countenances made 'em more fit for the School-Boy Exercises of Trap-Ball and Prison-Base, than to form a

Society,

Society, especially of Heroes in a Publick *Derby* Ale-House, where a parcel of Grave old Sots meet to tell old Stories, and young Ones come to hear them.

Should the dead Worthies from the Grave arise,
Shake of their Rust, and ope their drowsy Eyes,
And find their Glories, by the Sword obtain'd,
Sully'd by Blockheads, and by Boys Prophan'd,
They'd rend their Buskins, and their Helmets tare,
Renounce their Shields, and Curse the Toils of
                                        [*War.*

No more with Blood manure the dusty Plain,
But gaze upon their Lawrels with disdain,
To see those valiant Actions they have done,
The Kingdoms they've Subdu'd, the Battles Won,
The beauteous Captives, and the wealthy Spoils,
They've brought from foreign Courts, and distant
                                        [*Isles,*

Now Ridicul'd by those, whose Callow Years
Have ne'er been dispossest of Boyish Fears,
But want e'en Courage to attack Loves Fort,
Which, when 'tis taken, yields such pleasing sport;
Tho' only Linnen Walls the Place secure,
And feeble Woman Guards the Joyful Door,
Unable both to stand against a Storm,
Made by a Gen'rous Foe, that's Bold and Warm.

Therefore

Therefore how Wild and Silly muſt it prove,
In thoſe who're Cowards in Attacks of Love,
And when, perhaps, Invited, fear to Draw
God Cupid's Sword, tho' back'd by Natures Law,
To thus expoſe the Characters and Names,
Sully the Lawrels, and Ecclipſe the Fames
Of Worthies Dead, whoſe Actions ought to be
The brave Examples of Poſterity.
But 'tis, alas, Youth's Vanity to think
Themſelves undaunted Heroes o'er their Drink,
And to conceit that they're as wiſe and brave
As thoſe whoſe Lawrels bloſſom in the Grave;
Tho' ſhould they once the duſty Plains behold,
Where Lives for little Pay are bought and ſold,
And where ſwift leaden Meſſengers of Fate,
Make no diſtinction 'twixt the Poor and Great,
They'd fly the Danger, ſtand a Diſtance off,
And Reverence that Valour now they Scoff;
Tremble to ſee the Brave their Ground maintain,
And Honour thoſe whoſe Names they now Pro-
                                    [phane.

So have I heard raſh Coxcombs ridicule,
This Gen'ral for a Coward, that a Fool;
And o'er their Ninny-Broth pretend to ſhew
How eas'ly Sweden may the Czar ſubdue:
                                    But

But would thefe Heroes ferve but one Campaign,
Beneath thofe Gen'rals they fo much condemn,
View their Fatigues and Conduct, they'd adore
Thofe valiant Leaders they reproach'd before.

No fooner had our buffoonary Heroes done
pleafing one another with their Battles of *Ca-*
nada and *Pharfalia*; their Sieges of *Troy, Ba-*
bylon and *Jerufalem*, with as much Arrogance
as if they had been the very defunct Worthies
rifen from their Graves, who had been real
Commanders in the former Expeditions, and
that they had made an Elopement from their
Subterranean Grotto's to remind the World of
all their paft Adventures; but our *Græcian* and
Roman Reprefentatives would be apt to forget
themfelves over their ftupifying Wort, and re-
volt from their Princely Characters after fo co
mical a Manner, that the mechanick Dolthead,
and the *Scribere cum Dafho*, would fhew themfelves in Spite of all their fantaftical Bravery,
and thundering counterfeit Diftinctions: So
that the Noble *Julius Cæfar*, when grown almoft Boozy with a Repetition of his Nipperkin,
would lay afide his Battles, and drop into a notable Story of robbing his Grandmother's Or-
thard, and what a devilifh Fall he had, Head
and Shoulders to the Ground, off the *Bergamy*
Pear-Tree; and how fadly he was whip'd
at School for hazarding his Neck fo foolifhly.
The

The Great *Hannibal*, to shew himself conformable, would betray his Courage at once, by declaring to the Company how sadly he was Beaten, when a great Boy, by an angry *Turky-Cock*. The famous *Roman Scipio*, forgetful of his Fortitude, would up with a lamentable Tale how terribly he was frighted by the Parson's Py'd Bull, in crossing the Church-Yard to fetch his Mother a Pennyworth of Doctor *Dumbleton*'s *Aqua Vitæ*. The unfortunate *Pyrrhus*, quite thoughtless of the Pantile that crack'd his Crown at *Argos*, would be shewing his Conduct in robbing Hen Roosts, and how he us'd to cheat the Weasel by sucking the Eggs. And honest *Fabricius*, having digested his Cabbages would dwindle from his Integrity, and divert his Brother Heroes with a tedious Story of his catching Ducks with long Lines and Fish-Hooks, baited with young Frogs, or bits of *Hackney* Turnips. Thus one half Hour they would be rattling of their Battles, Stratagems and Sieges, like victorious Generals, and then ramble out of their Heroick Rapsodies into their School-Boy Adventures, and the unlucky Transactions of their greener Years; and from thence into their Love Intrigues with their Mistresses Chamber-Maids, when they were Clerks and Apprentices, that they were as good a Farce, to the rest of the Customers, as ever was acted upon *Windmill-Hill* by Mrs. *Mims*'s sworn Comedians. And that the Reader may be diverted with a *Dramatis*

matis Perfonæ of the Fools in the Play, for their better Information I have here inferted it.

Cæsar quod Damnum, a young Attorney.
Julius Fondlepunk, a Student at Law.
Antonius Coppywell, a Counfellor's Clark.
Maximinus Midnight, a young Curfitor.
Hannibal Spattle, a pert Apothecary.
Fabricius Block, a Periwig-maker.
Scipio Fippery, a Millaner.
Augustus Thimble, a Taylor.
Alexander Bounce, a Fencing Mafter.
Pompey Rhomboides, a young Mathematician.
Darius Scribble-Tony, a writing Stationer.
Calligula Chantwell, a Singing Spunger.
Ninus Lackwit, a young extravagant Heir.
Valerius Drinkwater, a Hackney Writer.
Crook'd-back Richard, a deform'd Beaux.
Clarentius Blazon, a young Herald.

The firft Parts of their Names were moft honourably confer'd upon themfelves, by the whimfical Majority of their Heroick Affembly: But the other additional Diftinctions, were adapted by a Gentleman who frequented the Houfe, in Order to make their fantaftical Socie ty the more ridiculous: For they were not only fo vain and foolifh to nick Name one another, during the Time of their Club, but whenever they met, would falute each other in all Companies by their Heroick Titles, or if they came into the Houfe at any other Time one
would

would be asking at the Bar whether *Julius Cæsar* had been there to Day; another, for *Hannibal*, or *Scipio*; so that in a few Months their
Lordships, Excellencies, and Majesties, became
such publick Laughingstocks to all the other
Gentlemen who were accustom'd to the House;
that they were made the common Banter of
every jocular Fuddlecap, who had a Mind to
make himself merry over his Nipperkins of Ale:
So that some of the leading Generals of the
martial Community, taking it in great Dudgeon, that their magnanimous High and Mighti-
nesses should be made the Scoff of every boozy
Jack-a-dandy, withdrew themselves not only
from the rest of their Brother Heroes, but forsook the Place of their Rendesvous, to betake
themselves to a House, where the Company
that us'd it should know better, than to make
a Mock of Merit, or to disturb the Peace and
Serenity of such an August Assembly. So that
when the greatest *Cæsars* had once made their
Retreat, the lesser Bravadoes thought it no
Dishonour to their unspotted Valour to folllow
the wise Example of their disgruntl'd Leaders,
but turn'd their Arses in contempt, upon their
unmannerly Opposers, and bolted after one a-
nother, like a Flock of Sheep through a Hedge-
Gap after their daring Ram into better Pasture;
upon which a pleasant Gentleman who had
frequented the House, and observ'd their Motions, thought fit to honour the offended Worthies
with the following Farewel.

K   *And*

And have the Heroes *in disgust turn'd Tail*
Upon such gen'rous Belch, such noble Ale,
That thus inspir'd them in Conceit to be
Soldiers *and* Worthies *of the first Degree?*
Since, in such Dudgeon, they are thus remov'd
From pow'rful Ale, which they so dearly lov'd,
And think it a Dishonour here to quaff,
Because the Warriers *see us* Cowards *laugh,*
E'en let the Heroes *to their Homes retreat;*
For Fools will sneer, when such a Congress meet.
Mosco's *Great Czar, who visited our Isles,*
Altho' in Cog could not escape our Smiles,
But was the common Jest of all the Town,
Who laugh'd the more to see the Tyrant *frown;*
Became the Scoff of e'ery Lady Bright,
Down to the Punk *he kiss'd so oft one Night;*
Nor cou'd the fam'd Ben-Hamet's *Phiz escape*
The grinning Manners of our English *Frape;*
Or the Black Bantom *shew his frightful Face*
In London Streets, *or any publick Place,*
But he was scoff'd and flouted by a Herd
Of Vulcan's, *Sons with Crock and Colly sneer'd.*

Why, then, should our Heroick Worthies *shew*
Their Anger at our Smiles; but since they do,

Let Brave Quod Damnum *to his Desk retire,*
There write i'th' Cold six Hours without a Fire,
Till his dock'd Pen from his num'd Fingers falls,
And his warm Breath supplies the want of Coals.

Let the fam'd Julius Fondlepunk *decline*
His Studies, for his Fencers, Whores, and Wine;
Get drunk o'er Night among a Rakish Crew,
That little have to Say, and less to Do;
Then doze next Morning till some lustful Dame,
Pats with her Fan, to cool his amorous Flame.

Let great Antonius Copywell *be ty'd*
To ingross Joyntures for each weighty Bride;
And on the lushious Tails of wanton Jades
Tag Settlements, before their Beauty fades:
And less the Keeping Cully's Mind should change,
Or some new Face incline the Fool to range,
Nod o'er his Parchment Skins from Noon to Noon,
To scrape for Expedition when he'as done.

Let Maximinus Midnight *mind his Scrawls,*
And loosely scribble quaint Originals;
Cover his Desk with swarms of useless Writs,
Get Drunk by Starts, and Bus'ness mind by Fits;

From *Dice* to *Whoring, thence to Wine adjourn,*
And thus persue each modish Vice in Turn,
That the Rakes Office *may secure it's Fame,*
And to the last, support it's ancient Name.

Let Hannibal *his* Spattle *nimbly use,*
And Plasters spread for crippl'd Whores in Stews;
Mix nauseous Vomits, gilded Pills prepare,
To purge both Ends of the Distemper'd Fair,
And to extinguish those Venereal Flames,
Kindl'd in Rakes *by over-heated Dames,*
That his long Bill's more than the Pox, may fright
His Patients from repeating Loves Delight.

Let Scipio Fippery, *mew'd up behind*
His shining Compter, be each Day confin'd
To draw on Gloves, to hide the Bacon Skins
Of Whores, that ply among the neighb'ring Inns,
Who, with hard Shillings newly earn'd, supply
Themselves with Nicknacks to invite the Eye,
And for small Pay their reeking Charms expand,
That Scipio *may be Clap'd at second Hand.*

Let bold Fabricius Block *court Servant Maids,*
And sooth them till he mows their sweaty Heads;

Then

Then flight the bald Pates, put 'em paft all Hopes,
And Wooe fresh Laffes who abound with Crops ;
Mix with his Whores Hair, Horfes Manes & Tails,
With Beards of Goats in Sachels brought from
                             [*Wales,*
That Carrot Pates in Borrow'd Locks may fhine,
And Beaus by Beafts be made profufely fine.

   Let Prim Auguftus Thimble *drefs and flrut,*
That his own Cloths may fhew his Campaign Cut ;
Frequent old Greys-Inn *Walks, that Beaus and*
                             [*Wits*
May fee how well his modifh Garment fits ;
Draw in young Fools to give his Shears the Vogue,
Becaufe they fee himfelf fo trim and fmug ;
That when he nicely fits an am'rous Rake,
Or hides with Pads and Wods, a Saddle Back ;
The Cully'd Spendthrifts may, without Difpute,
Pay double Bills for each commodious Sute,
And in a little Time their Pockets drain,
To make their Taylor much the better Man:

   Let Alexander Bounce, *with blunted File,*
Teach Cowards to Defend, and how to Kill,
And make his Pupils think they're brave at Heart,
Becaufe they Pufh fo well in Ters and Cart ;

                                   Till

Till by affronting those they can't withstand,
They fall, at last, by some more fatal hand ;
Or leave St. Giles's Church upon the Right,
For pinking some poor Watchman in the Night.

Pompey Rhomboides, *let the Rattle Chalk*
His Figures down, and o'er his Angles Talk,
On Ale-House Tables shew the nearest Way
From the North-Foreland *into* Hudson's Bay ;
Compute the Leagues betwixt the distant Poles,
And fancy all that contradict him Fools ;
Measure, with Ease, the Circle of the Sun,
And tell you, to an Inch, what Miles he'as run :
But never let him more perplex his Brains,
With the sharp Battle on Pharsalia's *Plains.*

Let dull Darius Scribbletony *write*
For Men of Law, to be a Beggar by't,
Whilst sharp Attorneys swallow all the Gains,
And scarce well pay him for his Skins and Pens;
But at low Wages keep him still a Slave
To this dull Sot, and t'other crafty Knave.

Let poor Caligula Chantwell *repair*
To Windmill-Hill, *or to some Country Fair,*

There,

There, among ſtroling Players, ſtretch his Throat,
In an edg'd Hat, fine Sword, but Thread bare
[Coat;
For 'tis by far more Honour to commence
Stage Songſter, than to ſpunge for want of Pence.

Let Ninus Lackwit *wed a homely Bride,*
Fit for no Mortal but himſelf to ride;
But let it be alone his Care to chuſe
One that's as Saving as himſelf Profuſe,
Who with her crabbed Looks, and noiſy Tongue,
May fright his Whores, and ſcare his Hangers on:
Then, thro' her Conduct, he may chance to ſave
Enough to bear his Charges to the Grave:
But if he Single lives, and ſtill ſhould run
The Courſe he ſteers, he muſt be ſoon undone:
Or if he weds a Damſel that is Fair,
His Follies will inſtruct her how to Err,
Teach her ill Humours, and provoke the Shrew
To make him both a Buck and Beggar too.

Let ſtarv'd Valerius Aquapote *take Care*
To drudge in Term, and ſtroling Punks forbear;
Work late, Riſe early, Scribble on like Mad,
And loſe no Time whilſt Buſineſs may be had;
K 4 *And*

Learn to be saving of his scanty Coin,
And mount his Cock-Loft e'ery Night by Nine;
Then in a long Vacation he may be
Exempt from Duns, and from his Hardships free,
And oft'ner change the Pump within the Rail
In Chanc'ry-Lane for Fullwoods fatt'ning Ale.

Let Crook-Back'd Richard, *in a faithful Glass,*
Behold his homely Shapes and Monkey Face,
Strip off the Taylor's prodigal Disguise,
And view his Person with impartial Eyes ;
Then would the crooked Pigmy boast no more
Of this fine Lady, t'other charming Whore ;
Or tell, where e'er he comes, how much the Fair
Admire his Wit, his Humour, and his Air,
But rather, when a beauteous Face he sees,
Blush at his own ——outh Deformities,
And prize the gen'rous Lady of the Town,
That will comply to lay her Honour down,
To such a quaint Babboon for half a Crown.

Let pert Clarentius Blazon *study hard,*
To tell us why such Arms were first confer'd,
And strive to prove it worth a wise Man's while
To know what Bastard Dukes have grac'd our Isle,
                                           What

What Nobles have been Traytors to their Prince,
And how their Coats came blotted Ages since;
What mighty Heroes, and what honour'd Clans,
Have been the spurious Broods of Curtizans;
That when grown learn'd in such old Tales as
                                    [*these,*

And skill'd in Guillim's *Curiosities,*
Then to reward the Knowledge of his Brain,
The Fool may starve in Little Charter-Lane,

C H A P.

CHAP. XV.

Of the BEAUS *Club.*

THIS finikin Society, or Lady's Lap-Dog Club, is now kept at a certain Tavern near *Covent-Garden,* where every Afternoon the fantaſtical Idols, ſo much worſhip'd and admir'd by our female Beauties, aſſemble themſelves in a Body, to compare Dreſſes, invent new Faſhions, talk luſhious Bawdy, and drink Healths to their Miſtreſſes. At the upper End of their Club Room, which is always kept as clean as a young Counteſs's Bedchamber, there ſtands a ſide Table, which is conſtantly furniſh'd with a Dozen of Flannel Muckenders, decently folded up for rubbing the Duſt off their upper Leathers, or an unfortunate Speck off the Scabbards of their Swords; that their *Spaniſh* Pumps, and their Hogs Skin Sheaths, may be kept as Spot-free as a *Dutch* Huſſife does the outſide of her Kettle: Upon the ſame Table, which is every Day cover'd with a freſh damaſk Cloth, there lies
Two

Two or Three Dozen of *Sevil* Oranges and
Lemmons; and by the Side of the Table, under a bright Pewter Ciftern, a white glaz'd
Bafon, that if any fpindle fhank'd *Narciffus* has
been contaminating his Fingers by any digitti-
zing Exercife, he may rinfe off the favory Remains with the acid Juices of the Fruit, and
mundify the defil'd Member, that has been
tickling the Honour of fome over frigid Lady
into an amorous Uproar. Next to thefe cleanly
Neceffaries ftands an Olive-Box full of the beft
perfum'd Powder, crown'd with three or four
mighty Combs., that their Crifpicapillary
Wigs may be new fented, and every ftraggling
Hair that has been ruffled by a Storm of their
Miftreffes Breath, or any windy Accident,
be timely reduc'd to Obedience, and carefully
reftor'd to it's primitive Station: Round the
Edges of the Table lies ftrew'd, by way of
Garnifh, Sifars, Tooth-Pickers, and Tweezers,
Patches, Effences, and Pomatums; Paints, Paifls,
and Wafhes; and all the ufeful Impliments that
Pride and Folly can invent to turn Men into
Monkeys, or to change the Features and Com-
plexions that God has given them, into artful
Countenances: So that the Sr. *Foplin Flutters*,
and Sr. *Courtly Nices*, are no fooner met, but
there is fuch tiffling of Wigs, wiping of Shoes,
brufhing of Stockins, and managing of Faces,
as if they were fo many Stage Players patching
up ftern Looks and Heroick Phizes, for Plumes,
Bufkins, and *Roman* Mantle, that they might
Rant

Rant and Strut, till they were foundly clap'd by fome of the Box Ladies, to reward their fham Fights, and bluftering Rodomontades. When every one has thus imbellifh'd his Effeminate Market-Place, and adorn'd his Body to the beft Advantage, then down they fit to their *Champaigne, Burgundy,* and *Hermettage,* pull out their gilt Snufh-Boxes of *Orangeree* and *Brazil,* that each may feed his Elephant's Trunk with odoriferous Duft, and make his Breath as fragrant as an *Arabian* Breeze to the Noftrils of a Seaman; and when they are thus made as fweet as fo many *Clove-July-Flowers,* then a delicious Health to fome celebrated Play-Houfe Wanton, *Hay-Market* Punk, or Court Curtizan, is, with abundance of eager Shews of his paffionate Luft and Affection, began with great Ceremony by the Cock of the Company, which is no fooner drank, but fucceeded with a long Lecture on her heaving Dumplins, her lufhious juicy Lips, and drowfy leacherous Pignies, with all the outward Signs that her charming Ladyfhip imparts, to fignify to the World, that fhe's an indefatigable Bedfellow, tho', perhaps, any Body, for half a Crown, may command the Ultimare of her Favours. Then a fecond gives his Toaft to fome Cherubimical Lady, whofe Name is purpofely introduc'd, that fhe may vie Beauty with the former; her Vertues, as well as Charms, being fo amoroufly exemplify'd, as if the Mention of her Graces gave him a counterfeit Enjoyment.
Then

Then a Third, to fhew his Brother Coxcombs, that he is not fo much a felf Admirer, but that he has fome Juvenile Sparks of Honour for the Charms of female Beauty, adminifters his Toaft to the Company by a fham Denomination; becaufe the Object of his Luft is a Man of Quality's Lady, and 'therefore her Name is to be kept facred. Thus every one, in his Turn, fhews his affectionate Devotion to fome cherubimical Fornicatrix or other, that he has felected from the reft of the tickle Fool Gender, to Idolize as his Goddefs, for Fear he fhould be thought, by his Companions, fo unfafhionable a Coxcomb as to want a female Conveniency. When they have pretty well tir'd each others Ears with their Encomiums on the Charms, Vertues, and good Humour of their feveral Punks, and Parramours, then the Scene changes, and another Act of the Fools Comedy fucceeds their former Vanity, wherein the admirable Cuts of their *French* Taylors; the airy Contrivance of their fkillful Periwig-Makers; the Courage of their Fencing-Mafters, and the Wit and Learning of our Modern Poets are rak'd up in Competion, that themfelves may fhew and magnify their own Judgments, in finding out, and expofing the little Faults and Blunders of every gingling Verfifyer: Of which notable Difcoveries they are as critically Proud, as if the Follies of an Author were the only Beauties of a Book, that afforded Pleafure to the Reader. Then a new Seffions of Poets

are

are moſt judiciouſly form'd by theſe fantaſtical
Criticks; where every poor Culprit of the Rhiming Fraternity is ſure to be condemn'd for
ſome Fault or other, tho' it be but for tranſgreſ-
ſing *D——s*'s new Mode of Spelling, or making an unfortunate Line half a Foot too long,
thro' the Neglect of an *Apoſtraphe.* Thus they
exerciſe their own Folly, by raking into the
Rubbiſh of other Men's Wit; and only examine Books, as Hogs do Dunghills, when they
rout for a Surreverence, to gratify their Curioſity; nor is the Play, or Poem, damn'd alone
for the Errors that they find in the Performance, but as often for the Faults that they
find in the Performer: For one Author ſhall Of-
fend 'em for being ſuch a filthy Sloven, that he
goes open Breaſted with a dirty Shirt, as if he
was the reverſe of all Beauiſh Nicety, and delighted to carry in his own Boſom a Linnen
Satyr againſt Cleanlineſs. A Second, perhaps,
decry'd for ſuch a confounded Sot, that his very Writings ſtink as ſtrong of *Derby-Ale,* as if
his only *Parnaſſus* was in *Fullwood*'s Rents;
and that he never was inſpir'd by any other
Muſe than his ſwanking Landlady. A Third,
deſpis'd for having ſo dull a Fancy in his libidinous Amours, that tho' he never thought any
Thing worth praiſing, beneath a Dutcheſs, or
a Counteſs, yet he never thought any Woman
worth kiſſing above a Cookmaid, or an Oyſter-
Wench. A Fourth, condemn'd for ſuch a
Clowniſh Blockhead, that rather than ſhew his
Poetical

Poetical Obedience, in waiting four Hours every Morning, for a Week or a Fortnight, in my Lord *Fondlewit's* Buttery, would chuſe to expoſe his Works naked, without the Armour of a Dedication, as if he was too Proud to ſcrape away the Soles of his beſt Shoes, and to loſe ten Guineas worth of Time, to get half the Value of ſome generous Mecænas. A Fifth, reproachfully cenſur'd for being ſuch a damn'd Jacobite, that he was not fit, in theſe pious Times, to write a Proteſtant Play for ſuch a ſanctify'd Stage, whoſe verdent Carpet has ſcarce been defil'd with the Foot of a Strumpet, ſince their laſt Reformation. Thus the Faults of the Author are made Errors in their Works ; and as Tryals are often canvaſs'd by partial Judges, the Cauſe is made bad, becauſe the Client is obnoxious ; but at laſt the Bays are given to ſome Poetizing Fop, for hammering out the inimittable Song of O *Happy Groves,* or ſome ſuch faſhionable Piece of *Lyrick* Poetry, that ſhews his modiſh Writings as fantaſtically Prim, as his nice effeminate Air, and his quaint Beauiſh Habiliments.

When foppiſh Apes preſume to judge of Wit,
Merit ſhould fly the Stage, and ſhun the Pit :
For partial Fools againſt the wiſe prevail,
And by the Dint of Number turn the Scale.
Where Beaus unite a Rhiming Fop is ſafe,
His Friendly Swarms without a Jeſt can Laugh ;
Commend

Commend a wretched Play without a Plot,
And clap the loudest when he's most in Fau't.
So when some Brewer for the Senate stands,
Whole Crowds of swanking Vict'lers he commands:
And the worse Man, the more the drunken Rout
Cry up his Vertues, and in Triumph shout,
Whilst honest Merit oft gives up the Day,
For some Sir Hops *and* Grains *to come in Play.*

When the modish Amarettoes have Drank
enough of sham Wine, instead of *Champaigne* at
Seven and Six-pence a Flask, to elevate their
Spirits, sublime their Wits, and put their
Tongues in Tune, that they may be every
way Quallify'd to attack the Mask'd Ladies,
who hang about the Theatre in their Second-
hand Furbiloes, to open the Wicket of Love's
Bear-Garden, to any bold Sportsman who has
a venturesome Mind to give a Run to his Puppy; then they pay their Reckoning, tiffle up
the Foretops of their Wigs with their Alaba-
ster Fingers, and walk Bare-headed to the Play-
House, where they commonly arrive about the
Third Act, by which time the Ladies, who
care not much to appear by Day-light, are
bolted from their Stews, and *Drury-Lane* Al-
lies, to sneak into the Pit and Eighteen-penny
Gallery, without Tickets, at the Curtesie of
the Door-Keepers.   When the cringing Peacocks

cocks are thus met with their Match, they Tattle away the Play-time among their Half-Crown Punks, and Intriguing Dulcibellas, till one of the Fraternity of sham-Heroes, makes an humble Bow to the Box-Ladies, and declares to the whole Audience the Title of the Fooleries they intend to present them with to Morrow; and then the Beauish Shallow-Wits, according to custom, divide themselves between Drinking, Whoring, and Gaming, till the next Morning.

To be a modish Fop, a Beau compleat,
Is to pretend to, but be void of Wit:
'Tis to be Squeamish, Critical, and Nice
In all things, and Fantastic to a Vice;
'Tis to seem Knowing, tho' he nothing knows,
And vainly Lewd to please his Brother Beaus;
'Tis in his Dress to be profusely Gay,
And to affect, Whore-like, a wanton Way;
'Tis to be charm'd with each new fashion'd Whim,
And to be modish to a vain Extream,
That each gay Punk a lustful Eye may rowl,
And for his Shapes admire the pritty Fool;
'Tis to attack the Ladies with a Grace,
And still transfer his Love to each new Face,
Flutter about her Charms, till, like a Fly,
Burnt by the Flame, he's scorch'd amidst his Joy;

L   *Then*

Then Curfing of the B——ch, is forc'd to cool
The Pocky Heat, by running oft to Stool;
Till with repeated Purges, by degrees,
The pricking Pains and Inflamations ceafe.

Then pleas'd to find that he fo Sound is made,
Refolves, in vain, to grow a cautious Blade:
So Wives in Travel vow to Kifs no more,
But foon forget the Torment when it's o'er.

Thus eas'd by Powders, Bolus, and by Pill,
He damns the Whore, and pays the Surgeon's Bill:
But foon forgetting the Venereal fmart
That teaz'd and bridl'd the unruly Part,
Renews his Courage, ftill perfues the Game,
Makes Luft his Leader, Maidenheads his Aim,
Till caught a fecond time by fome Lafcivious
                                    [Dame.

CHAP.

CHAP. XVI.
Of the WRANGLING,
OR,
HUSSLE-FARTHING *Club.*

THIS promiscuous Society of contentious Mortals, meet every Night at the two bowing Blockheads in *Shovel-Money-Street*, where they wrangle over their Claret about the Grand Preliminaries; and so earnestly dispute the New Articles of Peace, till, like Whores about their Vertue, they are ready to fall together by the Ears about their several Politicks; and the variety of Schemes they have projected upon their Pillows, by the help of their Wives, to bring those important Affairs, under a present Negotiation, to a Good and Prosperous Issue. When they have thus, for an Hour or Two, made the *French* King as lousy as an *English* Mumper; Shov'd the poor Pretender into the Arse of the Universe; Jostl'd *Phillip* out of *Spain*, and divided *Mexico* and *Peru* with such equitable Exactness, that we may have our Share; the

Talk

Talk of the *Indies*, and the Riches thereof generally infects them with such an Itch of Covetousnefs, that they can't forbear endeavouring to improve one anothers Pocket-Money, by filling into the *Tower-Hill* Sport of old primitive Huffle-Farthing; that, of a fudden, fuch warm Difputes arife about Crofs and Pile, fuch a confounded Roaring of Half-penny Betts, between thofe who are for Heads, and others who have chofen Tails, and thofe who, like Moderators, have taken a Chance, between both, hoping to win all by crying *Halves*; that it is common for ftrange Cuftomers, upon hearing the Noife, to enquire of the Drawer whether there is not a Cock-Pit kept above Stairs? And if the Cockers are not raving and betting in the Height of their Sport: For, when they are once begun fuch a Confufion of Tongues fills the wrangling Company, as if they were ambitious to make themfelves as noted as either *Babel*, or the *Bear-Garden*. For Nothing is heard among 'em, for two or three Hours together; *but, bide* Mr. Common-Councilman; *tofs up, Mr.* Alderman; *Crofs for a Penny, Mr.* Church-Warden, *Done with you, Mr.* Conftable; *you owe me Two-Pence, Mr.* Deputy; *give me Change, Mr.* Foreman, *and there's Six-pence, Hide fair Neighbour* Cloudy; *hold your Thumb out of the Hat; I fcorn your Words; do you think, Mr.* Scrapeall, *you're at Play in* Moor-Fields; *now, up Tails all, for Crofs is my Chance; the Devil take Fortune, all Pile by the Mafs; if it be fo, Brother* Burley,

Burley, *then take of your Glass.* Thus they make a Rattling with their Tongues, like fo many Red-Coats at a whimfie Board, and fuch a Clattering with turning down their *Famulus Numorum*, that inftead of grave Citizens, fit to attend a Lord Mayor in their-livery Robes, up-on the Day of his Triumphs, they would be better Companions for a Parcel of *Tower-Hill* Cripples, who are generally expert Gamefters at the fame School-Boys Sport.

Thus fome, who grow from Boys to Men,
Do into Children turn again,
And ftill delight to play the Fool,
As much as e'er they did at School.
Then, fince they're Infants, tho' they've Wives,
And ftill affect fuch Boyifh Lives,
They ought to bear the Mufes Flog,
When paft the Jirk of Pedagogue :
For when they are fo Big and Lufty,
So Difobedient and fo Crufty,
That no ftern Pedant durft to Thrafh 'em
It is the Poet's right to Lafh 'em.

When the latenefs of the Night has put a Stop to their Puerilous Paftime, and the Drawers old Hat, without a Lining, is, by the grave Confent of the Majority of the Company, moft thankfully return'd, with Two-pence for the

Lent

Lent of it: Every one, by pulling out his Pocket Furniture, begins to feperate his Silver from his Farthings, that he may readily determine, with the greater certainty, to what Purpofe he has Huffled away his time. One boafting of his Nine-penny Winnings; another fretting at his Five-penny Lofings; a third, pleas'd that he has fav'd himfelf; a Fourth, upon Thorns to be at Home with his Wife, for fear he fhould not be early enough in his Bride's Arms, to avoid a Curtain Lecture; a Fifth Ringing for the Reckoning in all hafte, that he may be in Bed time enough to Rife the next Morning by Five a Clock, to run with his Angle to *Hackney* River, that Mr. *Sly*, the Cuckold-maker, may be kindly Invited to a Fifh-Supper; a Sixth, wrangling for t'other Quart, contending for the reafonablenefs of one half-hour between that and Bed-time. Thus, when they have done Huffling, they fall to Buftling, that they are as bad a Plague to the Bar and the Drawers, by their Ringing and Rattling, as fo many *Northern* Attorney's, got half Drunk, are to a *Yorkfhire* Inn-keeper; fome ftealing down Stairs, having drop'd Eight-pence inftead of Nine-pence; others calling loudly after them at the Stair-head, to return up again, and pay t'other Penny; fome filling their Pipes with a Refolution to tarry one Pin-bafket Pint, and Peremptory Whiff, in fpite of all the Whifpering Summons they fhould receive from their

Wives, by the Mouths of their Apprentices.
Thus some fly the Pit, in seasonable time, to
avoid Nuptial Contention ; and others, inspir'd
with more Courage by the Wine, run the dangerous risque of a Weeks Clamour, for a little
Mid-night Enjoyment, which they are apt to
continue till the Vintner puts an Embargo
upon his Cellar-Door ; and then the Sottish
Remains of the Wrangling Society reel Muttering Home, for want of t'other Quart ; and
instead of rewarding the diligent Attendance
of the drowsie Drawer with a few Transitory
Half-pence, they give him an Angry Mouth-
ful of hard Words at Parting, because he cannot furnish them with a further Supply, so adjourn from Hustling of Stamp'd Copper to the
Jostling of Female Cruppers, that the exercise
of the Tail may allay the fury of the Tongue ;
and the forwardness of their Love excuse the
lateness of the Hour, which would otherwise
be Unpardonable.

> *Ladies who Love, as most good Women do,*
> *Their Husbands should the Nuptial Bonds renew,*
> *Are always Pert, and ready, if they've Sence,*
> *To take advantage of a Man's Offence,*
> *Knowing kind Nature, to oblige the Fair,*
> *Allows but one soft way when Husbands Err,* }
> *To sweetly reconcile the Marry'd Pair.*

L 4   *Therefore*

Therefore, when Men the Nuptial Laws tranf-
[grefs,

And angry Wives put on a moody Face,
Warmly attack the faulty Spoufe's Ear,
And Preach loud Lectures on the Wrongs they
[bear;
They Scold not to employ the reftlefs Sting,
But meerly Quarrel for the other Thing.

Why then fhould Man, whofe Fortune 'tis to
[take

A Female Partner for Enjoyments fake,
Fear Woman's teafing Tongue when he Offends, }
Since every Fool knows how to make amends, }
And with an angry Wife may be fo eas'ly Friends. }

CHAP.

CHAP. XVII.

Of the QUACKS Club:

OR, THE

PHISICAL SOCIETY.

THE Empericks of the Town, alias licens'd Phyficians, as to the Scandal of the College, they are pleas'd to call themfelves, that they might be the better able to promote the Intereft of Quackifm, thought it abfolutely neceffary, fome Years fince, to hold a Weekly Correfpondence at a certain Tavern near the *Change*, that by an amicable Club, they might not only be able to be of mutual Service to each other, but to defend their Pretenfions to Phifick, Chimiftry, and Pharmacy, againft the clamorous Infults of the regular Phyficians, Chymifts, and Apothecaries, who are the principal

pal Enemies that caſt their Dirt upon the paſ-
ſted Bills, as well as the Reputations of the
Mundungus Publiſhers of, not only ineffectu-
al, but deſtructive Medicines. Upon their firſt
meeting Dr. *Saffold*'s Succeſſor, becauſe he had
juſt at that Time the Impudence to publiſh a
Latin Book of Anatomy, in his own Name, in
Order to wipe off the true Aſperſion of his
not being able to read a Line of Engliſh, had
the Honour to be choſen, by the Majority of
High-German Coblers, *Dutch* Tumblers, and
Engliſh Rope-Dancers, Prolocutor of the Society, and took his Place at the Board in an El-
bow Chair accordingly, where he ſat in as
much State, as if he had been the learn'd Pre-
ſident of Phyſicians College, or a fat Ptiſicky
Alderman invited by Mr. *Foreman* to a Queſt
Treat: Every formal Student in the twin Sci-
ences of Phyſick and Aſtrology having ſo ſtrict
a Regard to the Gravity of their Profeſſion,
that they grac'd their ſolemn Juncto, with their
Ebony Canes and Bands, and all their Querpo
Formalities, as if they were going to Dine with
my Lord, and to beg Leave of the City to pull
down the Statute of King *Charles* the Second,
and to erect a Mountebanks Stage in the middle of the *Exchange*, that by ſelling Packets of
a noble Cathartick, call'd *Pilula Honeſta*, they
might purge all Manner of Knavery out of
the canker'd Conſciences of *Change*-Brokers
and Stock-Jobbers. When Rhimatical Doctor
John had thus aſſum'd the upper Seat at the
Table,

Table, furrounded with fuch an Emperical mixture of all Nations, that they were a perfect Refemblance of the Confufion of Tongues that happen'd once at *Babel.* The Poetical Purger of Town Sinks and Stallions, would be loudly repeating fome new Verfes, hammer'd out of his dull Noddle for his next Bumfodder Bill, that it might firft make People laugh till they were ready to Bedung themfelves, and then do 'em the Service of a Paper Muckender, to mundify their Funs. Doctor *Sal Volatile Oliofum,* would be Jabbering, in broken *Englifh,* fuch Hyperbolical Encomiums on his Chimical Infallibility, as if his all-Curing Secret was the very Quinteffence of the Philofophers Stone, moft wonderfully extracted by no other Heat than that of the Dog-Star, and therefore good to be taken in the Dog-Days, when Lunaticks are moft Mad, and Women moft Wanton. Dr. *Aurum Potabile,* with the Grace of a Stage Orator, would be fetting forth the Virtue of his golden Elixir, and would be ready to fwear 'twas the fame Cordial that *Venus* always adminifter'd to *Mars,* to prepare his Appetite, when the beautiful Goddefs had kindly invited the ftrong back'd Heroe to an *Old-Lang* Supper. Dr. *Pulvis Benedictus,* juft come from fimpling out of *Hamftead* Ditches, after he had rowl'd about his Eyes like a wild Cat, would, with a Tongue as loud as a Kettle-Drum, cry, *Here's a blefled Powder to Purge the Bug-Bears out of Children ; it brought forth a Monfter, the other Day,*

Day, from a Red Hair'd Girl, that had Horns like a Snail, a Head like a Snake, and was as long in the Body as half a Pound of Pack-Thread, and I have it now in my Study, quoil'd round upon a Sheet of blue Paper, that any Body may behold what wonderful Maggots often lurk in the Tails of young Wenches. Doctor *Aqua Te-trachimagogon,* your old Friend and Physician, would also blunder out the Fame of his *Græcian* Water, and swear that 'twould Conquer an inveterate Pox, in less Time, than a Sore-Ey'd Punk could cure her Sight or cool her Leachery, at *Crowder*'s Well, or *Lamb*'s Conduit. Dr. *Orveiton,* with a Voice as Hoarse as a double Curtil, as forward as the rest to magnify his Skill, and extoll his Medicines, to shew his Learning, would undertake to tell 'em, in false Latin, what a Number of *German* Princes he had Flux'd for the *French* Scurvy ; and how many foreign Queens he had infallibly Cured of the King's Evil, and all by that admirable Hodge-Podge, his *Orveitanum.* Amongst the rest, that famous Phisician, Doctor *Panacea,* whose generous Nostrum cures every Thing with as much Certainty, as it does any Thing. He, in an untelligible Jargon, between *Dutch* and *English,* would be Stuttering out the Infallibility and Universallity of his wonderful *Chatholicon,* and like a true *Low-Country* Protestant, ascribe to his Pill what he had deny'd to the Pope. At the lower End of the Table, paying Defference to the rest, sat an humbler Class of Quacking Operators, as Doctor *Couh-Fye,*

Eye, Doctor *Dentidraw,* Doctor *Cornucut, &c.*
One pulling out a handfull of nasty rotten
Stumps, most learnedly expatiating on the
manifold Defects which so oft had been the
Occasion of the Patient's Misery, and had cost,
among the Maids, more Sighs at Midnight than
the Unkindness of their Sweet-Hearts, or the
want of lusty Bedfellows, and made many a poor
Bride, in a Breeding Condition curse the unhappy Minute that ever she follow'd the Steps
of her Grandmother, since the amorous Pleasures of the Nuptial Bed, had so highly provok'd
her Tongue to complain of her Teeth : Next
him a famous Corrector of *Toe-Almanacks,* would
be pulling out a handful of the Horny Pearl
he had Dug out of the Pedestals of fine pinch
Footed Ladies, and old crippl'd Aldermen ; and
would hold Forth so Judgmatically, upon the
Extirpation of Corns, and the various Causes
of those Knotty Excrescencies, that a Stander-
by, from his quaint Terms and unintelligible
Speeches, might have thought there was as
much Conjuration in the Art and Mistery of
Corn-cutting, as there is in the mannual Ope-
rations of an expert Sow-Gilder, or in the dark
and intricate Mazes of that Blind Science,
call'd Judicial Astrology. Sir *William Couch,*
among the rest, would be brandishing his Nee-
dle, with his Heathen Blackamoor at his El-
bow, and would Exhibit to his Brethen, such a
Catalogue of Eye-sores he had Cur'd in his
Domestick Travels, that a Man might reason-
ably

ably have gueſt his Worſhip had gain'd his
Knighthood, by opening the Eyes of a Blind
People, who had not Senſe enough to diſcern the
difference between an illiterate Pretender, and
a learn'd Phyſician.

Thus the fam'd Quacks, who by their ſenſeleſs
                                            [Bills,
Proclaim the Vertues of their worthleſs Pills,
And Knaviſhly deceive the fooliſh Town
With Med'cines, even to themſelves unknown:
Met in a Body to contrive new ways
To Live, and Thrive by ſhort'ning others Days :
So Lawyers, ſkill'd in Quarrels and Debates,
From ruin'd Numbers draw their own Eſtates.

In this ſharp Age it is a ſtanding Rule,
For Knaves of e'ery kind to Bite the Fool.

When the Medicinal Coxcombs had exemplify'd, at large, the infallible Vertues of their
Popular Pills, Univerſal Powders, and ſundry
ſorts of *Panaceas, Noſtrums, Hodge-podges,* and
Catholicons; then, the wonderful Skill and
Cures of our defunct Mountebanks, ſuch as the
fam'd *Ponteus Salvator Winter, Rodocanace,* and
all thoſe Eminent Worthies who had, long
ſince, advanc'd the noble Art of Quackery,
were made the pleaſing Subjects of their Phiſi-
cal Diſcourſes, and were alſo Quoted upon all
Occaſions, with as much Reverence as a young
                                            Divine

Divine does St. *Gregory* and St. *Austin*; or a Learn'd Physician *Gallen* and *Hipocrates.* For as the High-Church are beholding to their Popish Saints and Fathers; and the Low-Church are justify'd by the Reverend Authories of their *Baxters,* and their *Bates's;* so our Modern Empericks have their Travelling Ancients, such as aforemention'd, to Countenance their Practices, Foreign Interlopers, who, with their Pills, Dentrifices, Worm-Powders, and Eye-Waters, perform'd, when they were Living, such inimitable Miracles upon Country Chubs, old Nurses, Sick Chamber-maids, and Lame Mumpers, that are never to be forgotten, whilst we have a worshipful Sir *William,* in his Coach and Six; or a famous Doctor *Gately* with his numerous Retinue of Vaulters, Tumblers, and Rope-Dancers, to support the Memories of their Emperical Predecessors. For when our Modern Operators mount their Country Scaffolds, with their Train of *Bartholomew* Fools, and *Parrot* Prating Orators, surrounded with a gaping Crow'd of Dary-Drudging Jugs, and Rural *Coridons,* then, that their Pacquet Speeches may be Larded with something that may seem Learned, *Cessante Tollitur, Causa effectus,* says the Plush Jacket Doctor, *was the great and good Maxim of that famous Physician, Doctor* Carleus, *who, for his Country's Good, Travel'd Publickly, as I do;* which is as much as to say, *If you Take my Physick you may be certain of a Cure.* Thus they back their own Impudence with

the

the Scandalous Authority of other Ignorant Pretenders, to whose Memory they ascribe abundance of Honour, that the People may learn from thence how to Reverence the Dunce who is Gulling them, at present, after the same manner. Among the rest of the Services that they did each other, when they were met o'er the Bottle, if any of the Fraternity, thro' their long Study, and Experience in Physick and Astrology, had happily discover'd a new Plaster for the Corns; a pretious Ointment for the Itch, or any other infallible Medicine much better than the Best, then the Assistance of the Society was most humbly entreated, to adapt some whimsical Name to the most admirable Secret, and to compose a Compendium of its singular Vertues, that the Infallible Aliquod might be usher'd into the World for the Benefit of the Doctor, much rather than the Publick. For the sake of these, and such like Advantages they continu'd their Weekly-meeting, during one whole Winter, but the Summer coming on, the greater Part drawing off to go their several Country Circuits, to distribute their Pacquets among the foolish Multitude, and the rest, in their Cups, contending about their Skill. and the Excellency and Efficacy of their never failing Remedies, fell together by the Ears on the first of *April,* and so, with black Eyes and broken Heads, contentiously divided, and put a Period to their Meeting, verifying the old Proverb, *That two of a Trade can seldom agree.*

agree. Thus they met like Friends; convers'd like Brothers; till, at length, they fell to Pieces like Enemies; fought like Drunkards; maul'd one another, like Butchers; parted full of Knocks and Bruises, like wrangling Clowns from a Cudgel-Playing, and so return'd, like Fools as they were, to their dark Alleys about *Moor-Fields*; where their Habitations are as well known to their Customers, by their Orbicular Sines, as themselves are to the World for their Ignorance and Impudence.

Of all the Plagues with which our Land is Curst,
The Frauds of Physick seem to be the worst:
For tho' the Law, 'tis true, abounds with Weeds,
And from Astrea's *Rules too oft receeds,*
Yet those keen Foxes of such sundry Sorts,
Who hang in Swarms about her awful Courts,
By their Male Practice, and Prolix Debates,
Can only hurt our Pockets and Estates;
But banefull Quacks, in Physick's Art unread,
To Weaving, Cobling, or to Tumbling bred;
Or else poor Scoundrels, who for Scraps & Thanks
Swept Stages for their Master Mountebanks:
These to the World destructive Slops commend,
And do their poys'nous Chents to Life extend;

M   *By*

By vain Pretences pick the Patient's Purse,
And with sham Med'cines make 'em ten times worse.
So the Quack Preacher, *who pretends to heal*
The wounded Conscience, scorch'd with too much
                                    Zeal,

For Want of Judging rightly of the Cause,
Inflaming Corrosives, from Scripture draws,
Which, wrong apply'd, for want of Skill and Care,
Fill the sick Mind with Horror and Despair.

CHAP.

CHAP. XVIII.

Of the Weekly DANCING Club:

OR,

BUTTOCK-BALL in St. Giles.

THIS capering Society confifted cheif-
ly of Bullies, Libertines, and Strumpets; alfo Quality's Footmen, who
had fhifted off their Mafters Live-
ries to appear Gentlemen, and Chamber-Maids, who had ftolen on their Ladies
Cloaths, to fet up for Gentlewomen. Tho'
I call it a Club, becaufe every Body paid alike
to the Mafter of the Revels, for his Trouble,
Candles, Dancing-Room, and Mufick, yet there
was no felect Company, or was there any Limitation as to Number, or Quality, but any
Perfon was free to fhake their Rumps, and exercife their Members to fome Tune, from the
Gentleman Rake to the *Water-lane* Pick-Pocket; and from the Lady's Confident, call'd her
Woman, to Oyfter *Moll*, whofe Cringerous Clift

was

was ready to run the Gantlope thro' a Regiment of Foot-Guards; so that all that would come were Welcome, in Masquerade, or otherwise, if they were but able to cross the Door-Keeper's Hand with Six-pence for their Admittance, which was all their Expence, tho' the Men Danc'd till they were as bad tir'd as *John* the Coachman with his Lady's Chamber Favours; and Women as much weary'd with their swimming Activity, as a fresh Whore, in a noted Bawdy-House, with a whole Days Exercise. The Variety of Figures that were to be seen, every *Thursday* Evening, were so well worthy of any Man's Observation, that, like a publick Meeting at *Port-Royal* in *Jamaica*, most of them look'd like the Purgings of our Goals, and the Spewings of our Bawdy-Houses. In would step a brawny Bully, equip'd, at second Hand, in *Monmouth-Street*, or *Long-Lane*, with his twisted flaxen Wig, just Comb'd and Powder'd, sold, perhaps, by the Hang-man into *Middle-Row*, and from thence bought by some of his Whores Pence, to adorn the Hector's Blockhead, with a lac'd Hat, Beaux like, under his Left Arm, and in his Right Hand a *Grays-Inn* Semptress tiffl'd up with taudry Laces, old Ribbonds, and black Bugles, as if she was Dress'd to act a Slatterns Part in some old slovenly Comedy. By and by, in would bolt my Lord *Scatterwit's* Butler, in a Cast-off Wig and *Spanish* Shoes, given him by my Lord's Vallet for making his Friends Welcome in my Lord's

Wine

Wine-Cellar, handing, in great State, my Lady *Firkinton*'s Waiting-Woman, most richly adorn'd in some of her Lady's best Rigging, which she hopes to defile before she goes Home, if her Mate has but Time to give her a Tavern Treat, and wants not the Courage, when he has her upon a Chair, to attack her Watering Place, which she has not Sense or Modesty enough to value; tho' that, with a few old Cloaths, are the utmost of her Fortune. Amongst the rest, a Lawyer's Clark, who had ventur'd to make a Loose from the Finger Drudgery of Pen Ink and Paper, would usher in the Buxom Daughter of some *Chancery-Lane* Victualler, in Hopes to be rewarded for his Trouble with a Taplash Maiden-Head, perhaps impair'd, long since, at *Pancras*-Wells, or by her Father's own Tapster. Next these a Beau Apprentice in his *Sundays* Cloaths, new Wash'd and Powder'd, handing in his Mistress's young Tallow Faced Kinswoman, that the Fortuneless Maukin, as soon as her Gallant has bury'd his Indentures, may decoy the amorous Nisey into the Matrimonial Shackles, and so prevent him setting Up for himself to the Dis-Interest of his Master. Besides these, who were the Top of the Quality that ever frequented this revelling Accademy, every now and then a fluttering Fool or two of both Sexes would bolt in, Masqueraded in strange Antick Dresses, borrow'd, for the Night, out of some *Moor-Fields* Musick-House, by such who were asham'd to appear

in

in their own Tatter'd Garments, or to fhew their fcandalous Faces without a Mafk; and to fwell the Number to a Spring-Tide of Confufion, fuch an Inundation of Shabby Rakes, Town-Sharpers, Weather-Beaten-Punks, and Young Strumpets, were perpetually flowing in, that the fweating Dancers could fcarce mind their Steps, for Guarding of their Pockets; or a *Libertine* fhake his Heels with his charming *Blowzabella*, without treading upon the Corns of fome other Trading Harlot. When the promifcuous Variety were thus met together, efpecially on a Summer's Day, when the Heat of the Weather requir'd Air more than Exercife, fuch an unfavoury Mixture of contrary Scents arofe from powder'd Locks, and plafter'd Ulcers; perfum'd Snufhes, and ftinking Breaths; fweaty Socks, and *Hungary*-Water Handkerchiefs; rotten *Old-Ling*, and odoriferous *Pomatums*; Fidlers Farts, and Ladies Sweet Bags; *Brandy* Belches, and Carway-comfits; fublunary Fumes, and fcented Gloves; ftinking *Gonorheas*, and *Harts-Horn* Bottles, that the Noftrils of the Company were at once faluted with all the Effences of a Perfumer's Shop, and all the Stenches of an Hofpital.

No Sick Man's Chamber, when a hard bound
         [*Stool*

Has eas'd his Brain, and does his Body cool,
         Whilſt

Whilſt Nurſe with flaming Roſem'ry *does diſguiſe*
The Nauſeous Fumes that from the Pan ariſe,
Could the nice Noſe with ſuch a Mixture touch,
And with ſtrange Whiffs confound the Senſe ſo
                                        [*much :*
Or could the fam'd Pandora's *pois'nous Box,*
That fill'd the World at firſt with Plague and
                                        [*Pox,*
Tho' mix't with ſulph'rous Vapours that are ſent
From Ætna's *Mountain to the Firmament,*
Met by a ſweet and ſalutory Breeze,
That from Arabian *Shores perfumes the Seas,*
With more Surpriſe upon our Senſes fall,
Or yield a Noſegay like the Buttock-Ball.
For there each Whiff that to the Noſtril comes,
From ſweaty Toes, foul Breaths, and pocky Bums,
Engender with Perfumes, that e'ery Minx
Wears to correct kind Nature's flowing Sinks,
And to confound the Noſe, beget a thouſand
                                        Stinks.

So ſavage Indians *luſtſul Brutes embrace,*
And oft amuſe us with a Monſtrous Race.

When a Set of Dancers were wantonly enga-
ged in their Shake-Tail Exerciſe, it was well
worth the while of a Sitter-by to obſerve their
ſeveral Motions. One ill-ſhap'd Clown, with

M 4   Mull-

Mill-Poſt Legs, much fitter to tread Mortar
than to ſtump it about after the celebrated
Tune of *Green Sleeves and Pudding Pyes*, would
be turning about his fat Partner, dripping hot,
with wadling like a Cow, without Step or
Figure.   Another, with an affected Air, as ſtiff
and as formal as a Moving Wax-Work Figure,
would be very buſie in recovering his Mate,
who, for Want of Skill, made as many wry
Steps in her Dancing, as ſhe had done in her
Modeſty ; and would give her ſuch Tugs to
him, and then ſuch Caſt-offs from him, as if,
like a loving Huſband, who has a handſome
Wife that Cuckolds him, he was neither plea-
ſed with her, or without her.   A Third, per ·
haps, would ſeem to be a finikin Drawer,
turn'd out of Place for his over Gentility, who
had got for his Part'ner a Tavern Cook-Wench,
diſtinguiſhably ſo, by her ſwelling Dugs being
burnt by the Fire to a Copper Colour, and by
the Lace of her Shoes being greaſily tarniſh-
ed with the Drippings of the baiſting Ladle.
A Fourth, by being bred in a Gentleman's
Family, would handle his Heels like an expert
Performer, and ſlide about the Room with ſuch
an Air of Quality, which he had learn'd of
his Maſter; that the ſlatternly Chamber-
Maid he had choſe for his Partner was as proud
to think ſhe was ſo nicely Gallanted, as if ſhe
had the vanity to fancy herſelf envy'd by all
the Whores in the Company.   A Fifth, being
a dapper Blade, would ſcorn to let his Heels
have

have any Contact with the Floor, but cocking
up his Chin would stretch his Body to its utmost Length, as if he thought, by Dancing upon his Tiptoes, to add a Cubit to his Heigth,
and would so bristle up to his light Huswife of
a Partner; as if he had made a Bargain before
Hand to take a Half-Crown Rubbers as soon as
Dancing was over. A Sixth would riggle about
his Rump, as if a Gentleman's Companion had
been preying about his Buttocks, whilst his Lady, to humour him in his fantastical Gestures,
would screw her Body into so many answerable
Postures, as if a Colony of Crabs had unhappily
taken Possession of her *Mons Veneris*; and that
she shuffl'd about her Arse to extenuate her Unea-
siness, for want of an Opportunity to remove her
Enemies by Scratching. A Seventh would tread
as gingerly upon the Floor with his Feet, as if he
was a *Roman Catholick*, enjoyn'd the Pennance,
by his Priest, of wearing Pees in his Shoes; and
that he had not been inspir'd with *Protestant*
Wit enough to give 'em true Boiling, match'd,
perhaps, with a Partner of the same Religion,
who was Lew'd enough to commit the Venial
Sin of Fornication, and Wise enough to conceal
it from the Ears of her Holy Father. An Eigth,
a merry *Libertine*, with a Heart as light as
his Heels, and his Countenance as chearful
as the Looks of a young Council that has gain'd
a Cause for his Client, united in Partnership
with a high-Church Whore, that would rather
chuse to be corrected with the Scourge of Re-

formation

mation, than contaminate her Honour with old
Juſtice *Sly-Boots.* A Ninth, with the ſolemn
Air and Gravity of a *Puritan,* with his Fingers
extended to their utmoſt Length, and his Arms
hanging down, like a Dead Criminal's upon a
Gibbet, would be Stepping to the Muſick, as if
he was Walking to the Meeting, moſt agreeably
link'd to ſuch a preciſe Counterpart, that the
Demurity of her Dreſs, and the Sanctity of her
Countenance made her look like the Great-
Grand-Daughter of *John* of *Leyden,* or his
Contemporary *Knipperdoling,* as if they were
only come to pry into the Vices of the Wicked,
on purpoſe to Reform them. A Tenth, with a
looſe Coat on, to ſhift off upon Occaſion, with
the out-ſide of one Colour, and the Lining of
another, Dreſs'd up *Parte per pale,* like a Moderator's Conſcience, who ſhuffl'd backwards
and forwards, and from one Side to the other,
as if he had a Maggot in his Head, and a Worm
in his Tail, and that he had a Mind to Dance
the amphibeous Part of an *Hermophradite* between both Sexes; yet had choſen out a Partner ſo very like himſelf, that ſhe had a Gown
on as white as a Surplice, and a Petticoat as
black as the Devil, and ſquinted ſo confoundedly, that when ſhe had one Eye upon her
Partner, the other was expreſſing her affectionate Tenderneſs to ſome more faſhionable Gallant. Thus the mottl'd Diverſity of Rakes,
Beaus, grave Hypocrites, and Apprentices;
Pimps, Bullies, Stallions, Vallets, Butlers, and
diſguis'd

difguis'd Livery-Men; Thieves, Gamefters,
Sweetners, Town-Traps, and Highway-Men;
Procurers, Punks, Cooks, Jades, and Chamber-
Maids; damn'd filing Whores, ftill Sows, and
Firefhips; lewd Widows, wicked Wives, and
whorifh Daughters; thefe larded, by Chance,
with here and there a Maid, but the feweft of
that Sort of any. The chief Motives that
induc'd fuch a Swarm of two Leg'd Caterpil-
lars to give their conftant Attendance at this
School of *Venus*, was, not fo much the Pleafure of exercifing their Pedeftals, and refrefhing Nature with a little wholfome Activity,
but to Ogle, Prattle, Wheedle, give convincing
Teftimonies, by their airy Agility, of their being charming Bedfellows; the Women to draw
in Cullies; the Men to furnifh themfelves with
new obliging Miftreffes, to put their Arfes by
one Sort of Dancing, into Tune for another,
and then to make Affignations; or for the hot
Codpiec'd *Libertines* to carry off their Doxies
to fome Bawdy-Houfe Conveniency, where,
without the danger of Surprife, they might
Dance *Adam's* Jig to no other Mufick than the
harmonious Creeking of a crazy Bedfted.
This *Buttock-Ball,* or *Diabolical Academy*, where
all Manner of Vice was promifcuoufly Taught
at a fmall Expence, by the Exemplar Levity
of fuch Perfons who were abfolute Mafters
and Miftreffes of all that was Infamous and
Wicked, was begun, above thirty Years fince,
by a half-bred Dancing-Mafter, over the Cole-
Yard

Yard Gateway into *Drury-Lane*; a Place fo
conveniently feated among Punks and Fidlers,
that the Mungril Undertaker was always fure
of Mufick, and equally certain of a Crowd of
Whores to Dance to it; and as to lewd Rakes
to match 'em, there could be no want of 'em,
for where fhould the Crows come but where
the Carrion's to be found? So that the Project
of Iniquity was no fooner put on Foot, but it
had fuch wonderful Encouragement from thofe
obliging Ladies, who delight to expofe their
Wares and Commodities to Sale at all publick
Market-Places, that the Eighteen-Penny Gallery at the Play-Houfe began to be as thin of
fat Bawds and Vizards, upon the Cole-Hole
Dancing-Nights, as the Church-Pews are of
loofe Sparks and wanton Ladies on an *Afhwed-
nefday,* who rather chufe to tarry at Home,
than to begin their *Lent* with Curfing one another; infomuch that the Undertaking took
mightily, and every Publick-Day was throng'd
with more Sinners than Doctor *B——s*'s Meeting-Houfe; fo that at length, the Mafter of
the Ceremonies thinking the Place too fcandalous for fo commendable a Vaulting-School,
took a more commodious Habitation in *King-
Street* in St. *Giles*'s, where he had not only the
Conveniency of a more noble Dancing-Room,
but alfo two or three fpare Retiring-Rooms,
where a Favourite Scholar, or Cuftomer, might
Whifper away a Night or two with a young
Lady upon a reafonable Confideration. Thus
the

the Undertaker of the Project went profpe-
roufly on with his Dancing *Bear-Garden* for
near thirty Years together, and got abundance
of Money without any Interruption, till at
laft, being perfecuted by the *Reforming-Society*,
he was forc'd to break up his Revels, and let
his *Firking-School* to an Independant Teacher,
that the unhallow'd Room might be cleans'd
of its Polution, and Attone, in its latter Days,
for its former Iniquities.

Thus all Terreflial Things of Courfe,
Soon change to better or to worfe.

Churches have heretofore, by Rebels,
Been turn'd to Garrifons and Stables;
And Schools to make Maids fit for Spoufes,
Have been reform'd to Meeting-Houfes.
The Godly e'ery Day we fee,
Will ftart from Grace to Liberty;
And the poor Whore fometimes Repents,
And claims a Place among the Saints:
Knaves, tho' unpunifh'd by Afflictions,
Turn Puritans by ftrange Convictions;
And Puritans, tho' near their Graves,
As oft turn Vice verfa Knaves;
So that in Spite of all our Nofes,
What wicked Satan one Way lofes,

To keep his Int'reſt at a Stand,
He gains again on t'other Hand :
So cunning Gameſters, Satan's Sons,
Recover by the Devil's Bones
What at his Books they've thrown away,
Or ſquander'd at ſome other Play.

The Coward who in one Kings Reign,
Is fearful of a ſharp Campaign,
Perhaps i'th' next his Weapon draws,
And ſwaggers in another Cauſe :
The Traytor may in Time, grow juſt,
And change into a Man of Truſt ;
Or he that's now ſo Juſt and Wiſe,
Turn Fool, or Rebel, e'er he Dies :
The very Prieſt that win's our Hearts,
Extol'd for Honeſty and Parts
May prove, in Spite of all his Grace,
A Janus *with a double Face :*
Religion, once a Popiſh Whore,
We ſee is now made very Pure :
Who knows but that again ſhe may,
One Time or other, run aſtray ?

Therefore,

Therefore, since Manners, Men, and Nations
Are subject to such strange Mutations,
Why should we wonder that a Place,
So infamously Lewd and Base,
Should now be made a Shop of Grace.

Nothing unalter'd long can rest;
All are but Changlings at the best.

C H A P.

CHAP· XIX.

Of the BIRD-FANCIERS *Club:*

And of their Annual Feaſt.

AMong the many whimſical Societies that, by the diffcrent Maggots of conceited Perſons in this Town, have been advanc'd and promoted, there are a ſelect Company of Gentle and Simple, Tag, Rag, and Bob-Tail, who have a Weekly Meeting, at a little Ale-Houſe in *Roſemary-Lane,* and are pleas'd to call themſelves the *Bird-Fanciers-Club,* none being admitted Members thereof, but ſuch, whoſe Affection to the Feather-Kind render them fitter Company for *Jack-Daws* and *Magpies,* than for their own Fellow Creatures, eſpecially thoſe who have ſhifted off thoſe Puerilous Recreations, of Searching Hedges for Birds-Neſts, and bringing Sparrows to Hat. When the Society are met, they generally conſiſt of as odd a Mixture as a Broker's Wardrobe in *Long-Lane,*

Lane, or *Monmouth-Street,* where a Beauiſh
Sute, ſold by a Gentleman's Vallet, ſhall hang
up in View between a Patch'd Doublet and a
Leathern Pair of Breeches ; and a fine Lac'd
Cloak be diſhonour'd with the ſcandalous Com-
pany of a Soldier's Louſy Coat, or an old
Thread-bare Livery ; ſo it frequently happens among theſe comical Admirers of the
Harmonious Quire ; for a well dreſs'd Gentleman, tho' with no more Brains in his Skull
than there are in an Owl's-Neſt, ſhall ſit
wedg'd in between a couple of Louſy Bird-
Catchers, whoſe Cloaths on their Backs are
ſcarce good enough to be remov'd from the
Dunghill into a Rag-Merchant's Ware-Houſe.
Next theſe a Cuckoldly Shop-Keeper out of
Cheap-Side, ſo in Love with Pidgeons, that
he keeps them in his Garret, hem'd in between
a couple of *Newgate* look'd Scoundrels, that
cry Singing-Birds about Streets, and make it
their Buſineſs to cheat Barren Wives, and fanciful Old Maids with Twittering *Green-Birds,*
Sick *Sky-Larks,* and Hen *Linnets.* Adjoyning
to theſe ſhall ſit a Maggotty Ale-Houſe-keeper,
who, to pleaſure himſelf much more than his
Cuſtomers, has turn'd his Publick-Room into
a great *Avery,* that the Birds may ſhite Flying upon Peoples Heads , and now and then
muddy their Drink with a *Hemp-Seed* Surreverence. Next him ſhall ſit, in great State,
a famous Bird-Doctor, who, after Twenty
Years Experience, by the Bleſſing of Providence

dence, can infallibly cure *Canary-Birds* of a Hoarseneſs; ſullen *Sky-Larks* out of the dumb Melancholy; all Feather'd Songſters of a molting Drowſineſs, or any other Diſtemper; Poultrey of the Pip; and. Pidgeons, when they are Louſy. Oppoſite to the Doctor, it may be, ſits a *Canary-Bird* Merchant, entreating his Aſſiſtance on the Behalf of a poor Cage Patient, who was frighted out of Song by the horrible Aſſaſſination of a terrible Boar-Cat. Next him, perhaps, is ſeated an Old Cobler who has taught, in his time, as many *Blackbirds* to Whiſtle *Walſingham,* as ever Dr. *Blow* did Boys to Sing the Church Litany. Among the reſt a Journeyman Flute-maker, with his Pocket full of Bird-Pipes, trying now and then a Tune, as if he whiſtl'd for a Cuſtomer. Next him, a Famous Projector of Wire Goals, otherwiſe call'd a Bird-Cage-Maker, Chalking out upon the Table the neweſt Model of wicker Building for an *Owl* or a *Magpy,* and Chattering as learnedly of Cage Architecture, as if there was as much Judgment in raiſing a little Cottage for a poor *Jenny-Ren,* as in the excellent Contrivance of a Pompous Eſcurial. Theſe mix'd with a noiſie Crowd of Neſt-Robbers, and Pidgeon-Merchants, Some talking of their *Spaniſh Runts, Rough-Foots, Copple-Crowns,* and *Carriers.* Others contending about the Harmonious Singing of their *Linnets, Wood-Larks, Finches, Nightingals* and *Canary-Birds*: A Third Sort boaſting of the admirable Elocution of their *Parrots, Magpies, Jack-Daws,* and *Sterlings.* A Fourth Cabal, Boasting of the excellent Beauty of their *Muscovy Ducks, Frizzl'd Hens* and *Peacocks.* Among the rest a Knot of Gardeners extolling the *Lapwing* above all other Birds, for an officious Worm-Picker; asserting they are as necessary in a Gentleman's Garden, as an *Owl* in a Barn, or Cat in a Cheese Loft. Thus altogether, like a *Dover-Court,* every one would be setting forth the great Acquirements, as well as the natural Qualifications, of those Kind of Birds which had most engag'd their Affections, whilst a fresh Supply of Full *Winchesters* were flowing every Minute to their several united Tables, which were patch'd together for the Entertainment of the Company, some higher, some lower, like the Stools and Chairs in a Country Farmer's Parlour.

How can we blame our Infant Sons
For loving Tops, and Inkhorn Guns :
Or think them foolish when they Cry
For this, or that fantastick Toy,
Since Fathers, old enough for Grandsires,
Of Silly Birds can be such Fanciers,
And, Children like, disturb their Brains,
About Tom-Tits *and* Jenny-Rens ?
'Tis true the Old Egyptian *Wizards,*
Paid Homage to their Bats *and* Buzzards,

N 2 *And*

And reverenc'd fair Minerva's *Bird,*
As if the Owl *had been a Lord.*
But in this Age, when Christian Souls
Adore their Gold instead of Owls,
And Men improve the Art of Thinking,
By little Study, and much Drinking,
'Tis Time that Man should bend his Mind
To Pleasures of a Nobler Kind;
And not to Whistle Time away,
With feather'd Voices Day by Day,
To teach poor silly Birds the Tune,
Of Pudding-Pies, *or* Bobbing-Jone,
When his apt Scholars may at last,
Perhaps, but break some Puss's *Fast;*
Who in one short, but fatal Minute,
May snap his Black-bird, *or his* Linnet,
For which, perhaps, the foolish Ninny,
Had just before refus'd a Guinea;
Then in a Passion swears the Tongue
That bid the Gold was ev'ly hung.

So when Goff Crump, *by* Gammer Brig,
Is bid the Value of his Pig,
And he the Money does deny,
Because the Beauty of his Sty;

Next

Next Day, perhaps, some fatal Murrain
Turns the poor Gaffer's Shoat to Carrion;
Then Crump *in Anger, runs to claw*
The Hag, that he her Blood may draw,
In Hopes to baulk the Witch, and save
His other Swine from Dunghill Grave.

Once in a Year, our Mufical Admirers of Cage-Harmony, who are charm'd so unaccountably with a little Twitter and Chearup, Entertain not only themselves, but any that will take Tickets, with a most sumptious Feast; where a Comedy, call'd, *Confufion*, is so naturally reprefented, that setting afide the Variety of Languages, *Babel* it felf was never acquainted with a greater. One half of the Company generally confifts of all Sorts and Degrees of infatuated Lovers of the Chirping Quire, from the fantaftical Efquire down to the merry Tranflator of old Shoes and Spatter-Dafhes; the other Moitie of the promifcuous Guefts are commonly made up of Men of large Stomachs, who have good Stowage; guzzling Carmen and Porters, who have wide Swallows; and fuch who out of Curiofity come to obferve the Diforder, and to Delight themfelves with the odd Variety that never fails to arife among the mix'd Rabble of fuch irregular Societies. The Houfe, in comparifon to moft that are converted to publick Ufes, is no bigger than a Bird-

Cage,

Cage, for which Reafon, I fuppofe, it was the
rather chofen by the *Bird-Fanciers*, for their
Place of Rendezvouz. So that, upon their Feftival Day, there is not a Nook in either the
Boozing Ken or the Yard big enough to hold a
Crooked Pigmy about the Height of a Nine-
pin, but what is occupy'd by fome Ticket Gueft
or other, who, rather than lofe their Twelve-
penny Dinner, will crow'd into an Auger-Hole.
every Room in the Coney-Borough Manfion,
upon this folemn Occafion, is ftuff'd fo full of
Seats and Tables, for the Victuals and the Company, that when they are crowded into their
Places, they fit as clofely wedg'd as a Firkin
of Figs, or a Barrel of Red-Herrings.   The
principal Table for the better Part of the Guefts,
fuch as the Worfhipful Efquire *Avery*, Mr.
Deputy *Love-Linnet*, Captain *Magpye* of the
Hamlets, and as many more of the *Bird-Fancy-
ing* Fraternity, and Heads of the Parifh, as can
crow'd in amongft 'em, is fpread up two pair
of Stairs, in the moft commodious Room, tho'
not much larger than a Brewers Copper: However, to make amends, thefe are honour'd with
whetted Knives, whofe Variety of Handles
difcover all the Diverfity that can poffibly be
found from the Elephants Tooth, and *Bucks*
Brow Antlers, to the Tip of the Bullocks Horn,
and Wooden Twopenny *Brumingham:* Alfo decently entertain'd with clean Linnen, that looks
of as many Colours, as the patch'd Sails of a
Newcaftle Collier refitted after a Tempeft:
Some

Some of the Napkins appearing as grey for
want of Whitening; fome as blue with over
Starching ; fome as yellow, with long Lying;
and others as white, with good Wafhing, as
if all the Huffwifes in the Neighbourhood un-
lock'd their Trunks to fupply the Feaft with
their Home-fpun Flaxen , which they had
carefully laid by againft the Marriage of their
Daughters.

In other Rooms, or rather Clofets, which are
feldom furnifh'd but upon this Occafion, the
Leaves of the Tables are rough Deal-Boards ;
fo full of ragged Splinters, for Want of Plain-
ing, that there is as much Danger in laying
down a Hand without Caution, as there is in-
grafping the Branches of an old ftubborn
Goofebury-Bufh; for the Ceremony of a Table Cloth was quite laid afide, as if it was as
obnoxious to the Company as a Surplice to a
Conventicle ; fo that Nothing appears befides
batter'd Plates, and crack'd Trenchers, to hide
the fhagged Boards, which are juft in the fame
Condition as they were brought from the Saw-
Pit, and only loofely laid upon empty Butts
and Barrels, that as the Gueft fit at their Tables, when over-gorg'd, they may pifs into the
Bung-Holes to make Room for more Liquor.
Whoever propofes to make a hearty Meal
ought to take fpecial Care to bring a Knife in
their Pocket; or, notwithftanding the Feaft, they
may chance to make a Faft-Day of it, if they
depend upon the Borrow ; their Seats have

N 4   hitherto

hitherto been an odd Mixture of little Forms, Crickets, Buffet-Stools, and Runlets; the laſt of which are commonly choſen by the greateſt Guzzlers, becauſe, when Nature is ſo oppreſt that they want Leakage, they may turn their Conduit Pipes into the Tap-Holes of the Caſks they ſit upon, without giving themſelves the Trouble of a Remove to the Chamber-Pot. Moſt parts of the Houſe, beſides the Club-Room above, and the Boxes below, are furniſh'd upon the Feſtival after the foregoing Manner, and I make no Doubt but ſome of the Society, whom my Landlord dare truſt, are glad to ſqueeze into the Cellar, there to ſtand among Tap-Tubs, devour their Dinner's upon But-Heads, and to wipe their greaſy Fingers betwixt their Legs upon their patch'd Breeches. Their Proviſions conſiſt always of the beſt Subſtantials, as Beef, Pork, and Mutton, for they are ſeldom troubl'd with ſuch ſqueamiſh Stomachs that require the Cookery of a *Pontac*, or *Locket*, to toſs up Dainties for their Appetites; there being ſome of the Company who, for their own ſingle Shares, would eat a *Rumford Calf* cut into *Scotch* Collups, beſides an anſwerable Proportion of forc'd Meats and Bacon; for which Reaſon the Bill of Fare, as it is order'd by the Stewards, is moſt commonly a true *Engliſh* Catalogue of noble Su-Loins, huge Thundering Legs of right *Hampſhire* Pork, and aſtoniſhing fat Giggets of rare *Leiceſterſhire* Mutton: As for Lady-Picking Wild-Fowl,

Fowl, Venfon-Pafties, and fuch expenfive Su-
perfluities, they leave them to the Court Quality, and rich gormondizing Citizens, who
have little elfe to do with their Money but
fool it away upon nice Bits, Raggoes, and
Kickfhaws : As to Liquors, like true and faithful Subjects, they never exceed the natural
Products of our own Country, but chearfully content themfelves with full *Winchefters*
of good Mild and Stale, the rare coroborating
Juice of wholefome Malt and Hops, fuch that
ftrengthens the Backs of Jolly Watermen, Porters, Coachmen, Carmen, and Black Thirfty
Vulcans, who drudge at the Nuptial Anvil, like
Slaves in a Plantation, to hammer out lufty
Boys for the Defence and Service of their
Country, and abandon all inglorious Lufts
after foreign Clarets, thofe coftly Occafions
of Feavers, Gouts, and Rheumatifms. The
laft Difh which is brought up two Pair of
Stairs to the principal Table, is a live Bird Pye,
which contains fuch Variety of feather'd
Songfters, that no fooner is the Lid cut up,
and the little Prifoners fet at Liberty, who
lay before immur'd between Pye-Cruft Walls,
but the Room, in an Inftant, is turn'd into an
Avery, whilft the Company, like Wild-Cats,
tumble all into Confufion, and madly leaping
over one anothers Heads, claw, fight, and
fcramble, in their Hair-Brain'd Perfuit of their
poor frighted Quarry; who, to efcape the
Hands of their contending Enemies, dodg them
for

for a Time till some of the Fatteft of the Company, quite tir'd with the Chafe, are forc'd to give out, and fit Puffing, Hawking, and Coughing, ready to difcharge their full Stomachs of thofe greafy Dabs they had fo plentifully Eaten, whilft others, who have more Breath, and are more active, catch the beft of the Birds, that they may carry them Home as Tokens of their Affections to their Wives and their Daughters; upon the Difpatch of this Ceremony, which is commonly attended with broken Shins, much Laughter, and abundance of Diforder, the Dinner is concluded, and then the Plate is handed about for the Relief of the poor Widow of fome Deceas'd Bird-Fancier, which has no fooner made its Way thro' the feveral Branches of the well ftuff'd Society, but a Period is put to the grand Solemnity; and, *You are Heartily Welcome Gentlemen.*

How fond is e'ery Fool to be a Gueft,
Where wild Diforder Crowns the noifie Feaft?
As if indecent Scrambling with each Clown
And rude Confufion makes the Meat go down:
Sure Wife and Children, whom we ought to love,
Vexatious Mefs-Mates to the Hufband prove,
Or elfe no Spoufe would rather chufe to Dine
Among fuch greedy Herds of two Leg'd Swine,

Where

Where dirty Boards on musty Vessels lye
As Tables, some too low, and some too high;
And where course Towels of a Groat a Yard,
Are only to the Parish Dons prefer'd;
Whilst those of lower Rank have neither Cloth,
Or Napkin, but are destitute of both;
Yet all sit easy o'er the Fare they find,
And gladly lick their Fingers when they've Din'd;
Drink with their Lips unwip'd till greasy Oil
Glazes the Surface of their powr'ful Swill:
Yet no nice Guest, like squeamish Beau finds Fault,
But swallows down the Fat that Crowns the
                                        Malt;
Why not? Since each Man, left the Proverb Lyes,
Must Eat a Peck of Dirt before he Dies.

But if at publick Feasts we can agree
With such course Usage and Indecency;
And tho' we pay, yet be content to bear
With Slights & Failings when our Hosts shall Err.
Why then at Home, when Trifles prove amiss,
Should we grow angry and disturb our Peace?
What tho' the Capons are in Roasting spoil'd;
Or the Calves-Head too Much, or Little boil'd?

What

What if the Cloth be neither clean or fine,
When some dear Bottle Friend's brought Home
[to Dine:
Or that your Wife should at the Table Frown,
Because, perhaps, Undrest, in Morning Gown,
For want of Timely knowing she should be
Oblig'd to Entertain strange Company;
Why should such Female Follies vex our Hearts,
And make us Mad at Home by Fits and Starts?
Since we Abroad, at our Expence, can bear
A Thousand Faults that more provoking are,
To the proud Madams of the Bar Bow low,
But to our Wives Moross and Slighting grow:
Wink at great Errors for a Vict'ler's Gain,
But oft at Home without a Cause Complain.

Therefore, since guzzling Spendthrifts can
[dispense
With Dirty Ale-House Slights without Offence,
When Maudlin Drunk they from their Revels
[come,
They should not Crow and Tyrannize at Home:
For he that snubs his Wife he ought to prize,
Is Born to be a Cuckold e'er he Dies.

CHAP.

CHAP. XX.

Of the LYING Club:

And how it came to be Establish'd.

SIR *Harry Blunt*, a Witty Gentleman, and very famous in the Art of *Mendaciloquence*, being under an Obligation to give a Tavern Treat to some foreign Travellers, who were come over into *England*, to make themselves acquainted with our Customs and Curiosities, did accordingly Invite, in the Year Sixty Nine, his Out-Landish Guests to the *Bell-Tavern* in *Westminster*, to a plentiful Entertainment; Their Dinner consisting of a huge over-grown *Carp* stew'd; three Brace of *Partridge* and a *Leveret* in the Middle, for the second Course, and a Butter'd Apple-Pye to conclude the Feast. When each of the Company had suffic'd Nature, and their Tongues began to be at their usual Liberty, the Dainties which so lately had oblig'd their Appetites, occasion'd them to fall into a Discourse of Fishing

ing, Fowling, and fuch Sort of Sports, as 'tis reafonable to believe the Creatures they had eaten muft naturally introduce, efpecially among fuch Perfons that happen'd to be Sportsmen; fo that every one being fond of amufing the reft with fome extraordinary Adventure, as an Evidence of his Skill in thofe Rural Recreations., a forward Gentleman, who was willing to break the Way, begins the following Story, to fhew what miraculous Succefs he had once met with in his Hunting, *viz.*

About feven Years fince, when I liv'd in *France*, a few Leagues from *Mompellier*, in the County of *Languedock*, an unhappy Gentleman, who was my near Neighbour, happen'd to be murder'd by his own Servant, who alfo broke open a Cafket, and carry'd off fome Jewels of a confiderable Value; but publick Intelligence being immediately difpatch'd throughout the whole Kingdom, there was no Poffibility of attempting to get over Sea from any of the Ports but he muft, of Neceffity, have been Taken. About a Week after this horrid Villany was perpetrated, the Seafon being agreeable, I had a ftrong Defire, mov'd by fome fecret Impulfe, to take out my Dogs, being inwardly affur'd, that in fuch a diftant Wood I fhould meet with a Wild Boar that would yield us excellent Sport, accordingly, one Morning an Hour before Sun Rife, having given my Huntfman Notice over Night, we were all in a Readinefs to take the Field; and pre-

poffeffed

poſſeſſed of Infallible Succeſs away I Mar-
ched, with only my Huntſman, a Relation and my Servant, in Queſt of the Game
I had already rowz'd in my Fancy, we
had not long been enter'd into the Avenues
of the appointed Wood, but the Dogs,
who were beating in one of the thickeſt Cop-
ſes, began to Open, and no ſoooner had the
Huntſman given them Encouragement, but
away they went full Cry, tho', what Game
they had met with was but as yet Conjecture,
at length, hearing them all Open in the Middle of the Wood a long Time together without
any Ceſſation, and much about the ſame Place,
as near as we could gueſs, we judg'd, by the
Eagerneſs of their Mouths, that they had ſomething at a Bay, upon which, fir'd with the
Reſolution of keen Sportſmen, we bolted
thro' the under Wood, leaving here a Bit of
Coat, and there a Bit of Skin, to back the Dogs
againſt their powerful Adverſary, who, as we
thought, was defending himſelf with his
Tuſhes; at laſt, after many painful Scratches,
and other implacable Difficulties, we came in
to the Hounds, who were all ſpending and
tearing at the Bottom of a high Tree as if the
Devil had poſſeſs'd them; but finding no
Signes of any Thing that could warm the
Dogs with ſuch unuſual Fury, we were ready
to conclude they had hunted ſome old Witch
in the Shape of a Boar, who had given them
the Drop in that Place, by Mounting upon a
Withe,

Withe, and Riding o'er the Tops of the Trees
to take Sanctuary in her own Cottage; but,
as we were thus standing under the Umbrage
of the Oak which the Dogs had surrounded,
all strangely amus'd at this uncommon Disappointment, down drops a Surreverence from
the Top of the Tree upon the Withers of my
Horse, just under my Nostrils, which, in plain
English, stunk much worse than ever I smelt
a *Pole-Cat* ; Morblu, thought I, what unlucky Bird is this that has dishonour'd my Galloper with such an ignoble Crest? And with
that, looking upwards, I beheld a huge bald
Pair of Buttocks, with the other Appurtenances hanging dangling down like a Lyon's
Tongue when he has been well Hunted, per-
ched upon a crooked Bow instead of a House-
of-Office, to prevent the unsavory Fruits of
his Labour from dripping into his Trouzers.
How now, Sirrah, said I, Trees were made
for Birds to Perch upon, and not such Beasts
as you are, who cannot elevate your unmannerly Rump, but you must pour down your Den-
delyon Dung upon the Heads of your Betters.
Pray Sir, forgive me, crys the poor Fellow, *it was
nothing but the Overflowings of my extraordinary
Fear ; and I thought a cleanly Stool would be much
more comfortable than a foul Pair of Breeches.*
Sirrah, said I, come down, and let me know
who and what you are, or my Man's Fusee shall
fetch you off your Perch ; upon which Threat,
he only beg'd Leave to Buttton up his Breeches,

ches, faying, he would then defcend, and fub-
mit himfelf to our Mercy; accordingly the
frighted Refugee quitted his lofty Station, and
flid down the Trunk with as much Agility as
a Monkey; but, no fooner had he drop'd himfelf upon *Terra Firma*, e'er I prefently difcover'd him to be my Friend's Servant who
had Rob'd and Butcher'd his Mafter; upon
which, I pofitively charg'd him with the Fact,
and with a forrowful Countenance he confefs'd himfelf Guilty, I then enquir'd of him
what was the meaning that the Hounds perfu'd him, to which he anfwer'd he could
affign no Reafon, but thefe Two; the Firft
was, *That his Pumps were made of the Tan'd
Hide of a Wild-Boar, and by the Heat of his
Feet left a Scent, as he fuppos'd, upon the Ground,*
which the Hounds had been us'd to; or elfe,
*That Providence had ordain'd that a Man who
had kill'd his Mafter fhould be Hunted by Dogs
into the Hands of Juftice*; fo, in this Miraculous Difcovery we ended the Sport of the Day,
and deliver'd the Offender into the Power of
the Law, who, in a little Time, was broke upon the Wheel, as he juftly deferv'd, for his
moft treacherous Villany.

No fooner was this Story ended, but another Gentleman, with the Licenfe of a Traveller, fucceeded it with a fecond, no lefs remarkable for its furprizing Contingencies, than
what might be obferv'd in the preceding
Amufement, *viz.*

O   About

About Nine Years fince, being order'd from *Holland* to negotiate fome Bufinefs in *Nova Hollandia,* in the *Eaſt-Indies,* I was oblig'd to refide, for feveral Months, in the *Dutch* Factory; in which Time, being curious to infpect a little into the adjacent Country, I got an honeſt Fellow, who was a Neighbouring *Indian,* that could fpeak a little *Dutch* to bear me Company; and willing to give my felf fome Diverfion in my Ramble, I took with me fuch Fifhing-Tackle as the Country afforded, that we might pleafe ourfelves, by the Way, with an Hour or Two's Recreation by the Sides of fuch Rivers as we fhould chance to meet with, Angling being a contemplative Paftime that I always delighted in. When we were thus equip'd for our wandring Expedition, away we jog'd upon our Pedeftals, till at laft we came to a pleafant River which the *Indian* was acquainted with, who told me, it abounded with a delicious *Fiſh* in the Language of the Natives call'd a *Powton,* which fignifies a Glutton; fo nam'd, becaufe a voracious Fifh that would frequently prey upon its own Kind; Walking by the Banks to pick out a fhady Place that might give us a little Umbrage from the fcorching Sun-Beams, we at length came to a curious Bed of Ofiers, where we might ftand with Pleafure, and there accordingly we prepar'd our Tackle, and refolv'd to try our Fortune. The *Indian* being but a Bungler at this fort

of

of Sport, could not get himself in a Readiness
so soon as my self; so that I was enter'd upon
my Pastime, whilst he was very Busie in fumb-
ling out his Implements; nor had I laid into the River above two Minutes, e'er I found
by my Float I had a swinging Bite, but, as ill
Fortune would have it, I happen'd upon my
Head to have a feather'd Cap, much worn in
that Country, and as my Noddle was moving
among the Tops of the Osiers, a swinging
Hawk, which are generally very large in those
Parts, hovering aloft just over me and taking,
I suppose, the Plumes upon my Noddle to be
some strange sort of Bird, and having a Mind
to taste whether 'twas good Food or not, came
sooping down, and made such a furious Stroak
at her new Quarry, that I thought, for a Minute or two, she had left my Shoulders Head-
less; under which Surprize I drop'd my An-
gle-Rod and so lost my Fish; but coming by
Degrees a little to my self, I began to scratch
my Ears to feel whether I had a Head on, and
in groping after that, I found I had only lost
my Cap; I was very much amaz'd at this unaccountable Assault, and gazing around me to
discover the Assailant, but seeing no Body near
me but my *Indian* Companion on the other
Side the River, I turn'd my Eyes upwards,
and at a considerable Distance, there I saw the
feather'd Thief sailing upon the Wing to the
next Wood, I suppose, to examine into his
Booty; my Fishing Mate was so busie that he

perceiv'd

perceiv'd not the Difafter, and was as much
furpriz'd when I told him what had happen'd,
as I my felf was who had furviv'd the Danger; However, having no great Dammage, I
ftood again to my Tackle, and apply'd my
felf to my Sport, but remember'd the Sportfman's Saying, *viz. Ware Hawk,* and kept my
Eyes about me, for fear the hungry Raparee
who had fnatch'd away my Cap, when fhe
found herfelf difappointed, fhould come again
for my Head, which, as empty as it is, I was
very unwilling to fpare her; I had not long
been return'd to my Paftime, e'er I had another Bite, but juft as I ftruck I found a ftrange
Flouncing in the Water, and fuch a Weight
pulling at the End of my Line, that I did not
dare to weigh what I had faften'd for fear of
fhivering my Tackle, fo that I play'd with my
unknown Supper down the Stream, till at
length we came to a Gravelly Shallow,
where, with eager Eyes, I beheld the Monfter I had tir'd with my Management, upon
Sight of which in ftept my Companion, and
it was as much as he could do to give him a
Heave upon the Shoar; when we had thus
fecur'd him, he had fo gorg'd my Hook, that
I was forc'd to rip him open, or muft have
broke my Line, but found upon the Defeċtion
that the leaft of feven Fifh had firft taken the
Bait, and being well faften'd was fwallow'd by
a bigger; thefe two by a third; the three by
a fourth; the four by a fifth; the five by a
fixth,

fixth, and all thofe by an over-grown large
one, which compleated the Number aforemention'd, fo that I caught a Neft of Fifh one
within another, at one fortunate Stroak, to
make my felf amends for the Lofs of my feather'd Cap, at which Succefs I was fo highly
pleas'd, that we put up our Tackle and retur-
ned homewards with abundance of Satisfaction; but that which happen'd to be the moft
fortunate Miracle that attended our Adventure, was, that juft as we came within Sight
of the Factory, my Cap which I had loft after
fo odd a Manner, came tumbling down in a
perpendicular Line, from a lofty Diftance, and
chuck'd as clofe upon my Noddle, as a new
Hat fitted on by an *Englifh* Haberdafher; being ftrangely ftartled to find fomething clap'd
upon my Head and my Companion before me,
I pull'd off my Bonnet in a great Surprize,
and perceiv'd it to be the very individual
Cap which the *Hawk* had rob'd me of, and
viewing it all over for my better Affurance,
found that the merry Bird had muted in
the Lining, and, either through Defign or
Accident, had crown'd me with a Surreverence: I prefently recollected the old *Englifh*
Pioverb, *viz. That fhitten Luck was good
Luck*, and highly commended the good Humour of the *Hawk*, that would not fuffer me
to return into the Factory with a callow Pole,
which being new fhav'd was as bare as a Birds
Arfe, fo I wip'd off the Soil, put on my fea-

O 3   ther'd

ther'd Mounteer, and was pleas'd I had met with a Bird of Prey that had much more Honesty than some of my Fellow Creatures. Upon the Conclusion of which Story, *Indeed, Sir,* says Sir Harry Blunt, *had not the* Hawk *been so civil as to return your Cap, I would have given you mine, for I think you deserve, for the Wonders you have told us, all the Caps in the Company.*

Sir *Harry* being a Gentleman of ready Wit, and quick Invention, and it now falling to his Turn to entertain the Company, considering it highly concern'd his Reputation to oblige them with something that might be worthy of his Character, accordingly he presented them with a Specimen of his Genius after the following Manner, *viz.*

As for my Part, Gentlemen, the only Exercise that I particularly delight in, is drawing the long Bow, in which Piece of Archery, by continual Practice, I am so expert, that I have oftentimes, with an Arrow, taken a single Jack-Daw from the Weather-Cock of a Church-Steeple, so that I, as frequently go a Fowling with my Bow and Arrow, as other Gentlemen do with their Nets or Birding-Pieces, and as often return Home with unaccountable Success. It happen'd, no longer since than Yesterday Morning, that my Man and I cross'd the River into *Surrey*, to try if we could meet with any tollerable Sport on that Side the Water, where we rang'd the Woods and Fields

for

for feveral Hours, before we met with any
fort of Game that was worth our Shooting at,
infomuch, that we were quite tir'd with our
Fruitlefs Endeavours, and to eafe our Legs,
had taken up our Sitting upon the pleafant
Bank of a narrow Rivelet; alfo to confult
which Way we fhould fteer our Courfe, that
we might mend our Fortune; as we were
thus Talking and Refiefhing our weary Limbs,
cafting my Eyes around me, I happen'd to efpy a *Wood-Pecker* very bufie at Work upon
the Trunk of an Apple-Tree, whofe Boughs
were laden with very beautiful Fruit, growing by chance in a Meadow on the other Side
of the River, fo that, tho' I very well knew
a *Wood-Pecker* was no Food, yet, to exercife
my Hand, I refolv'd to let fly at her, accordingly drew my Bow, at which Inftant up leap'd
a fwinging Carp, a great Height above the
Stream, in a Diametrical Line to the Mark I
had taken Aim at, that my Arrow very luckily took the Fifh in the Head, carry'd that to
the *Wood-Pecker* and peg'd them both faft into the Body of the Apple-Tree, being greatly
overjoy'd at this unexpected Succefs, by the
Help of my Man's Grane-Staff I took a Running Jump and fprung over the River, and
pulling out my Arrow with fome Difficulty,
down drop'd my Fowl and Fifh both as dead
as a Herring; upon this, ftooping for a little
Grafs to wipe off the Blood from the Peg of
my Arrow, I happen'd to catch a young *Leve-*
rite

rite by the Ears, who finding himſelf taken did ſo claw my Hands in Struggling for his Liberty, that, being vex'd at the Smart, I gave his Neck a Twiſt, and Flinging him in a Fury a few Yards from me, caſt him by good Fortune among a Covy of *Partridges*, and by the Violence of the Throw kill'd three Brace. Being ſtrangely aſtoniſh'd at this Miraculous Event of one ſingle Shoot, I toſs'd back the Staff that my Man might come over to me, who, with lifted up Hands, beheld the bleeding Wonder, and picking up the Game put them into his Hawking-Bag. By this Time the Heat of the Day and our tireſome Walk having made us drowthy, we began to remind our ſelves of the Apples over our Heads, ſo that I order'd my Man to climb the Tree, who mounted accordingly and ſhook down as much Fruit as we could well bring off with us; thus highly ſatisfy'd with our unexpected Succeſs, we return'd Home laſt Night on purpoſe to entertain this good Company with the Fruits of our Labour; ſo that the *Carp*, the *Partridges*, the *Leverite* and the *Apple-Pye*, which were brought to the Table this very Day, I hope will convince you, that I ſcorn to tell leſs Truth than the reſt of my Neighbours.

Pray, Sir Harry, ſays one of the Gentlemen, *what did you do with the* Wood-Pecker *?* Poh, poh, replies Sir *Harry*, I intend to dry him in an Oven, then hang him up in my Hall with

a

a Parchment Label about his Neck that fhall convey the Miracle to fucceeding Generations.

A fober grave Gentleman fitting next to Sir *Harry*, who had no extraordinary Talent in fuch fort of Stories, but it being his Turn to continue their Mirth, the Company were very importunate with him to oblige them with a Relation of fome Adventure that might be a-greeable wi' the former; but the Gentle-man, confcious of his own Infufficiency, and perceiving the reft to be all Mafters of the Art of Amufement, defired to be excus'd, but they ftill perfifted in their troublefome Entreaties till they teaz'd him into a Paffion, infomuch, that he wraps out a great Oath, and breaths out this Expreffion, *viz. I verily believe every Tittle you have faid to be infallibly True, and that, fince I muft be conformable, I think as great a Lye as any I have heard yet.*

The foregoing Sarcafme being fpoke with Warmth, it put the Company into a Fit of Laughter: *Well,* fays Sir *Harry, Since we are all Travellers, and fo happily met together, let us conftitute a Meeting once a Week in this ve-ry Houfe we are now fo Merry in, that we may refrefh Nature with a chearful Bottle, and ex-ercife our Faculties to one anothers Satisfacti-on*; to which Propofal the whole Company affented: *But hark ye, Sirs,* fays the Gentle-man whom they had teaz'd with their Impor-tunites, *a Society without a Name, is like a Book without a Title*; therefore, *if we intend*

to

to hold a conftant Meeting, it is neceffary we fhould affume fome certain Denomination; upon which, one would have it the *Gentleman's Club*, another the *Traveller's Club*: *No, no, fays the fleering Satyrift, let us call it the* Lying-Club, *and chufe Sir* Harry *for our Chair-Man:* Being all very Merry over their Wine, they were beft pleas'd with the laft Diftinction, accordingly refolv'd themfelves into a Club under the fame Title; and before they parted fettled all the Preliminaries, and agreed to be govern'd by the following Orders, *viz.*

Orders to be obferved by the LYING-CLUB, *holden at the* Bell-Tavern *in* Weftminifter.

I. THAT the *Chair-Man fhall be oblig'd to wear a Blue Cap with a Red Feather in it, or, upon his refufal to do the fame, fhall, for fuch Contempt, be turn'd out of the Society.*

II. *That no Perfon fhall be admitted as a Worthy Member of this Worfhipful Society, till he has given fufficient Teftimony of his Qualifications to the whole Board.*

III.

III. *That whoever shall presume to speak a Word of Truth between the establish'd Hours of Six and Ten, within this Worshipful Society, without first saying with an Audible Voice, be your Leave, Sir Harry, shall, for every such Offence, forfeit one Gallon of such Wine as Mr. Chair-Man shall think Fit.*

IV. *That when any worthy Member shall Modestly introduce any stupendious Improbability, beyond what the* Chair-Man *shall be able to parallel, that then the said* Chair-Man *shall resign his Cap, and deliver up his Chair to so deserving a Member, who shall Hold the same, till some other Member, by his extraordinary Merits shall happen to oblige him to the like Resignation.*

V. *That any worthy Member of this Worshipful Society, who shall presume to Swear during Club Hours, except to grace a Lye, shall, for every such Offence, forfeit one Bottle of such Wine as the* Chair-Man *shall appoint.*

VI. *That if any Member of this Worshipful Society shall neglect to appear upon the Club Night, between the aforesaid Hours of Six and Ten, that every such Aggressor, upon the succeeding Club Night, shall, for such Contempt, be a-merc'd four Rhodomontades off Hand, or forfeit Five Shillings to the Servants of the House, and in Case he doubles his Neglect by not atten-*

ding

ding the Board upon the next Club Night, then to be amerc'd upon his next Appearance, as many thumping Lies as the Chair-Man shall think fit, or to be expell'd the Society.

VII. *That no Parson be admitted as a Member of this Worshipful Society, except Doctor Oates, or such as shall bring under the Doctor's Hand and Seal a Testimonial of their Quallifications.*

VIII. *That this Worshipful Society be duly adjourn'd at Ten of the Clock, or the Chair-Man to forfeit a Gallon of Claret to the Board, and his Cap and Feather to his Right-Hand Neighbour.*

Upon this Footing the *Lying-Club* was at first establish'd, over which Sir *Harry Blunt* presided as *Chair-Man* above a Twelve-month, till at length, a merry Gentleman, who was an absolute Master of the Lying Faculty, disrob'd him of his Authority; but Sir *Harry* in a little Time recover'd his Reputation, and re-instated himself in the Chair, which he held successively for several Years after, till he had the Honour to become the Patron or Mæcenas of all the Fictions in the Town, therefore, since I have given you the Rise and Constitution of this Memorable Society, I shall now proceed to some of their fabulous Stories, delivered by certain Members upon their first Initiation,

ation ; alfo feveral remarkable Extravagancies
that pafs'd too and fro, between the famous
Knight, and fuch of the witty Members as
contended for the Chair.

In a fhort Time after the Society was eftablifh'd, came a Couple of young Gentlemen to
defire their Admittance, being well qualify'd,
as they thought, to perform their Exercife according to the Cuftom of the Club, upon
fending up their Bufinefs by a felect Drawer
that attended the Society, they were admitted
to the Board, to give Proof of their Endowments; upon which, the moft forward of the
Two began to exercife his Talent, (after paying his Compliment) in Manner following,
viz.

Gentlemen, about five Years fince, I had
the ill Fortune to Marry a very beautiful
Woman, in whofe delightful Embraces, for a
confiderable Time, I thought my felf not only
fecure, but extreamly happy, till at length, as I
was Walking early one Morning in my own
Grounds, according to my Cuftom, I happen'd
to meet with an old Woman, who was Saun-
tering towards my Dary-Houfe to beg a Pitch-
er of Butter-Milk, *Good Morrow to ye old Mother,* faid I, *Good Morrow Mafter,* quoth the
Beetle Brow'd *Beldam,* adding, if I would crofs
her Hand with a Piece of Silver, fhe would
tell me my Fortune, which accordingly I did,
but more out of Charity, than any Curiofity
I had to hear my Deftiny ; no fooner had fhe
receiv'd

receiv'd a Token of my Bounty, but, in plain
Words, she told me I was a Cuckold, you're a
Lying old Hag, said I; and I could find my
Heart to have you lash'd at the next Whipping-
Post. *Since you will not believe me,* crys the
surly Witch, *I'll make you see your Horns,
e'er you go much further*; and so we both
parted muttering at each other, but I had not
gone above Two Hundred Yards, before I
came to a curious Spring, which tempted me
to refresh my Eyes with some of the Running-
Water, which I had no sooner done, but stoo-
ping to the Stream to repeat the same, I saw
my self in the Water perfectly transform'd into a mighty Buck, with a Load of Antlers upon my Head sufficient to have set up a Knife
Cutler; I was strangely astonish'd at this unaccountable Change, and began to consider
that I was certainly bewitch'd, by that confounded Sorceress, who had told me my Fortune; for I still found I had my Memory left,
tho' I was depriv'd of Speech, and totally di-
vested of my Humane Appetites, so that my
Brains run upon Nothing but shady Woods and
fresh Pastures; and were so strangely possess'd
of unaccountable Fears, that the Barking of a
Dog frighted me much worse than a Clap of
Thunder; I now, to hide my self from the
Sight of the Passengers, made the best of my
Way to a Neighbouring Cover, where I lay in
Solitude for several Days and Nights, and
was glad to nibble oft the Bark of my own
Trees,

Trees for a Starving Suftenance: In this unhappy State of a Timorous Brute I liv'd for
feveral Months, till it began to be Rutting-
time with me, that I found my Dowfets Itch
as much after a Doe as ever my Concupi-
fcence did after a Woman, and was grown of
a fuddain fo Horn-mad withal, that I was ready to run a Tilt at every thing that came
near me; fo that I left my Cover in the Night
and Jump'd ver the Pales into my own Park,
in hopes to Match my felf with a Mate, where
I had not been above a Quarter of an Hour,
but I heard a ftrange Voice over my Head,
crying, *Marcum, Marcum, draw Blood of thy
Rival, and the fame fhall reflore thee to thy former Shape:* I liffen'd, you muft believe, with
all the Ears I had, and was glad to be inform'd,
that there was any poffibility of being once
more recover'd into a State of Humanity, but
was ftill as Ignorant which way to profecute
the Advice that the Witch or Devil had given
me, as I was, before I was inftructed, how to
fhift off my Brutality; fo that I was ready
to fancy, the Hag had only Scoff'd me, for I
could not forefee any profpect that I had of
perfuing her Directions; but the next Day
proving exceffive Hot, and I, who ought to
have been the Mafter Buck, being a Stranger to
the Herd, was beaten by my Horned Brethren,
from all the Covers of the Park, that for my
Eafe as well as my Security, I ventur'd to leap
over a lofty Pale, that fenc'd in an Orchard
adjacent

adjacent to my House, there couch'd my felf
amidft a Thicket of Curran-bufhes, where I
had not lain long, but my Rival and my Lady came failing along the Grafs, link'd fo amoroufly together, as if they were retir'd with a
mutual Defire of giving their Arfes a Salat:
Juft as I imagin'd, fo it prov'd, for no fooner
had they fkreen'd themfelves behind a thick
Holly Hedge, but down he lays my Lady, and
juft as he was going to add one Sprout more
to my unmerciful Creft, up roufes I, and with
the revengeful Fury of a Horn-mad Cuckold,
run full tilt at the Pofteriors of my Rival, and
Goring his Brawny Drivers with my Brow-
Antlers, I was immediately reftor'd to my pri-
ftine Humanity, which the Adultrefs beholding
in a ftrange Confufion, fkip'd as nimbly from
the Ground as a *Dutch* Tumbler; and flying
in a fright with her Gallant halting after her,
happen'd to plunge into a deep Well, over-
grown with Nettles, and her Spark upon her,
fo I clap'd on the Lid, for fear they fhould
ftruggle out again, went into my Houfe, reconcil'd my felf to my Servants, and came to
Town on purpofe to Oblige you ingenious
Gentlemen with this amufing Relation, in
hopes to become a Member of this worfhipful
Society.

Truly, Sir, replies the Chairman, *this Story
may pafs for a fubftantial Lye amongft fome
Ignorant Pretenders, who are not able to diftinguifh between Truth and Falfehood; but we*
ᴄannot

cannot here, by the *Laws* of our *Society, admit any Gentleman who is so Careless, in the Performance of his initiating Exercise, as to corrupt his Genious with the least Probability:* No adulterated *Lie, dash'd and brew'd with Truth, will pass Currant in this Eminent Society;* tho' *a great part of your Story is fabulous enough in Reason, yet nothing is more likely than that you may be a Cuckold, and the probability of that destroys the Incredibility of all you have reported; for as Truth out of a Lyar's Mouth ought scarce to be credited, so nothing can deserve the Sanction of a Lie, but what is refin'd with Judgement from all manner of Probability; therefore* I hope, *Sir, you will excuse us, for we cannot possibly admit you.*

This unexpected Disappointment so dash'd the poor Gentleman out of Countenance, that he had nothing further to offer in his Defence, but up he started, and stepping abruptly out of the Room, *Z——ds,* says he, *if such Lies as these will not pass Muster among you, the Devil himself is only fit to be your* Chairman; so went hastily down Stairs, left his Friend behind him, and march'd off, Muttering, very much dissatisfy'd.

No sooner had the Society dispatch'd this Gentleman, but Silence was commanded, and his Companion that came in with him was call'd upon to report to the Board what he had to offer, that might recommend him to the Society; upon which, tho' he was a little dispirited

pirited

pirited to fee his poor Friend come off fo un-
fuccefsfully, yet, having a pretty good Affurance, he refolv'd to give them a Specimen of
his Talent, and thus began his Amufement,
viz.

My Father, being a *Darbyſhire* Gentleman,
happen'd to have an old Seat near the *Peak*,
and a plentiful Eftate in that County ; behind
the Houfe, among other Wonders, there remains a deep Well, into which, not only our
own Family, but many of the Neighbours, in
the inteftine Wars, caft the beft of their
Treafure to fecure it from the Rebels; but,
when the Troubles were over, attempting to
recover what, as each believ'd, they had fo
carefully difpos'd of, they found upon their
Search, the Gulph that had fwallow'd up their
Wealth was of fuch an immenfurable Profun-
dity, that all the Cart Ropes in the Country,
join'd together, were not long enough to fa-
thom it; upon which my Father, being troubled at his Neighbours Loffes as well as his own,
fent up to *London* for a Waggon Load of Hemp,
and had it fpun and twifted into a ftrong Line
in Order to reach the Bottom; when he had
thus far proceeded, he erected a *Windlefs* over
the Mouth of the Well, had a Bucket made
as large as *a Graveferd* Tilt-Boat, furnifh'd it
with a good Feather-Bed, a Runlet of *Derby-
Ale*, a Peck Loaf and a *Chefhire* Cheefe, Pipes,
Candles, and Tobacco, and offer'd five Pound to
any Country-Fellow that would venture to
Travel

Travel to the End of this Infernal Thorough-
Fare; but notwithstanding the Provision he
had made, and the Reward he promis'd, yet
the Country People had such frightful Notions of this terrible Descent, that none of them
would engage in the Subterranean Expedition;
at length, a poor *Scotch* Pedlar, being robb'd of
his Goods, as Travelling to a Fair, came in
great Distress to my Fathers Door, and beg'd
for a hard Onion and a little Oatmeal to help
him forward in his Journey, upon which my
Father told him the whole Story, offer'd him
the Gratuity aforemention'd, and, for his further
Encouragement, a Tythe of all the Riches he
should happen to recover; these joyful Propo-
sals so readily prevail'd with the indigent Pedlar, that he presently undertook his perpendicular Journey, and swore, were it the Fundament of Hell, and he should meet the De'il
by the Way, yet, if it were possible, he would
earn the Money: Upon this his Resolution, my
Father bound him to his Bargain by an Earnest of Ten Shillings; so the Tackle was got
ready, and after a little Repast, the Pedlar, without Fear, stept into his Cabbin with his empty
Wallet upon his Shoulder, and was let down
Gradatim for two Days and two Nights, and
then the Line slacken'd, from whence we concluded that he was arriv'd at the Bottom,
where we suffer'd him to remain the best part
of a Day to gather up the Riches; at last, we
found he gave the Rope a Pull as an Item of

his

his willingnefs to Return, accordingly we
wound up, and to our great Satiffaction, found
him much more ponderous than in his Paffage
downwards, from whence we reafonably conjectur'd he had difcover'd the Wealth, and
made a profitable Voyage; by this Time the
Neighbours were collected in a Body, all gaping for the fortunate Refurrection of the
bold Adventurer, like the Rabble waiting at
the Foot of the Mountain for the Sight of a
ftrange Monfter; fome enliven'd with the
pleafing Hopes of fharing the wealthy Returns
he had recover'd from the Deep; others ex-
pecting to hear wonderful News from the
Neather-Receffes of the Lower World; all e-
qually importunate to behold the Undertaker
of fo dangerous an Expedition; at laft, after
three Days Labour to reduce him from the
Deep, up came the Vehicle, and out ftept the
Scotchman, with his Pack upon his Back very
richly laden with *Muflins, Callicoes,* and *Silk
Handkerchiefs,* but without a Tittle of the
loft Treafure for which he had been Diving;
we prefently attack'd him with a Thoufand
Queftions, about what Difcoveries he had
made in his Subterranean Travels, particularly how he came to be fo well furnifh'd with
fuch a Stock of Commodities; in Anfwer to
which, he told us, he had met with nothing
remarkable in his long dark Paffage, till he
came among the *Antipodes,* where he happen'd
to find a Parcel of *Indian* Weavers felling their
Goods

Goods at a Fair, so that he improv'd the Opportunity by buying good Penny-worths, and
had replennish'd his Pack with several *Indian*
Manufactures, at the small Expence of what my
Father had given him; but, as for the Treasure
he went in Search of, what had been pour'd
In on this Side the Globe, was taken Up on the
other Side, and past all Recovery, so that every
Body was forc'd to be content with their
Losses; as soon as he had given us this sorrowful Account, beholding himself surrounded
with such a Number of Spectators, he fell to
opening his Pack, and all People present, being
curious to purchase something of what was
gain'd so miraculously, bought up all his Wares
at his own Prizes; upon which, the Pedlar
was very importunate with my Father to give
him the Liberty of going a second Time to
Market; but my Father, being a Man of a covetous Temper, deny'd the *Scotchman*'s Request,
and resolv'd to go himself, but the Tackle
breaking in the middle of his Descent, let him
drop at once to his Journey's End, beyond all
Recovery; so that I lost my Father, but got
the Estate, and am now come up to *London* to
offer this *New-found Passage,* upon reasonable
Terms, to the *East-India* Company.

His fictitious Story being thus ended, *Truly,*
young Gentleman, says the Chairman, *conside-*
ring your Youth, I think you have given a suffi-
cient Testimony of your Qualifications, and, be-
cause so promising a Falsiloquent should not be

baulk'd

baulk'd of his Matriculation, we admit you as a Member of this Worſhipful Society; ſo my humble Service to you, and you are welcome Brother.

Upon another Night, when there was a full Board, and the Fumes of the Wine had inſpir'd the Society with much Wit and Pleaſantry, ſome, who were ambitious of being ſeated in the Chair, reſolv'd to make a home Puſh at Sir *Harry Blunt,* and by the Dint of extravagant Lying to thruſt him out of his Authority, the *Chairman* being oblig'd to reſign his Poſt, if he attempted a Tale that he could not make paſſable, or when another told a Lye that he could not readily parallel. Purſuant to this Deſign which was agreed on by ſome Travellers, one of the Undertakers, who was warm'd with Emulation, began as follows, *viz.*

As I was once Travelling upon the *Weſt-India Continent,* I happen'd to behold a Cabbage whoſe Leaves were ſo extenſive, that it was at leaſt a Months Journey for a *Snail,* or a *Slug* to croſs the leaſt of 'em; and that one ſingle Leaf, in Caſe of a Famine, was ſufficient to ſubſiſt a whole County for a Week, but that which was moſt remarkable, the Stalk was as thick as a Church-Steeple, and as high as the *Monument;* out of the Sides of which, beneath the Cabbage that grew upon the Top of the Stem, ſprung a plentiful Excreſcency of ſuch delicious Sprouts, that a Meſs of them

Boil'd

Boil'd with a Gammon of *Bear-Bacon*, was the beft Victuals in the Univerfe.

'Twas a thumping Cabbage, indeed, reply'd Sir *Harry, but I once met with as great a Won-der in my late Travels through* Prefter John's Country, viz. As I was Riding upon an *Eli-phant,* with my Man behind me upon the fame Beaft, in my Paffage from *Chimaza* to *Tottimoza,* I happen'd, by the Road fide, to efpy a Brazen Wall of fo ftupendious a Height, that I got a Crick in my Neck by gazing at the Top of it : When we had Rid by the fide of it about a League and a half, we came to a very tall Ladder erected againft the Wall, and pitch'd againft a Hole half a Mile below the Cornifh, thro' which I imagin'd the Inhabitants of the City, fo miraculoufly Fortify'd, pafs'd In and Out; being ftrangely amus'd at this wonderful Sight, I ftop'd my *Elephant,* and leaving the peaceable Brute to the Care of my Servant, mounted up the Ladder to fatisfie my Curi-oufity by a peep on the other fide, and having Climb'd to the Port in about half an Hour, with an aching Heart and a giddy Brain, I caft my Eyes downwards from my Lofty Promon-tory, but could difcover nothing at fo great a diftance, but a great number of Little Black things, who were pecking like fo many *Rooks* in a new-Sown *Peas-Field*; but finding ano-ther Ladder on the contrary fide, I took Heart of Grace and defcended down amongft 'em, and when I came there, what above I took to be *Crows,*

I found below to be *Tinkers* very hard at
Work; and what I had foolifhly conjectur'd to
be the brazen Walls of fome Rich and Popu-
lous City, prov'd nothing more, upon a clear
Enquiry, than an old *Caldron,* about a League
in Diameter, which had fuftain'd fome Dammage by carelefs Ufage, and fo an Army of
Tinkers were imploy'd by the Owner to ftop
its Leaks. *A Caldron,* cry'd the Author of the
foregoing Story, *a League in Diameter too!
Nouns, Mr.* Chairman, *pray what could it be
for? Sir,* reply'd Sir *Harry, it was made on
purpofe to Boil your great Cabbage in.* By
which witty return Sir *Harry* maintain'd his
Honour, and fecur'd his Chair from the inva-
fion of his Rival.

Upon this Difappointment, another of the
Combinators, to back his Confederate, thus began his extravagant Fiction, in hopes to win
that Honour which his Friend had fail'd of.

Being fent into *Perfia,* fome Years fince, to
Negotiate an Affair concerning the Silk-Trade,
with an Eminent Merchant of that Country,
and hearing, when I was there, an incredible
Account of the *Sophy*'s Palace, I had a great
Curiofity to behold the fame, accordingly gave
my felf the trouble of a Days Journey to gra-
tifie my Defire; but when I came within
Sight of the magnificent Pile, I was much
more aftonifh'd at its wonderful Appearance,
than I was at the Defcription; for the *Alps*
are no more to be compar'd to it in Height,
than

than a Mole-hill to Mount *Caucasus.* The *Sophy* being retir'd to his Rural Palace, by feeing of a Servant I had an Opportunity of viewing the Infide; but the Foundation of the Edifice was fo vaftly deep, that it coft me a Weeks time to go down into the Wine-Cellar, where we could hear the *Antipodes* hallow over their Liquor, as if they had been Hunting: From thence we were fix Weeks time in Climbing into the Garrets, which ftood above all the Clouds fo extravagantly high, that the *Moon* had Until'd the Houfe, but the Night before, by knocking her Horns againft the Rooff of the Building: I took but little time in looking about me, for our Provifions falling fhort, we were forc'd to return haftily, for fear of being Starv'd before we got down again; and though we trip'd it as nimbly as a Ploughman from Church to a Bag-Pudding, yet we made it a full Month before we could recover the Ground Floor; fo I thank'd my Conductor for his great Civility, and return'd to my Merchant's Houfe as heartily tir'd, as if I had been Rowing fix Months in a *French* Gally.

I confefs, Sir, replies the *Chairman, this is as ftrange a Palace as ever I heard of: But as I was once Travelling in the Country of* Maurufia, *I happen'd to take a view of a Giant's Caftle, which had formerly been the noble Seat of that monfter of a Man,* Antæus, *who was flain by* Hercules, *that he might Kifs his Wife* Tagenna, *who, as well as her Hufband, was about*
feventy

seventy Cubits high; and there, indeed, to my great wonder, I saw one Banqueting-Room, where they us'd to entertain their Friends upon Festival Days, which, to oblige my Curiosity, I measur'd exactly, and found it to be something above a Mile in length, but that which was more remarkable, it contain'd a Table which, upon full extention, was two Miles long.

Now, Sir Harry, cries his Laughing Antagonist, *I am sure we have caught you: How can a Room that's but a Mile long, contain a Table that is two Miles long? I must tell you, Gentlemen,* replies Sir *Harry, you may quit your hold, for it was a Drawing-Table, and happen'd to be shut in half a Mile at each end.*

No sooner had Sir *Harry,* by his witty Come-off, preserv'd his Reputation, and defended his Chair, from the Usurpation of his Rivals a second time, but a third renew'd the Challenge by the following amusement, *viz.*

As I was Travelling in the *East-Indies* from one of our Factories further into the Country, I happen'd to meet upon the Road an over-grown *Tyger,* as big as *Homer* reports the *Trojan* Horse, with as many Fortune-tellers Riding upon his Back, as ever the other carry'd Warriers in his Belly, yet the Beast was so very Tame, that he bore 'em all quietly without the Government of a Bridle, and went Puring along like an old Cat, as if he was proud of his Servitude; I took the liberty to ask them what they had fed him with, to Nurse him

up

up to that prodigious Magnitude? To which they anfwer'd, That they never gave him any thing, for that he only lived by Licking his Whifkers.   There happening in the Company, to be a lufty Gentleman with a huge pair of Whifkers, who had fpent his Fortune by con-fulting the Stars among *Gadbury,* *Cooley,* and the reft of the Wife-akers, who pretended to Aftrology, and was often forc'd to depend up-on the Society, for want of Money to pay his Club, who, finding the Story fo applicable to himfelf, fteals down Stairs, and Shaves off the Ornament of his Upper-Lip at the next Bar-bers, returns again to the Company, who pre-fently obferving the mighty alteration, took the freedom to afk him what was become of his Whifkers ? *Z——s,* fays he, *that honeft Gentleman in his Story of the* Tyger, *gave me fo hard a pull by 'em, that I went immediately and cut them off, to fpoil his hold for the future.*

Sir *Harry,* according to the Cuftom of the Chair, now enter'd upon his Story in anfwer to the Challenge, *viz.*

I confefs I never beheld fuch a large Tyger as that worthy Member has reported to the Board, but I have often feen in the Weft-Indies, *to my great Admiration, what has been equally wonderful, which are a fort of monftrous Bees of fuch a prodigious Magnitude, that they are commonly as big as our* English *Bull-dogs, and have their Arfes fortify'd, Dragon like, with*

fuch

fuch extenfive Stings, that they can dart a Man through at one Thruft, as if he was ftuck with a Rapier. Pray, Mr. Chairman, fays a Thwarting Member, *what fort of Hives have they in that Country?* Juft fuch, replies Sir Harry, *as our Bees have in* England; with that the whole Society burft into a Laughter; crying, *how can fuch monftrons Bees creep into fuch little Hives?* Nay, nay, crys Sir Harry, *let the Bees look to that.*

In thefe fort of merry Jefts, and extravagant Fables, the Rodomontading Society us'd to fpin out their Club-Hours, Judging the largenefs of a Man's Genious by the mightinefs of his Lyes; in which prepofterous Talent they fo plentifully abounded, that they furnifh'd the whole Town with their fictitious Stories, and rais'd their fabulous Society to fuch a pitch of Reputation, that fcarce a Lye could pafs Mufter that had not the Honour to be father'd upon their judicious Affembly. Thus they made themfelves famous for feveral Years, till at length, Sir *Harry*, who was the principal Supporter of the Diabolical Faculty, pik'd over the Perch,, and then the Club dwindl'd into publick Contempt for want of the great Example, as well as Direction, of fuch another *Chairman.*

A

A Poem in Praise of the Art of
LYING: *Written by a*
Member of the Lying Club.

O Muſe! Inſpire me with a Brazen Face;
For good Aſſurance is a Lyar's Grace;
No painful Studies can our Thoughts refine,
Or gild our Wits, like Impudence and Wine:
Such Powers united, bleſs us double Fold,
One makes us Bright, and t'other makes us Bold:
O! Let me neither Want, that I may praiſe
The Art of Lying in Romantick Lays;
That ancient Art, which has in Faſhion been,
E'er ſince fair Eve was Monarch Adam's Queen:
That Noble Art, which taught them firſt to know
Forbidden Springs where Tides of Pleaſures flow,
And how, by mutual Struggles, to improve
The Force of Dalliance, and the Joys of Love.
What, tho' it is by Saints and Prieſts decry'd,
And by the Great to meaner Slaves deny'd?
Yet well-bred Lying is an Art that's us'd
By thoſe the moſt, by whom it's moſt abus'd,
It hides a Thouſand Faults from publick View,
And adds a Grace to e'ery Act we do;

It

It is the Statesman's *Friend, the* Lawyer's *Plea,*
The Poet's *Muse, the* P——'s *Security,*
The Trader's *Conscience, and the* Woman's *Veil,*
That hides the Failings of her wanton Tail:
It conquers Beauty, carries on Intrigues ;
It leads to Battle, and consummates Leagues ;
It Merit gives to Fools of high Degree,
And yields the Pope *Infallibility* ;
It draws the Crowd into a wild Belief,
Quickens our Joys, and moderates our Grief ;
It does the Bibliopolæ's *Wealth encrease,*
And starves the Author to enrich the Press ;
It paints the Patron of a glorious Hue,
And makes him learn'd in Arts he never knew;
It gives a Sanction to the wealthy Knave,
Bleeches the Dowdy, *makes the* Coward *brave* ;
It shews the Harlot in a modest Dress,
And weavs a Cov'ring for her foul Disgrace ;
It oft appeases Jealousies, and finds
Pleasing Excuses, and a Thousand Blinds,
Preserves the Comforts of a Nuptial Life,
And makes the Cuckold *hug the Jilt his Wife.*

What tho' of Hellish Race, as some do hold,
And the first Lye was by the Devil told?

Yet,

Yet, should the Art of Lying be suppress,
And us'd no more in Earnest or in Jest,
A Thousand hurtful Truths would then arise,
Which now are skreen'd by necessary Lies:
My Lady *could no more with* Cousin *hide,*
And by her Maids *and* Footmen *be deny'd;*
Our Teachers *no fictitious Tales impose,*
To lead believing Thousands by the Nose;
No fullsome Praise, from Poets Pens *would flow,*
To flatter this rich Knave, *or that fine* Beau;
No nauseous Adulations shame our Schools,
To raise the Fame of undeserving Foolls:
In short, the greatest then must low'r their Pride,
And hear those Truths they would be glad to hide:
The Lady *then that feasts her* Lover's Arms,
Would seem no more all Innocence and Charms,
But her Brib'd Confidents, when ask'd, betray
The shameful Secrets of each sinful Day;
Nor could the honour'd Fool, *or wealthy* Ass,
Thro' the whole Nation for a Solon *pass;*
But all appear, if stript of their Disguise,
Empty and Vitious to the Vulgar's Eyes:
Then why should busy Mortals be enjoyn'd
To follow Truth, since in this Age we find }
Officious Lyes so useful to Mankind?

C H A P.

CHAP. XXI.

Of the BEGGARS Club.

THIS Mendicant Society of old Bearded Hypocrites, Wooden Leg'd Implorers of good Chriftian Charity, Stroling Clapperdudgeons, Lymping Diffemblers, fham-Difabl'd Seamen, Blind Gunpowder blafted Mumpers, and Old Broken Lim'd Labourers, hold their Weekly Meeting at a famous Boozing-Ken in the middle of *Old-Street*, where, by the Vertue of found Tipple, the Pretenders to be Dark are reftor'd inftantly to their Sight; thofe afflicted with feign'd Sicknefs recover perfect Health; and others that Halt before they are Lame, ftretch their Legs without their Crutches. When the Jovial Crew are met, no fooner are their Aching Heads unbound; their dirty Handkerchiefs and Night-Caps flip'd into their Pockets, and their crippl'd Legs and Arms taken out of their Slings, and return'd from their Cramping

Poftures

Poftures to their Eafe and Liberty; but every drowthy Mortal whips off a *Winchefter* at a Draught, that they may drown Sorrow at once; wafh away the Thoughts of Beggary, and the terrifying Fears of Juftice *Moody* and the *Whipping-Poft*, and wholy refign themfelves to Mirth and Jollity without any interruptions.   When their extended Gullets are pretty well liquor'd by a hafty Repetition of large Go-downs, and their Hearts begin to be light with the powerful Effects of rare found Beer, delicioufly improv'd with a Dafh of humming Two Threads: Then he who is, amongft 'em, the moft celebrated Songfter, to exhilerate the reft, begins to open his Pipes, rumbling out a Groaning-Board Bafe, with running his ftubbed Fingers along a fmooth Table, whilft his merry Companions by bearing a Bob, make up the Hogftie Harmony, which is generally fo fingular, and the Songs they Sing fo well adapted to themfelves, that I think it not amifs to Entertain the Reader with one of their neweft Ballads, which had the Honour to be Lyrick'd over by a blind Fidler and fome of the Jolly Members at their laft Quarterly Feaft, *viz.*

> *Tho' Begging is an honeft Trade*
> *That Wealthy Knaves defpife,*
> *Yet rich Men may be Beggars made,*
> *And we that Beg may rife.*

The

The greateſt King may be betray'd,
And loſe his Sov'reign Power;
But we that ſtoop to aſk our Bread
Can never fall much lower.

C H O R U S.

Then on with your Night-Caps, and tye up
[your Legs,
A Begging let's go for the Smelts and the Megs;
When the Mauts and Rum Culls have recruited
[our Store,
We'll return to our Boozing. O Pity the Poor.

What louſie foreign Swarms this Year
Have ſpoil'd the Begging Trade?
Yet ſtill we Live and drink good Beer,
Tho' they our Rights invade.
Some ſay they're for Religion fled,
But wiſer People tell us,
They're only forc'd to ſeek their Bread,
For being too Rebellious.

C H O R U S.

Then on with your Night-Caps, &c.

We

We hug our Eafe, fecure from Care,
  Whilft Numbers lofe Eftates;
And fome who our kind Mafters were
  Become our Jolly Mates.
If thefe good Pious days fhould laft,
  As moft believe they will,
Hard Times will others Fortunes blaft,
  Whilft we are Beggars ftill.

CHORUS.

Then on with your Night-Caps, &c.

Let heavy Taxes greater grow,
  To make our Army Fight,
Where 'tis not to be had, we know,
  The Queen muft lofe Her Right.
Let one Side Laugh, and t'other Mourn,
  We nothing have to fear,
But that Great Lords fhould Beggars turn,
  To be as Rich as we are.

CHORUS.

Then on with your Night-Caps, &c.

Q 2   *Then*

What tho' we make the World believe
  That we are Sick or Lame;
'Tis now a Vertue to deceive,
  The Righteous do the same.
In Trade Dissembling is no Crime,
  And we shall Live to see,
That Begging, in a little Time,
  A common Trade will be.

CHORUS.

Then on with your Night-Caps, &c.

Come fill a Bumper, Brother Mump,
  And let us be as Merry
As Cavaliers *that burnt the Rump,*
  And Sung, Hey down-a-derry.
Let Soldiers Fight, and Saylors Cruse,
  Whilst Cowards Curse the Taxes,
We'll stay at Home, Tope humming Boose,
  And hug our Mauts and Doxies.

CHORUS.

Then on with your Night-Caps, and tie up
                       [*your Legs,*
A Begging we'll go for the Smelts *and the* Megs;
When the Mauts and Rum Culls have recruited
                       [*our Store,*
We'll return to our Boozing. O Pity the Poor.
                            When

When with Drinking and Singing they have given Nature a Fillip, and Elevated their Beggarly Souls far above the pitch of their scandalous Profession, then up starts the nimblest of the Jovial Crew, and, to make Sport for the rest of his Mendicant Brethren, entertains them with a Dance, wherein he expresses, by variety of Grimaces, and comical Gesticulation, all the several Circumstances of a Beggar's Life, sometimes affecting a sorrowful Look, and a dissembled Lameness, haulting along the Room, Cap in hand, as if he was at the Arse of a miserly Alderman; then biting his Nails, and shaking his Head, puts on a grinning Countenance, as if he Curs'd him in his Heart, because he had not the Charity to reward his Prayers with a loose Half-penny. Next flinging away his Crutches with abundance of Contempt, he cuts as many wild Capers as a Punch-Drunken Seamen, shewing his Musick-House Activity before the Mast, to pleasure his proud Commander; then suddenly, as if bitingly attack'd by his Eight-Leg'd Enemies, he falls to fingering his Collar, conveying his Little Foes that he happens to take Prisoner between Finger and Thumb, from his Neck to his Mouth, that he may bite the Biters, which he dispatches so naturally, that it is hard to distinguish whether he is in Jest or in Earnest: Thus he recreates himself, and diverts the Company, who cannot forbear Shruging at the Lousie performance, as if they Itch'd by Simpathy.

Q 3

No

No fooner is this Scene ended, but the Stewards of the Club require every Member to fhew his manner of Mendication, that by an ingenious difcovery of their feveral Shams and Wheedles, they may prevent their interfeering with each others way of Begging; fo that every poor Stroler may be the more fecure of the Pity-moving Whedles he commonly makes ufe of, as if the fame were his own Right and Property: Upon which demand of the Stewards, the Oldeft Mumper being allow'd the precedency, each takes his turn according to their Standing; fo, purfuant to their daily Practices in the Streets, every one, in his way, fhews a diftinct method of opening his miferable Cafe to excite Chriftian Charity: The Firft, with an *Abrahamick* Beard down to his Leathern Girdle, thus begins the Comedy, *Good your Worfhip caft an Eye of Pity upon a poor decay'd Tradefman, who has been the Hufband of Three Wives; the Father of Thirty Children; the Mafter of Eighteen Apprentices, and has kept Six Journy-men at Work for many Years together, till at laft, Undone by long Sicknefs, and fevere Creditors, was kept a Prifoner in* Ludgate *for Sixteen Years; and now, in the Winter of my Age, forc'd to Beg my Bread thro' down-right Poverty and incurable Lamenefs.* Then follows a Second, whofe Legs are difmaliz'd with artificial Ulcers, a dirty Handkerchief bound about his Head, and his Face gilded of a *Turmerick* Complection, *viz.*

Good

Good Christian People *shew your tender Hearted Charity to a disabled Wretch, who has been troubled this twenty Years with the Running-Evil: Pray look upon my deplorable Condition: I have been Touch'd by two Kings; have been in all the Hospitals about* London, *but turn'd out as incurable; have been brought to Beggary and Want by ill Surgeons and unkind Relations; and am now in a starving Condition, left the Lord opens the Hearts of some Good Charitable Chistians to relieve a poor distressed Creature under a load of Miseries.* After him a Third, who has lost one Eye in a Flux, and Counterfeits Blindness with the other, leaning upon a Quarter-Staff, and turning up the Sight of the best under the Upper-Lid, thus exhibits his deplorable Story, *viz. Pray pity the poor Blind, who lost his pretious Sight in the late Wars at Sea, by a blast of Gun-powder; bestow your Charity upon a poor Soul who has lost his Eyes in the Service of his Country, and now wanders about the World in perpetual Darkness.* Then a Fourth, dress'd up like a decay'd Shopkeeper, with his Right Arm bound up in an old Silken Sling, thus sets forth, in a soft Voice, the humble manner of his Hypocritical Complaint. *Pray, worthy Sir, compassionate the Sufferings of a poor decay'd Citizen, who, after many Crosses in his Family, and Losses by Trade, had his House burnt Down by the carelessness of a Servant, and the use of his Right Arm taken from him by the Dead-Palsie;*

Q 4   *and*

and now forc'd to ask the Charity of well dispo-
sed Persons, not only on the behalf of my poor
self, but a distressed Wife, that has lain Sick,
and Bed-Ridden above these two Years. A
Fifth, with a Wooden-Leg and but one Eye,
having lost the one by Wrestling, and the
other by Boxing, with a Thrum-Cap upon his
Head, a pair of Mittings upon his Hands, and
a Seamans Handkerchief about his Neck, makes
a blunt repetition of his fabulous Oration, *viz.*
God bless you, noble Captain, *remember a poor*
Seaman, who has lost a Limb in the Service, and
an Eye in the Battle; was I able to Fight I'd
scorn to Beg; I have been a whole Man in my
time, therefore, pray, Captain, bestow your Chari-
ty upon what the French *have left of me.*
Next these a Sixth, to shew his Qualification
in the Art and Mistery of Begging, by screw-
ing up his Limbs, seems to dislocate his Joints,
and crumples his whole Body into such a
Lame distorted Posture, as if he had been
broke upon the Wheel, and his Life afterwards preserv'd by some *Dutch* Mountebank,
puts on a sorrowful Look, like a Play-House
Ghost, and in a frightful Tone thus informs
the rest how he implores your Charity, *viz.*
O pity a poor Labourer, who, by falling off a
Scaffold from the Top of Pauls *had my Bones*
broken, my Scull crack'd, my Limbs crippled, and
in one moments time, was made this miserable
Spectacle, who is now forc'd to crawl upon his
Crutches to beg your tender Charity. After
                         him

him a cleanly old Fellow, with a copper Countenance, silver Hairs, a broad brim'd Hat, clean Band, but a Coat patch'd with as many different Colours as are to be seen upon a *Herald*'s Mantle, starts up among the rest, uncovers his Grey-head with abundance of deliberation, makes an humble Bow, and with singular Formality begins the following Story, *viz. Pray, Sir, vouchsafe to look upon a poor decay'd Gentleman, who was once blest with a good Estate, kept an Hospitable-House, and had many Servants, but by my over-Kindness to an ill Wife; my Friendship to poor Relations, and being Bound for ungrateful Friends, have unhappily brought me to Want and Misery in the Winter of my Age.* Next to this Lying Hypocrite up starts a Ragged old Fellow, with a Lousie Look, whose Beard is shap'd like an old Stable-Broom, and rowling about his Eyes, without saying a word, down he drops at the end of the Table, clinches fast his Hands, foams at Mouth like a *French* Prophet in a Fit of Inspiration, and beating his Head against the Floor, most artificially dissembles the Falling-Sickness, till at length recovering, up he gets upon his Breech, sets his Back against the Wall, and sweating with the Pains he had taken in his Mimickry, falls into abundance of *God help mes, and Lord bless ye's*; and then re-assumes his Seat at the Board among the rest of the Society.

Thus every one, in Turn, Acted his Begging Part, using such agreeable Gestures,

apt

apt Words, forrowful Looks, and moving Ca-
dencies, performing their Hypocrifies with fo
much Humour, Art, and Livelinefs, as if fome
had been Educated in *Drury-Lane* Theatre,
and others Train'd up in fome Fanatical Semi-
nary. By that time they have concluded this
Diverting Part of their Evenings Exercife, their
Six-pence a piece, which is their common Club,
is pretty well exhaufted; then thofe who,
thro' the badnefs of their days Work, are a little deficient in the Pocket, begin to exclaim
againft the Pulpit Cacklers for not exciting the
Rumcullies to more Charity. One crying,
*That he had known the time when he could but
have ftep'd into* Moorfields *for an Hour, and
have pick'd up a Hog with more Eafe than he
now could eight Jacks upon an* Eafter Holiday.
A Second, fhaking his head, crying, *Ah,* Tom, *I
fhall never forget King* James's *Reign; thofe
were bleffed Times, when a Man might have
Hopp'd to* Wild-Houfe, *about Eleven a Clock
ftep'd in, and crofs'd himfelf with a little Holy-
Water, ftood at the Chapple Door, when Mafs
was over, and have got half a Crown before
Dinner; and now a Man may put on a fanctify'd
Look, and wait a whole Afternoon at a Meeting-
Houfe Door and not get enough to buy a* Knap-
per's Nul *for Supper.* A Third Mumper, of a
more ancient Date, faying, *He had always obferv'd, That when Vice was moft rampant Charity was moft fluent,* extolling *King* Charles's
*Reign for the moft glorious Days, when Trading
flourifh'd,*

flourifh'd, and Whores could afford to be Charitable, and when Great Men fpent their Eftates, and Beggars got 'em. Thus the poorest of the Crew turn Commentators upon the Times, and are glad to try their Credit for eight Jacks, or a Tefter, among their richer Brethren, fo that tho' their Club is adjourn'd when their Sixpences are in, yet every one has the liberty of running into fuch exceedings as himfelf fhall think fit, provided he wants neither Money nor Credit to fatisfie the Maut, that is, the Miftrefs of the Boozing-Ken: So that they commonly Tipple on till as Drunk as Lords, and then fome to Hufle-farthing, and others to All-fours, till by Wrangling and Squabbling, they wake the Children, and difoblige my Landlady, fo that the Smiths Daughter is turn'd in a huff upon the Cellar-Door, and then away Hop the Jovial Crew, upon their Wooden-Legs and Crutches to their Ally-Habitations, where they Sleep contentedly without the danger of Theives, or the noifie Interruptions that attend much Bufinefs.

Since Begging Vagrants, who alone depend
On Providence, that Univerfal Friend,
Can be content to glean their Daily Bread,
And blefs the bounteous Hand by which they're
                                                    [*Fed;*

Sing

Sing and be Joyful when their Store's but small,
And with a Gen'rous freedom spend their All,
How wretched must the Miser be, who Lives
In dread of Want, and neither Spends or Gives,
But vainly hugging of his useless Store,
Starves, tho' he's Rich, thro' fear of being Poor.

The Beggar for to Morrow takes no Thought,
Thinks himself Rich if Master of a Groat,
Because, when Hunger craves, he dares to part
With his whole Substance to revive his Heart.

The Miser, tho' encompass'd round with Gold,
Doats on his Bags of Wealth that lie untold,
In fetter'd Trunks the tarnish'd Dross secures,
And pines beneath those Wants his Gut endures:
T' improve his Hoards does Nature still abuse,
And vainly Worships what he ought to Use.

The Poor Man needs but few things to com-
[*pleat*
A happy Life, and make his Labours sweet;
Has the true relish of his homely Food,
And thinks his mouldy Scraps extreamly good.

But

But he that's *Rich*, and *Coveteously-bent*,
Wants all that's *Needful* by his own *Consent*;
Denies that *Sustenance* which *Nature* craves,
And makes himself to *Wealth* the worst of *Slaves*.

The *Beggar's* wishes seldom are profuse;
He only covets what he dares to use;
Limits his *Hopes* according to his *Sphere*,
And when he's able will enjoy good *Chear*;
Ne'er *Starves* to multiply his *Pence* to *Wealth*,
But gladly drinks his *Benefactors Health*.

The *Miser's Lust* to greater *Sums* aspires,
The more he has, the more he still *Desires*:
Is ne'er content, but still improves his *Pounds*,
And grows most *Stingy* when he most *Abounds*;
Torments his *Body* till his *Sands* are run,
Then leaves his *Hoards* to some unthankful *Son*,
Who finding *Bags* on *Bags* in *Coffers* heap'd,
Profusely squanders what the *Niggar'd* scrap'd.

Then who'd not chuse a *Gen'rous Beggar's Fate*,
Much rather than a *Miser's Wretched State?*

CHAP.

CHAP. XXII.

Of the SCATER-WIT *Club.*

A Few Years fince a parcel of young Gentlemen, who were pretenders to Wit, and great adorers of the Mufes, form'd themfelves into a Society, which they kept at the *Rofe* Tavern in *Covent-Garden* chiefly, becaufe it happen'd to be fo near a Neighbour to *Apollo*'s *Seffions-Houfe*, where our celebrated Wits are forc'd to take their Trials, and abide by the Judgment of a herd of Criticks, who affume to themfelves the judicial Power of *Damning* or *Saving* any *Stage-Author*, according to their Prejudice or Partiality; fo that, upon every Occafion, they were ready to ftrike in with any Pit-Faction, that by the additional Affiftance of their Claps, or Hiffes, they might be able to over-rule the more Candid part of the Audience, and, according to the mode, put a Modeft Poet to a Repenting Blufh, or advance the Reputation of fome forward Block-head above the

Standard

Standard of his Merit. When the Scatter-Wit
Society were met over the Flask, and the Wine
had infpir'd them with a ftrange Conceit of
their own pregnant Genioufes, then a Pipe of
Tobacco could fcarce be fill'd, a Glafs of Wine
drank, or the Drawer Snuff the Candles, but
a Pun, or a Diftick, was hammer'd out upon
the Occafion. One, perhaps, having furnifh'd
himfelf with a notable Collection of *Swan's*
old Cunnundrums, which he had mufter'd up
at Beau *Coffee-Houfes*, and *Gaming Ordina-*
ries. A Second, by the witty Converfation of
Dan Gummut Flat had acquir'd fuch an admirable knack of turning upon a Syllable, that a
Man fhould not fay Cant but he would inuen-
do the *a* into a *u* Vowel, to make the Company
Laugh. A Third, perhaps, had pick'd up fo
many fcraps out of the *Diverting-Poft*, and the
Plain-Dealers Mifcelany, that he would have
fome Dogril or other to apply to all Purpofes,
and could not fpeak a Sentence but he muft
tag it, like the end of an Act, with fuperexcel-
lent Couplets. A Fifth, having made himfelf
fuch an abfolute Mafter of old celebrated *Hu-*
dibrafs, that he could no more forbear tickling
the Ears of the Society with the Silver Hairs
he had pick'd out of *Butler's* Beard, than a
Country Pedagogue can decline a Latin Sentence, without giving the Authority of a Rule
in Grammar. Thus every one had his peculiar Talent, either in fafhionable Banter, punning Wit, ready Rapertee, or dull Repetition;

and

and now then, perhaps, when their Thoughts
were elevated to a Poetical pitch, then the
Drawer was call'd in haste to bring Pen, Ink,
and Paper, that they might unburthen their
Brains of some seraphick Ditty upon cherubimical *Cloris*; a Lampoon upon my Lady *Suck-
bottle*, for enriching her Nose with Carbuncles,
by drinking *Cold-Tea*. A piece of Lyrick
Bombast in praise of *Juniper-Ale* : A comical
Dialogue between Whig and Whiffler : Or a
quaint Prodigy of a Poem upon some such like
Subject, that might shew, at once, the Nicety of
their Choice, as well as the Greatness of their
Wit, and the Sublimity of their Invention :
And that some of their singular Performances
may be made known to the Curious, I have
here inserted some of their whimsical Products,
for the Entertainment of the Reader; the first
being written by the Cock of the Company under the following Title :

A Hobby-Horse Ditty in praise of Juniper-Ale.
To the Cow-Dance Tune of Gallup and Shite.

I.

Come all ye grave old Gouty Dons,
   Lame Aldermen and Beadles,
Clap'd Beaus and Rakes, by butter'd Bums
   Inflam'd with Pins and Needles.

II.

II.

Come ye Mi∫ers that find
  You have nothing but Wind
In your Guts, by negle&t of good Eating;
  And you Tun-belly'd Swine,
  Who, as oft as you Dine,
Stuff your Bellies with more than is fitting.

III.

If Cholick Pains, or aking Brains,
  The Drop∫y, Stone, or Gravel,
Brui∫es, or Smarts, i'th' Upper-parts,
  Or Ails below the Navel;
Or if Hard-bound by Toping round
  Bad Punch, or Co∫tive Clarets,
Or Midnight Joys, have made your Eyes
  As Blood-∫hot as a Ferrets.

IV.

Drink my Juniper-Ale,
  Not too Mild, or too Stale;
It gives Ea∫e in the wor∫t of Conditions,
  Mends the whole Ma∫s of Blood,
  And will do you more Good,
Than the Colledge of Quacks & Phy∫icians.

R   V.

V.

Come all ye merry Dames that drink
  Too much Cold-Tea, *or* Coffee,
And baren Jezabels *that think*
  All Fruitful Women scoff-ye.

VI.

Come ye Wither'd old Jades,
  And ye Tallow Fac'd Maids,
Who are Sick for a lusty young Lover,
  And ye Saint-looking Tits,
Who are wicked by Fits,
And repent when the Pleasure is over.

VII.

Come you that find, by being Kind,
  Your Guts begin to grumble;
And you that cry, when Kiss'd, O Fie.
  But yet will backwards tumble.

VIII.

Come High-Church, Low-Church,
  Trimmer, *no* Church,

Libertines

Libertines and Quakers,
I'll Cure you all, both Great and Small,
From Lords to Kennel-Rakers.

IX.

CHORUS.

Drink my Juniper-Ale, *and 'twill open the Tail,*
 Turn a Hypocrites Zeal into Farts;
Make a Canting old Cuff, if he drinks but enough,
 Out Chatter a Master of Arts.
It will cool a Mans Veins, purge his Belly & Reins,
 And infallibly root out the Scurvy,
Give a Husband new Life, make him Smuggle
        [*his Wife,*

 Till he tumbles her Topsie-turvy.
It is brisk in the Mouth, very good to quench
        [*Drouth;*

 Is most excellent after a Fuddle :
Take a little 'twill cool any Feaver by Stool,
 And a Dose will Climb into the Noddle.

When such a merry Piece of Drollery, as the
foregoing Whim, had been lug'd out and Read
to the satisfaction of the Company, it commonly put the rest upon producing some Deform'd
Off-spring or other, left one, above the rest,
should plead a Title to the Bays, which they
had the Equity to think ought not to be in-

gross'd

grofs'd, but fhared among the Society: So that no fooner had the former been Conn'd over with applaufe; but it was feconded by the following Rapture, which was Compos'd by one of the Members, as he was cooling his Intrails upon a Clofe-Stool, after he had taken Phyfick, *viz.*

I.

O that my Rump had but an Eye to weep,
And that my Farts like mighty Guns could roar,
  My Arfe no Councils for the Great fhould keep,
But echo Wonders from the Britifh Shore.

II.

Some Night-man's Doxy would I dub my Mufe,
She fhould my Guts, inftead of Brains, infpire.
  A Painter's Pencil for a Pen I'd chufe,
And dawb whole Fools-Cap *Reams with* T——d
                                          [*and Mire.*

III

My Tail Prophetick Poems fhould excrete;
I'd Rife Arfe upwards e'ry Day by-times;
  On Boghoufe Walls I'd digitize my Wit,
And fhitten luck fhould wait upon my Rhimes.

IV.

IV.

The Pope with Heath'nish Scandal I'd besmear,
And with Dutch Morals poyson Jews and Turks;
* I'd make each modern Saint a Knave appear,*
And H——y H——ls, should Pyrate all my Works.

* I'd sing of Lady Jilts, and Lustful Kings,*
Justice to Knaves, and Wit to Blockheads teach,
* At Stool I'd fizzle out a Thousand things,*
And with Quack's Bills, then mundify my breech.

The next Member in his Turn, perhaps, of a more amorous difposition, would fignalize his Art in a moft exquifite Sonnet upon fome bouncing Doxy, who, with the Glance of an Eye, or a Jut of her Bum, had kindled more Fire in his Heart, than he could vent out at his Codpiece; and therefore could not be eafy without plaguing his cherubimical *Dulcibella* with fome of his Rhiming Impertinence: As for Example,

I,

Tho' Phillis my requeft denies,
* I'm fure fhe hugs me in her Thoughts,*
Sh'as Nefts of Sparrows in her Eyes,
* And in her Heart a Herd of Goats;*

For

For when I afk her to be kind,
  Tho' her deceitful Tongue crys no,
Yet to the Joy fhe feems inclin'd,
  For fomething elfe crys yes below.

II.

O that fhe would but let me know
  How much fhe does the Blifs defire,
With balmy Drops, as white as Snow,
  I'd add frefh Fuel to her Fire:
Therefore, fince fhe my Flame can cool,
  And with new Pleafures fan her own,
Is not the filly Nymph a Fool,
  To long for Man, yet lie alone?

III.

I fee by e'ery Step fhe treads,
  And e'ery Glance the Gypfie throws,
That tho' fhe's rank'd among the Maids,
  She Sins in Fancy as fhe goes:
Her Bubbies heave, her Buttocks move;
  Her Belly cleavs the yielding Air;
Her winking Eyes diffolve in Love,
  And fhew the Joy fhe finds elfe-where.

IV.

IV.

O how her lusheous Charms will melt,
  When she the nuptial Dart receives.
What Man, for Millions, would be Gelt,
  Whilst such a lovely Creature lives ?
What tho' she's Coy, and does withdraw
  Her Smiles, when I entreat and pray,
Yet Virtue, when she's warm will thaw,
  And drop like melting Ice away.

No sooner was this salacious Ditty lyrick'd
over to some Tune, but another Member of
this *Scatter-Wit* Society, to shew his poetical
Knack in tagging Metor with a little Sonivi-
ous Gingle, would be tendering to the Board
the newest Off-spring of his working Brains,
that the rest might pass their Judgment upon
his Brat of Fancy ; which happen'd to prove
the following piece of Monstrosity, by way of
Riddle, *viz.*

I.

There is a Thing that's seldom Seen,
  Felt, Heard, or Understood ;
Yet 'tis a place we've all been in,
  E'er we were Flesh and Blood.

R 4   II.

II.

It's *a warm pleasant House that has*
  Seven Chambers on one Floor;
And tho' it is so wide a place
  It opens but one Door.

III.

It is an Easie Mansion, where
  Both Sexes live and dwell;
It has no Window, I aver,
  But is as dark as Hell.

IV.

The Door three Quarters of a Year
  It very oft keeps shut.
And then what enter'd Lifeless there,
  From thence comes Living out.

V.

Whoever dwells within its Walls,
  Meat, Drink, and Cloathing find;
But when the Dame that keeps it calls,
  They leave it all behind.

VI.

VI.

Tho' Moneyless, to Food they're free,
But never chew one Bit;
They Live and Thrive, but cannot See
What 'tis they Drink or Eat.

VII.

They often kick their dearest Friend,
Till they can bear no more,
Who then does for Assistance send,
And turns them out of Door.

VIII.

But when the Tenant's forc'd to quit
Their warm and thriving Station,
The Messuage in a Month is fit
For further Occupation.

A Fifth, unwilling to be behind the Ligh‑
ter, being skill'd enough in Flattery, to be a
Gentleman Usher to some Countess Dowager,
would oblige the Company with a most accu‑
rate Panegyrick upon my Lady *Fizzleton's*
Lap‑Dog, which ought, for its Singularity, to be
honour'd with a place among the other notable
Performances

Performances of his Brother Poetasters; therefore I have here recommended the Rhimatical Fangle to the Judgment of the Reader, *viz.*

Jewel, how Charming is thy cole-black Nose;
How Moist it looks; how prettily it grows;
Shap'd like an Æthiopian *Lady's Snout,*
And shines like polish'd Ebony, *or* Jut;
Flat in the Middle, rising at the End;
Cool as the Waters that from Rocks descend,
And to the sweaty Palm a pleasing Friend.

Contiguous to this beauteous Feature hangs
A lovely Mouth, well arm'd with Ivory *Twangs,*
Whose Lips are honour'd oft with kind Salutes,
To Man deny'd, tho' granted thus to Brutes:
A Mouth whose Tongue my Lady's Wants supplies,
But never tells the freedom it Enjoys;
Pleases much better than the Spanish *Art,*
Tickles at once, and Mundifies the Part.

Large rowling Eyes the fav'rite Puppy wears,
Whose flowing Juices Gum the neighb'ring Hairs,
Which Miss, to shew how far her Love exceeds,
Wipes with her Tongue to cleanse the pretty Beads,
Kindly rewards the little Four-Leg'd Beau,
For secret Service he performs below;

Who

Who at the Monster does half frighted stare,
And crys Baw-waw, as Butchers Dog at Bear.

 Like modish Wig, his flapping Ears hang down
Below his Nostrils, from his Curling Crown,
Comb'd e'ery Hour with so much Art and Care,
'Tis difficult to find one straggling Hair ;
But fall so Nice, are such a charming Grace
To e'ery Feature of the Puppy's Face,
That no Bel's Pinner tiffl'd half a Day,
Can make the am'rous Wanton look more Gay.

 His pretty Paws, like Hoofs of Flanders Mare,
Or something else, are cover'd o'er with Hair,
That as he treads 'twixt Chimney and the Door,
Like little Brooms they sweep the dusty Floor ;
And gather in his Range the nimble Fleas,
That hop for Air from Madam's Thighs & Knees ;
And when he's Comb'd are by the Whelp convey'd
To th' flabby Bosom of her wither'd Maid,
Who shakes 'em off upon the Coachman John ;
So thro' the House the high-bred Vermin run,
Lest a wet Finger does their Lives betray,
And Thumb Destruction meets 'em by the way.

His

His Body does a Party-Liv'ry wear,
Made up of White and Liver-colour'd Hair,
Oft trim'd by S — gw——k, *that the Cur may*
          [*prove*

An Object worthy of his Lady's Love;
Who with her own soft Fingers parts his Crest,
And Curls the Rudder of the fondl'd Beast,
Whose Stern, to make amends, must bear the
          [*blur,*

When Madam drops by chance a gentle Slur:
So cunning Statesmen to preserve their Fame,
Find Puppies, when they Err, to bear the blame.

O happy Jewel, to be thus Carest,
And by so fair a Dame so highly blest:
Pamper'd at Table with the nicest Bits,
And made Partaker of expensive Treats;
Hug'd in the Lap of Pleasure by the Fair,
As if God Priapus *himself was there:*
Stroak'd as thou Slumberst 'twixt thy Lady's
          [*Knees,*

As if thou hadst some secret Power to please;
Fondled all Day, and then at Night prefer'd
To Sleep in Holland, and be Honour's Guard,

         That

That none without thy Notice should approach
The Seat of Joy, which thou hast leave to
[touch,
And with thy Icy Nose presum'st to Kiss,
Without Offence, the very Gates of Bliss.

O that I might thy happy Place supply,
Where many a Christian would be glad to lie.
Like thee I'd start at e'ery noise I heard,
And snarl at each new Rival that appear'd;
Ingross those Charms which you so oft salute,
And hang thee for a bold aspiring Brute.
For who that loves without Revenge can see
A Cur enjoy more Happiness than he,
And not expel thee from the Sheets design'd
Only for Mortals of a Nobler kind.
And should the Charming Dame that hugs thee
[now,
At my Commands, but shew an angry Brow,
I'd scorn the Quane that should so foolish be,
And wholly give her up to Dogs like thee.

For she that does her Beauty such disgrace,
As in her Bed to give her Whelp a place,

And

And tho' her angry Lover does Complain,
Will still commit the Folly o'er again,
E'en let her Live with Dogs despised by Men. }

Thus the whole Society were such notable Versifyers, that when any one ventur'd to pull some new excrement of his Brains out of the poetical Side of his Spanish Breeches, the rest as naturally follow'd his Example, as the Beaus do at *Man's* Coffee-House; when any one diffobulates his Watch to enquire nicely after an Assignation Minute; or as Sheep do, when one bolts a Hedge all the Flock run after. Thus when every Member, to shew the wonderful Respect he had for those old fashe-on'd Gentlewoman, call'd the Muses, had either read or repeated one of the newest of their Products, they began to be pretty well tir'd with their whimsical Performances; so adjourned their Club till the next succeeding Night, and commonly had recourse early enough to the Play-House to furnish their Memory with new Theatrical Jests, and their libidinous Desires with taudry half Crown Mistresses.

Riming's become a London *Plague,*
That spreads like Knav'ry at the Hague;

Mechanicks,

Mechanicks, whom Apollo knows,
Ought only to Romance in Prose;
Have now improv'd the Gift of Lying,
Into the Knack of Versifying,
As if, cause Trading is no better,
They were resolv'd to starve in Meter.

The Bankrupt Trader, heretofore,
Us'd to turn Law Solicitor;
Manage bad Causes in the Hall,
To gain at last the Dev'l and all;
Bribe Witnesses to Say and Swear,
What's useful in a Legal War,
That an ill Cause mayn't want a Lye
To steer the honest Jury by.
But now, as soon as left his Shop,
And giv'n his Creditors the drop,
He tags his Brains, and up there starts
A Poetizing Ass of Parts,
Who storms the Church with grinning Satyr
And so becomes a Saint like Creature.
For he that would be reckon'd witty
By the grave Goose-Caps of the City,
Must learn of F—— to scandalize
All Truth and Honesty with Lies:

Then

Then shall the Saints his Cause espouse,
And fix the Lawrel on his Brows;
For 'tis not Wit, in these dull Days,
But Malice, that must gain the Bays:
Therefore those Scatter-Wit *Buffoons,*
Who deal so much in Church Lampoons,
Cannot do less, to please their Party,
Than damn themselves to shew they're hearty;
And then to make his Fame the Brighter.
They'll swear he is a Saint like Writer.

CHAP.

CHAP. XXIII.

Of the FLORISTS Club.

THIS Odoriferous Society of *Pink* and *Tulip* Worshippers, who can walk ten Miles to see a new Stripe in a *Clove-gilli-flower*, or gaze away whole Hours upon an odd Colour'd *Dasie*, preserve an amicable Conversation, at the Sign of the Bloody-King of the *Quadrupedes*, near *Hoxton*-Hospital, it being a noted House where our Uxorious Citizens carry their plump Wives and buxom Daughters to Feast them, in the Holidays, with Hot-Cheese-Cakes, that themselves may have the opportunity of stuffing their own Guts with rare *Lincoln*-Ale, which the Jolly Landlord keeps on purpose to fatten up Lean Shop-keepers to the Graceful Bulk of a Church-Warden or Alderman, as he has puft'd up himself, by the same Liquor, to the Ostentatious Stature of a *Train-band* Lieutenant, that his Tuny-belly might become a Marshal-Sash as well as a Hogshead does a Hoop, or a Vintner, made a Military Commander, does the print

S

of his Apron-ftrings.   Thefe Knights of the
Nofegay, or Floriferous Gentlemen, who are
as feldom to be feen without a Flower in their
Mouths, or ftuck into their Button-holes, as a
Horfe-Courfer without a Swich, or a Gentleman's Footman without a Tag'd Shoulder-knot,
Affemble not themfelves Weekly like other
Clubs, but have their feveral Feftivals Dedica-
ted to the Honour of fuch certain Flowers
which are highly efteem'd by the moft Judicious Worm-pickers, and other whimfical Gar-
den-gropers, for excellent Beauty, and reviving
Fragrancy; as in particular, they have their
Tulip, their *Auricula,* their *Rofe,* their *Gilli-*
flower, their *Carnation-Feafts,* &c. which are
held Annually at the *Marygold* and *Colliflower,*
the *Snail* and *Cabbage;* the *Artichoke* and
Thiftle; the *Radifh* and *Dungboat,* or at fuch
fort of Houfes, kept in the Neighbouring Villages by fome of the Muck-hill Brethren, who,
finding it difficult to pick up a fweet Penny
out of a T—d, are glad to Sell *Brandy, Ale,*
and *Cyder,* that the Town Sparks and Ladies
may have recourfe to their Gardens, and there,
without the danger of a Reforming *Conftable,*
give their Arfes a Salat.   But the principal and
moft flourifhing of thefe fragrant Feafts, being
held in *Hoxton*-Fields, at the Sign of the four
Leg'd Emperour aforemention'd, I fhall therefore only entertain the Reader with the Diverting Humours of this particular Society:
For who would Treat feparately of a Bear-
baiting,

baiting, Bull-baiting, and a Mercenary Combat between a couple of Gladiators, when all may be handsomely included in the Natural Description of one noisie Bear-Garden. About the meridian Hour, upon the Day of their Triumphs, Tickets having been given out, and Provision made by the Stewards of the Feast, the scatter'd Members, with prepar'd Appetites, begin to Assemble themselves at their general Rendezvouse, from the Military Major to the *Snail*-Crushing Adamite; and from the honest High-Church Doctor, who dares *to* speak Truth in the worst of Times, to the little Low-Church Ignoramus, who has scarce Sence enough to know a *Primrose* from a *Holly-hock.* The Doctor stepping in with a *Carnation* in his Mouth, as big as the Rose of his Canonical Hat-band; the Major with an *Auricula* tuck'd into his Button-hole, as Beautiful and Gay as his Sash and Feather, and as flourishing as the *Colours* of his own Company; the *Hoxton* Gardiner with a *Clove-gilli-flower* in his Hand, blown as big as a *Colliflower,* and the principal Director of *Whores-Ditch* Parish with a huge double *Marygold* stuck under his Chin, adorn'd like a piece of *Bull-Beef* in the Shop-Window of a *Boiling-Cook,* in *Chick-lane-corner.* A fifth, as tall and as upright as a Staff in the powerful Hand of a stern Midnight *Constable,* with a *Rose* as large as an *Artichoke,* so nicely supported between Finger and Thumb, as if he had forgot himself, and fancy'd he was handing

ding up a Bill to his Fanatical Teacher, to desire his Prayers for a desponding Sister, who
had been preach'd Mad the last *Lords-Day.* A
Sixth, a notable Defender of *Revolution Princi-*
ples, with a *Sweet-William* sticking under his
own Hawk-Nose, which beloved Flower, tho'
it was but a paultry one, was respectfully introduc'd, and admir'd by every Body; not at all
for its Beauty, but for its Name's sake: So that
Bull-Beef with his *Marygold,* and Old *Cant*
with his *Sweet-William,* had the Honour to be
Seated at the upper End of the Table, because
they reviv'd the Blessed Memory of the *Pro-*
testant Partners, by bringing into Company two
such pretious Flowers. Thus, in a little time,
the Company drop'd in one after another, each
having robb'd his own Garden, or his Neighbours, of the most beautiful Ornament that
prolifick Nature had prepar'd for their Hand;
so that the Variety of their Nosegays, when
they were assembl'd in a Body, made them look
like so many *Cow-Keepers* met together to dress
up *Flowry Garlands* for their Cherry-Cheek'd
Milk-Maids against *May-Day*; or that they
were so many *Pagans,* instead of *Christians,*
come, in a solemn manner, to pay their heathenish
Adoration to that lascivious Goddess, *Flora,* a
worse *Roman* Strumpet than the very Whore of
Babylon. When they were first met and seated
on all the Sides of an Oblong Union of *Spanish*
Tables, for want of rightly considering who
and who should be together, they were as ill
match'd

match'd, and as promifcuoufly accompanied, as Hogs, Hens, Geefe, and Turkies, in a Farmers Yard; for here fat a *High-Church* Parfon, a Man of Wit and Learning, between a couple of Fanatical Hum-drums, that whenever they fpoke 'twas like a Groaning Board; there fat a *Tacker*, a Man of Honour and Refolution, wedg'd in between two *Sneakers*, who look'd as fickly in the Face, by over charging their Confciences with *Occafional Oaths* and *Sacraments*, as if they had weaken'd the whole Frame of Nature by cafuiftical Vomits to fetch 'em up again; next thefe fat an honeft Church-Man, of found Principles and unfhaken Fidelity, among a parcel of Double-Looking Saints, call'd *Moderators*, who fpit Oil out of one Side of their Mouths, and Vinegar out of t'other, whofe Palats agreed beft with Ale and Stale-Beer, becaufe it was fweet and fouie: Oppofite to thefe fat a rigid *Prefbiterian*, next to a jolly *Quaker*, who look'd at one another, over their Neighbouring Shoulders, as if *Thee* and *Thou* was angry to fee the *Geneva* Saint above him, and that *Jack Prefbiter* was as vex'd to fee the *Quaker* fo near him: Next thefe fat a Confcientious *Non-juror*, and an All-fwallowing *Williamite*, who leer'd at one another, as if *Jack* thought *Will* a very Conformable Knave, and that *Will* thought *Jack* as Obftinate a Fool, to be even with him; next thefe fat an honeft well-meaning *Hoxton* Gentleman, and a ftingy querimonious Grumbletonian Shop-

keeper,

Keeper; one in his Converfation eafy, pleafant, and facetious, and the other, hanging down his Head, with his Snout in his Bofom, look'd like a Hedg-Hog rowl'd up in his own Briftles : Oppofite to thefe fat a jolly young Libertine, who talk'd as if he had never entertain'd one Thought of Religion, fince the Time of his Baptifm : Next him a *Seeker*, who had been a Man of as many Opinions, in Matters of Faith, as there are fpecify'd in *Rofſe's View of Religion* ; but thofe two fat Cheek-by-Jole, and were as well coupl'd as any Pair of my Lord Mayor's Hounds. In fhort, when they were all together, there were as many different Churches in one Room, as ever were difcovered by St. *Paul* in *Ephefus.* However, by degrees, to prevent Difputes, and to make themfelves the more eafy, they chop'd and chang'd Seats, upon every chance Removal, till at laft thofe of the fame Kidney got clofe to one another, and fo Birds of a Feather flock'd together; and then, by that Time the Company had taken a pretty handfome Whet, the Dinner was ready for the Table; but I fhall not trouble the Reader with a Bill of Fare, left I fhould happen, with a dull Entertainment of grofs Food, to overcharge his Stomach; therefore I fhall only touch upon two or three Difhes, which, by great Accident, gave Abundance of Diverfion: The firft was a Side of *Salmon* very palatably drefs'd with *Shrimps* and *Oyfters*; infomuch that one of the Members, who had a

Body

Body like an *Elephant*, a Stomach like a *Tyger*,
and a Mouth like an *Allegator*, as he sat shov'ling
in the Fish, as a Scavenger does Soil into his
dirty Vehicle, happen'd to be highly commending the excellency of the Sauce. *Nouns*, says
a merry Fellow that sat directly opposite, *don't
you know one of the Stewards is a Kitchen Gar-
dener; and the Rogue, to save Charges, has
put in Worms instead of* Shrimps, *and* Snails *in
the Room of* Oysters : Which unlucky saying
put such a sudden Check to the voracity of the
Glutton, that he mumbl'd about the Morsel he
had in his Mouth with as much Leisure, as a
Cow does her Cud, or an *Ass* a Thistle, till at
last forcing it down with as great Difficulty
as a Patient does a Bolus, he forsook the Fish,
and reserv'd the Remainder of his Appetite
for some other Dainty.   This luxurious In-
troduction to their further Plenty, was succee-
ded with Variety of more substantial Food,
such that was sufficient to pacifie the craving
Stomachs of industrious Gardeners, who had
dug six Hours, before they came, to get good
Appetites to their sumptuous Feast, which was
so wonderfully garnish'd with all Sorts of
Hortelage ; that after the Company had Din'd,
a Drove of Hogs might have made a very good
Meal of their Green Fragments : The last
Course that was brought to the Table consist-
ed of *Cheese-Cakes* and *Lobsters*, both which
went as merrily down, as if every Member,
by smelling to his Flower, had begot him a

fresh

fresh Appetite. But, no sooner had the Florists gutted their Shel-Fish, e'er a warm Contention arose amongst 'em about the Lobsters Claws, and how they should be divided, that every one might have some to hang over his Flowers to trepan the *Erwichs:* The Major urging, that as he was a Military Officer, and the Lobsters being Red-Coats, he ought to command 'em, the Parson asserting, *That as they were black Coats before they were boil'd, they ought to belong to the Church, and therefore he, as a Priest, had the best Right to 'em.* A Third, who had no Garden of his own, pointing to his opposite, said, *his Neighbour* Mutable, *was once a Fanatick, tho' now a Churchman, and therefore, since he had chang'd his Coat, as the Lobster had his Colour, he ought to have the Claws for his Flower Pots.* A Fourth, starting up amongst the rest, said, *That his Father was a Captain, and his Mother a Parsons Daughter, and therefore, as he was nearly related to both the Lobsters Colours, had the best Title to both the Lobsters Claws;* at length up rises a Quaker, with as much Deliberation, as an independant Teacher craves a Blessing upon his Food; *Verily,* crys *Annanias, your Mouths were so nimble, I could catch none of the Fish; therefore the Spirit moves me to tell ye I have the best right to the Shells.* The Quakers Argument proving the most cogent, every one of the Company withdrew their Pretensions, tenfions, and fo the Claws were refign'd to the primitive Contender, *Nemine contra dicente.*

The Dinner being now ended, and the Doctor having given a *Quietus* to the Teeth of the Society, the Flowers began to be handed about that every Man's darling Beauty might be nicely infpected by thofe who had the Vanity to fet themfelves up as the moft diftinguifhing Judges. When, like a parcel of conceited *Antiquaries* tumbling over a Bag of Rufty *Roman* Trinkets, they had begun their View, one Flower was highly applauded for its white Edging, which look'd as pretty round the frizzl'd *Carnation,* as a Silver Purle round the Scarlet Edges of my Lady *Plump*'s Neck-Handkerchief, and was Chriften'd, for its Beauty, together with its Fragrancy, *Dulcibella,* which fignifies *Sweet* and *Fair.* A Second was greatly admired for having a Stripe of yellow upon a crimfon Ground, and was notably compar'd to the Gold Galloon round Gammar *Gurton's* red Petticoat, and for its remarkable Singularity, was nam'd, by the learned, *Zelotypia,* becaufe Nature had tinctur'd it with a Badg of Jealoufy. A Third was very much approv'd for the largenefs of its Bloffom, and the diverfity of its Colours, and was faid, by fome of the Company, to be like *Great Britain,* becaufe it was adorn'd with fuch a mottl'd Variety; but happen'd to be Chriftned by the glorious Name of *Tolleration,* for Reafons beft known to thofe that were its Godfathers. A Fourth, tho' it

was

was pifh'd at by fome, was very much commended by others for the Contexture of its
Leaves; the Conftancy of its Colour; the
Sweetnefs of its Scent; the Livelinefs of its
Looks; and for Blowing without burfting in
fo bluftering a Seafon. This fome of the fober
Judges, it being a Beautiful Bloffom of one in-
tire Die, compar'd to a Man without Blemifh,
that had no fpots in his Reputation, or
blots in h', Scutcheon, but was as unchangeable in his Principles as the Flower in its
Colour; then fays the Doctor, *As 'tis the Off-*
fpring of my Garden, no-body fhall Chriften it
but my felf, accordingly he fmil'd upon the
flourifhing *Gugaw*, and Baptiz'd the Darling
by the Name of *Tacker*; then convey'd it
to his Nofe, that he might refrefh his Senfes
with the wonderful fweetnefs the Name had
added to its Odour. The Fifth was a *Double*
Couflip, every diftinct Bloom being of a different Colour, which, together, were compar'd
to the many Sectaries that now Bloffom'd in
the Kingdom; but for holding down its Ears,
which is the Nature of that Flower, it was call'd
a Sneaker. The next fragrant Curiofity that was
handed up, was an *Edmington Tulip*, of fuch a
changeable Colour, that, like the Feathers of a
Woodpecker, turn it one way it would feem to
Blemifh another way Glewifh. Thus according
to the different Reflection of the Lucid Rays,
would change its tincture like the Beautiful

Camelian;

Camelian; fo that none were able to determine
what was its Natural Colour; therefore it was
faid to be like a *Cunning Trimmer,* who manag'd
himfelf fo, that no-body could difcover what
fide he was moft affected to, for which reafon
the *Tulip* was honour'd with the Name of
Moderator. The *Quaker,* as they commonly
affect Singularity, having ty'd up a huge Nofegay of common *Pinks, Dafies, Bluebells* and
Butterflowers, fome out of his Garden, and
others gather'd in the Fields, till he had bun-
dl'd up enough rifraf to have fill'd a couple
of Flower-Pots; which thundering Pofie, according to cuftom, was handed up very merrily, to be view'd by the Judges as a great Ra-
rity, who, in looking upon the Variety he had
prefented to the Board, happen'd to efpy abundance of Little, Black Infects, with which
Flowers are oft infefted, Crawling up and
down his fine flourifhing Mefs-of-medly; upon
which, cries a fkilful Florift, *You have brought
us nothing, Mr.* Sly, *but a parcel of Beggarly
Trumpery not worth our looking at: Befides,
they are fo confounded Loufie, that they are
enough to infect all the Flowers in the Company: For which reafon,* replies the Quaker, *I
fhall call my Nofegay the* Palatine Proteftants,
*and the more Lice thou findeft the fitter it is to
bear the Name I have given it.* Thus they
went on, pleafing themfelves with their Effeminate Toys, till they had run thro' the
Flowers of the whole Company, and then every

ry one returning his gay Bauble to his Button-
hole, fell to Drinking and Smoking, nothing
being heard, for an Hour or better, among the
Flower-croping *Vertuofos,* but fome new Difcovery or other, for the further improvement
of *Auriculas,* and *Carnations, Daifies, Butterflowers,* and *Primrofes,* &c.   One averring
Mole, Lime, and Afs-Dung to be the beft
Earth in the Univerfe for a Pot-Flower.   Another afferting Cow-Pifs to be an excellent
Cordial for a fick *Clove-gilli-Flower.*   A Third
humbly prefuming, that a Tin Extinguifher,
provided it be clean Scower'd, and made the
Crown of a Flower-Stick, is as good a Trap
for an *Erwick,* as either a Lobfter's Claw, or
the Head of a Tobacco-Pipe.   A Fourth al-
ledging, that nothing is better to Lay a *Clove,*
or a *Carnation,* in either Bed or Pot, than the
inflexible Stumps of an old Stable-Broom.   A
Fifth undertaking to blow a Flower to twice
its ufual expanfion, with only a few additional
Puffs of a pair of Mathematical Demifnorters.
Thus they rambled on for a little time, each
vending his own Whimfical Notions, like a
parcel of *Alchymifts* flip'd into the talk of the
Tranfmutation of Metals, tell at length they
chang'd their Subject, and fell into a Conteft
about what was the beft Flower that a Garden
produc'd: One faying *an Auricula;* another, *a
Carnation;* a third, *a Tulip;* a fourth, *a Rofe;*
and fo on, till at laft up ftarts Friend *Amindab,*
and tells them, according to his Opinion, *Of*

all the Flowers in a Garden, a good Colliflower *was the beft.* Thus they paft away their time over fome Wine, much *Lincoln* Ale, amidft a Cloud of Smoke, and many thwarting Claps of Verbal Thunder, till at laft, when every one was well fatisfy'd with his plentiful Entertainment; then away went the *Major* with his *Dulcibella*; Old *Fumble* with his *Zelotypia*; Mr. *Occafional* with his *Tolleration*; the *Doctor* with his *Tacker*; Mr. *Cant* with his *Moderator*; 'Efquire *Safe* with his *Sneaker*; and the Merry *Quaker* with his Loufie Nofegay of *Palatine Proteftants*, attended with a Croud of Salat-pickers, Cabbage-Merchants, Slaves, Knaves, and Flower-Fanciers, who, with full Guts and dizzy Brains, took an amicable Leave of one another; mutually wifhing Happinefs till their next merry Meeting.

> 'Tis ftrange that Men of Sence fhould Doat
> Upon a gaudy Fading Toy,
> Beneath a Wifemans fober thought;
> In all its Bloom not worth a Groat,
> It does fo quickly Die,
>
> Man fhould delight his penfive mind
> With things more permanent and bright,
> Wherein the active Soul may find
> Enjoyments of a nobler Kind,
> That reach beyond the Sight.

Flowers

Flowers are Gugaws only fit
　To gratify a Womans Pride,
And Man that boasts superior Wit,
Should leave those Toys so Fair and Sweet,
　To th' study of his Bride.

Adam, first Master of the Spade,
　Who did in Eden Dig and Live,
Altho' a Gard'ner by his Trade,
We never read that e'er he made
　One Nosegay for his Eve.

Such blooming Trifles ne'er imploy'd
　One careful Hour of Adam's Life;
They only grew in some back-side,
The Privy-Garden of his Bride,
　Inclos'd to please his Wife.

'Tis true, much Beauty we may find,
　In blushing Roses and Carnations;
But what are they to Woman kind,
Who yield the Body and the Mind,
　Much sweeter Recreations?

But

But Man fhould elevate his Thought
   To yet a much fublimer pitch,
And not, like Maids, on Flowers doat ;
Or too much on the Petty-Coat,
   But curb the foolifh Itch.

But if a Man muft pleafe his Sight,
   And be a Slave to Beauty's pow'r,
Give me the Lafs that's Young and Bright,
Full of good Humour and Delight,
   Take you the gaudy Flow'r.

CHAP.

CHAP. XXIV.

Of BOB WEDEN's *Cellar Club.*

B OB *Weden*, univerfally fo call'd, was the younger Brother of that unfortunate Gentleman, who, after he had given a new Turn to Old *Jackanapes-Lane*, and to his great Expence had defign'd and promoted many ufeful Projects, for the Benefit of the Publick, convey'd himfelf out of a jarring World, to the peaceful Grave, by the Mifapplication of an ignominious Halter which he had never deferv'd. *Bob* being the Pin-Bafket of the Family, was put Apprentice to *Greenhil* the famous Painter, but before he had acquir'd a fufficient Perfection in that ingenious Art to get his Bread by his Pencil; a Fortune of two Thoufand Pounds falling into his Hands, e'er he was Mafter of fo much Difcretion as to make a right Ufe of it, he prefently put a Stop to his further Progrefs in the Art of Painting, and totally refign'd himfelf to Wit and Pleafantry, in which himfelf had a very fpritely Genious; fo that

m

in a little time, he had not only wasted his Patrimony, in a persuit of his Pleasures, but so far disabl'd himself, by a neglect of Business, from living in the World by any creditable Means, that he was forc'd to depend upon the Bounty of his Friends, and the Extravagance of his Companions, for an uncertain Subsistance, being every way qualify'd for the Conversation of such Gentlemen who valu'd not their Expences, if they had but a Song or a Jest to give the better rellish to their inebrious Excesses. Having, by this time, acquir'd the Airy Reputation of a Pleasant Companion, he was highly celebrated for a Wit, by all the Rakes in the Town. And now, that he might be constantly found, by all that were desirous to have a taste of his Conversation, he settl'd an Every-Days Meeting at the Sign of the *Still* in the *Strand,* where they had a little Cellar, about six Foot under Ground, which they had converted into a Fuddling-Room; and this being judg'd as the most secure Retirement from the surprize of Bailiffs, and the fittest Apartment for their Midnight Revels, was therefore chosen by *Bob,* as the most convenient Sanctuary, not only for himself, but such as he had selected for his daily Companions, who were generally Gentlemen of Fortune, Petticoat-Pensioners, *Irish*-Captains, and such sort of improvident Sharpers, who, as they Got their Money over the Devils Back, neglected no opportunity of Spending it under

T   his

his Belly. Their time of meeting was generally in the Evening, *de Die in Diem*; the Liquor that they drank, commonly bumpers of *French* Brandy; and their time of parting, the next Morning by Daylight, tho' some times they sat, without any adjournment, for half a Week together, scorning any other Refreshment than a Nod in a Chair, or a Sleep upon a Bench, till at length the emptiness of their Pockets forc'd 'them home to compose themselves, that every one, in his way, might be able to excercise his Talent for a new Supply; which was no sooner obtain'd Cunningly, but as Foolishly wasted, after the foregoing manner. Their principal Divertions, when, like Ghosts and Spirits they were Revelling at Midnight in their Subterranean Cavern, were Jesting, Punning, Singing, opening their Intrigues, Lusheously telling Bawdy Stories; Wittily Prophaning Scripture; Merrily Despising Vertue; Impudently Ridiculing all that was Good and Pious; and blundering out Bulls Foolishly, in which the Non-Commission Captain *Mac*'s, had so excellent a gift, that they could no more tell a Story without fifty *Irishisms*, than a Fanatick Pray without as many Grimaces. Sometimes they had a Harp, to add a sprightlyness to their Mirth, and sometimes a celebrated Musician would drop in amongst 'em, to enliven their Hearts with a new Play-House Song, or merry Spur-bottle Catch, made by some whimsical Rake, and sung as an applicable

plicable Encouragement to their prefent Extravagance. Every Mans Pocket was in common
to the Company, for if any one wanted, and
another had it, he that Abounded was defpis'd
as a Niggard, when the Reckoning came to be
paid, if he refus'd to make up the Deficiency.
When a frefh Rake was Decoy'd into their
Company, who, perhaps, had an ill-got Eftate
fallen into his Hands, by the long wifh'd for
Death of an old miferly Father, to be fure he
was fet up as the very Idol of the Society, and
fo hug'd and carefs'd for a Worthy Accomplifh'd Gentleman, till, in a little time, he was
forc'd to make ufe of the wicked Wit he had
learn'd, and turn as fharping a Town-Shift, in
his own defence, as if he had been bred up
from his Cradle to Cut, Sham, and Wheedle.
When their Brains were elevated, and the
fumes of the Brandy had robb'd them of their
Modefty, which fhould have conceal'd their
Infamy, one, in a Bravado, to fhew his Gallantry, would fwear there was not a Vintners
Book between *White-Chappel-Bars* and *High-
park-Corner*, but what his Name was Regefter'd
in for a round Reckoning. A Second, would
laughingly Affert, That there was not a Hack-
ney-Coach in the whole Town, but what he
had Bilk'd two or three times over. A Third,
would merrily Affirm, That there was fcarce
a Stroling Punk in all *London*, but what, at
one time or other, he had Pawn'd for a Tavern Treat. A Fourth, would jeftingly Main-

T 2

tain,

tain, That he had as many Whores Masks in
his Closet, which he had snatch'd from 'em in
the Streets, as would make a Stage-Mounte-
bank a Velvet Jacket. A Fifth would Report,
under a thumping Oath, That he had never
worn a Waftcoat this seven Years, but what
had been made of a Silk Petticoat; or any o-
ther Nightcaps, than Womens Cambrick Handkerchiefs. A Sixth would rap out a Curse,
upon the whole Female Gender, and Swear,
That he never got any thing by the Sex but
a damn'd Clap, or a Baftard Child; affirm,
That he had not been one year free from
either Pox, or Parifh, since he left the Univer-
fity. A Seventh, the extravagant Son of a
parfimonious Doctor, would fcoffingly Infinu-
ate, That what his Father had got by Praying
and Preaching, he had Generoufly flung away
in Drinking and Whoring. An Eighth would
be commending his Taylors, for the honefteft
Fellows in the Univerfe, for that he always
wore as good Cloths as 'Squire-any-Body, yet
they never coft him above half a Crown a Suit,
and that he gave to the Finifher, whom
he always appointed to bring his Cloaths
Home upon a *Sunday* Morning, fo that he had
Time to make Ufe of a double Advantage, and
and at one Stroak bilk his Lodging and his
Taylor. Thus, in their Cups, they us'd to
make themfelves merry over the fcandalous
Impofitions they had put upon others; and
their drunken Rendefvouz ftanding juft

upon

upon the Bounds of the *Savoy* Liberty, and the Sparks taking Care to keep themselves in Fee with the Bailiff of the Dutchey, bid Defiance to the Law; and being safe over their Liquor, made a Jest of their Villanies, and a Scoff of their Creditors. *Bob Weden,* who had happen'd, in a severe Salivation, to catch an incurable Hoarfness from the Excoriations of the Mercury, never car'd to talk much, because it was painful to express himself so loud as to be heard; but when he did, to be sure it was to entertain the Company with some biting Sarcasm, or ill natur'd Jest; for he was a perfect Satyr in his Temper, and had Wit enough at Will to command an Apt Thought, and to make his Words darting: He was but little in Stature, but never fail'd to add some Inches to his Height, by the extravagant Heels of his rather Stilts than Shoes, for which he was remarkable. Though his Tongue, in his Cups, was too keen and piercing, and his galling Repparties very oft provoking, yet he always wore a very pacifflick Sword, which was often without a Point, and sometimes adorn'd with no other Handle than a Rusty Ribbon. As his Life was a Contradiction to all humane Prudence, so, in his Dress, he was commonly a Diffenter from all modish Observancies; for in Summer he was usually equip'd in Cloth or Frize, and in Winter thin Clad, in a *Sarge* Suit, or some of *Doyly's* Manufacture, caft off by some new Acquaintance. When the

different

different Seafons of the Year requir'd a change
of Apparel, his Hat, Wig, Linnen, and all his
other Appurtenances were fo agreeable to the
former, that they all help'd to compleat an In-
dex of his unhappy Circumftances; for whoever was Herald enough to blazon the Sym-
toms of decay'd Gentility, might very eafily
read Pride, Poverty, and Carelefsnefs, in the
Threadbare Contexture of his unfeafonable
Rigging; yet, Philofopher like, he made a Virtue of Neceffity, and feem'd to make many
Things his Choice, which were the Refult of
his Misfortunes. As he was under the Indi-
gency of *Diogenes,* fo he wanted not his Vanity, for he was always infolent to his Betters,
and only affable to thofe who were as neceffi-
tous as himfelf: Whilft over the Bottle he was
a perfect *Democratus,* for his higheft Satisfaction was to Laugh at the reft of the World, but
without Liquor, was as fad as *Heraclitus,* who
always Wept when he went abroad, to amufe
others that laugh'd at him. A Bed he valu'd
as little as a *Gypfie* or a *Hermite,* and thought
it great Extravagance to contract for a Lodging
above Twelve-Pence a Week, tho' he never
paid a Farthing, fince he could refrefh himfelf as heartily with a found Knap upon a hard
Bench, or a Cole-Heap. This Sort of Life he
affected for many Years, without any Endeavours to refcue himfelf from a long Succeffion
of Folly, Madnefs, and Neceffity, till at length,
Captain *Ruffel* being appointed Governour of
Barbadoes,

Berbadoes, who, having some little Knowledge of *Bob's* diverting Qualifications, at the Request of his Brother, made him one of his Retinue, and so remov'd him out of God's Blessing, into the warm Sun, and did him the Honour, when he had him there, to make him his Table Jester; the only employment that he was truly fit for: So that being thus oblig'd to take Leave of his Companions, for the comfortable Assurance of hot Liquors, and hot Weather, of both which he was a great Lover, he proceeded his Voyage to the Oven of the Universe, and left the rest of the Society to bemoan his Absence. He had not been long sweating out the painful Remains of his Old *English* Debauches in his new Humums, before he sent a comical Letter to his Friends at the *Still*, to acquaint 'em with the present State of Felicity he was now settl'd in, and what a curious warm Climate he was destin'd to spend the Remainder of his Days in; and the Epistle being something Singular, as well as Witty, I have thought it not improper to introduce it here, for the Satisfaction of the Reader.

Gentlemen, I have little News to tell you, but that I am Lacquer'd with the Sun, till grown as yellow as a Termerick *Pudding, and my Skin as crackly as a* Bartholomew *Fair Pig's twice Roasted. I have these Three Months enter'd into an everlasting Sweat, and am forc'd to be rub'd down every Hour, like a*

T 4   *New-*

New Market *Race-Horse after a four Mile Course.* Our Cooks here have a very easie time of it, for we bake, roast, and boil all our Victuals in the Sunshine. As to my own Part, in Spite of all I can drink to moisten my Clay, I am perfectly burnt up into a brown Crust, and expect, in a little Time, to be crumbl'd into Ashes. I am become a perfect Sieve that can hold no Liquor, for as fast as I pour it in at my Mouth, it runs thro' my Pores before it reaches my Bladder. We have rare Melossas Spirits for our Mornings Draught, powerful Medera, to drink at Meals; and she Devils to beget young Saints upon, for the next Generation. Our white Ladies, as they call themselves, are but meer Marygold Beauties; and tho' they go almost as cooll drest as Granny Eve in her Fig-Leave-Apron, yet they are always dripping, like Bacon in wet Weather. Our Island is heavily afflicted with the dry Belly-Ach, tho', I thank my Stars, I have never been troubl'd with any Thing but the Heart-Ach since I have been in the Country. We have as Rakish Conversation as a Man of my Vertues can desire to be happy in, for our Parson and I are look'd upon to be the two soberest Men in all our glowing Paradise, except the Governour. We have Plenty of Provisions, but slender Appetites, abundance of Women, but no Desire; and rare Liquors, had we but a cooll Place to drink 'em in: But that is such a Phœnix, that is not to be found in this Climate. In short, by the extraordinary Heat in these

Parts

*Parts there fhould be but a thin Partition be-
tween us and Hell. Therefore, if any of you
chance to go that Journey, pray call by the Way,
and take a Bottle with your Friend* Bob, *who
is your fweating humble Servant.*

In a little Time after he had oblig'd his old
Companions with the foregoing Letter, according to his own prophettick Saying therein, he
fell a much lamented Victim to that Kill-Devil
Liquor, *Rum*, fo that he went as a Harbenger
into the Subterranean Territories, to provide
an Apartment for his kind Mafter, who foon
after follow'd him into the dark Mazes of an
unknown Futurity. Therefore, as my Friend
Bob was an Original in his Way, a witty pleafant Companion, and a Man of fingular Deportment, thro' all the Changes of his Life, I
am willing to dedicate the following Elegy to
the Honour of his Memory.

*Mourn all ye Nibblers at a Jeft or Pun,
Dabblers in Wit who live as if you'd none;
Infernal Rakes, who, with inebrious Bowls
Of* Stygean *Spirits, drown your thirfty Souls.
Weep o'er your Bumpers of the Hell-born Juice*
*Drank now by Ladies, down to Whores in Stews,
Till your warm Tears into your Cups defcend,
Then Swill to th' Mem'ry of your Abfent Friend,
That he your Sorrows, for his Lofs may know,
And kindly pledg your burning Draughts below.*

Let

Let the Curs'd *Still your craving Lusts supply,*
Like Weden *drink, till you become more dry,*
That your parch'd, shrivel'd Intrails may require
A Flood of Water to abate their Fire;
Then may you find that strange unbeaten Road,
Which surely none but Weden *ever trod,*
Who in a Sea of Brandy *drown'd his Care,*
And seem'd to only live by Fire and Air.
With flaming Quarts he boldly would engage,
And was the Salamander *of the Age;*
Victuals he slighted as a useless Toy,
But Draughts united he would hug with Joy;
With Spirits fill'd his Veins instead of Blood;
For Brandy *was alone his Drink and Food.*

Brandy *i'th Morning did his Stomach heal,*
That and Tobacco *was a Princely Meal;*
I'th Afternoon a Bumper chear'd his Heart,
Liquor'd his Brains, and made his Wits more
                                    [*Smart;*
Inspir'd his Fancy with a Thousand Whims,
As Fiery Zeal *does* Calvin's *Saints with Dreams.*

At Night it rais'd him to a nobler Pitch,
Made him not only Wise, but Great and Rich;
                                    Proud

Proud as a Prince, whom Slaves *and* Vassals
        [dread,
And gave him large Dominions in his Head;
So th' Cobler, when good Ale has warm'd his
        [Brains,
In Fancy forms new Worlds, o'er which he
        [reigns;
Among fat Ale Wives, does exert his Pow'r,
Till Sleep abates the drunken Calenture,
Then with a drowsy Noddle full of Pain,
Old Cæsar *to a* Cobler *turns again.*

 Weep all ye Midnight and insatiate Sots,
Who Sacrifice your Ease to Gills *and* Pots,
That Bob *the Glory of this drunken Age,*
Should in his Prime forsake the publick Stage;
He, whose strong Breath, less fragrant than his
        [Toes,
Was like a Harts-horn *Bottle to his Nose;*
And with Tobacco, Brandy, *and the* Pox,
Out stunk the Poysons of Pandora's Box,
But now, alas, he Lies imbalm'd in Rum,
Whilst Swarms of Crabs *invest his Sandy Tomb;*
There let him rest, to Brandy *once a* Slave,
Unmatch'd on Earth, unequal'd in the Grave.

        CHAP.

CHAP. XXV.

Of the MOLLIES *Club.*

HERE are a particular Gang of *Sodomitical* Wretches, in this Town, who call themselves the *Mollies*, and are so far degenerated from all masculine Deportment, or manly Exercises, that they rather fancy themselves Women, imitating all the little Vanities that Custom has reconcil'd to the Female Sex, affecting to Speak, Walk, Tattle, Curfy, Cry, Scold, and to mimick all Manner of Effeminacy, that ever has fallen within their several Observations; not omitting the Indecencies of lewd Women, that they may tempt one another by such immodest Freedoms to commit those odious Bestialities, that ought for ever to be without a Name. At a certain Tavern in the City, whose Sign I shall not mention, because I am unwilling to

fix

fix an Odium upon the Houfe ; where they have
fettl'd a conftant Meeting every Evening in the
Week, that they may have the better Opportunity of drawing unwary Youth into the like
Corruption. When they are met together, it is
their ufual Practice to mimick a Female Goffi-
ping, and fall into all the impertinent Tittle
Tattle, that a merry Society of good Wives
can be fubject to, when they have laid afide
their Modefty for the Delights of the Bottle.
Not long fince, upon one of their Feftival
Nights, they had cufheon'd up the Belly of
one of their *Sodomitical* Brethren, or rather
Sifters, as they commonly call'd themfelves,
difguifing him in a Womans Night-Gown,
Sarfnet-Hood, and Nightrale, who, when the
Company were met, was to mimick the wry
Faces of a groaning Woman, to be deliver'd of
a joynted Babie they had provided for that
Purpofe, and to undergo all the Formalities of
a Lying in. The Wooden Off-fpring to be afterwards Chriften'd, and the holy Sacrament
of Baptifm to be impudently Prophan'd, for
the Diverfion of the Profligates, who, when
their infamous Society were affembl'd in a Body, put their wicked Contrivance accordingly
into practice.

One in a high Crown'd Hat, and an old Bel-
dams Pinner reprefenting a Country Midwife,
another bufy Ape, dizen'd up in a Hufwife's
Coif, taking upon himfelf the Duty of a very officious Nurfe, and the reft, as Goffips, apply'd
themfelves

themfelves to the Travelling Woman, according to the Midwife's Direction, all being as
intent upon the Bufinefs in hand, as if they had
been Women, the Occafion real, and their Attendance neceffary. After Abundance of Buffle
and that they had ridiculoufly counterfeited all
the Difficulties that they fancy'd were accuftomary in fuch Cafes, their Buffoonary Maukin
was at length Difburthen'd of her little Jointed
Baftard, and then putting their Shotten Impo-
ftor to Bed upon a double Row of Chairs; the
Baby was dreft by the Midwife; the Father
brought to Compliment his New-born Son;
the Parfon fent for; the Goffips appointed; the
Child Chriften'd, and then the Cloth was
fpread; the Table furnifh'd with cold Tongues
and Chickens; the Guefts Invited to fit down,
and much Joy exprefs'd that my Gammar
Molly had brought her honeft Gaffer a Son and
Heir to Town, fo very like him, that as foon
as Born, had the Eyes, Nofe, and Mouth of
its own credulous Daddy. Now for the further promotion of their unbecoming Mirth,
every one was to Tattle about their Hufbands
and Children: And to ufe no other Dialect
but what Goffips are wont to do upon fuch
Loquacitous Occafions. One would up with a
Story of her Little *Tommy*, to fhew the promi-
fing Genious of fo witty a Child, that if he let
but a Fizzle, would prefently cry out, *Mammy
how I tink.* Another would be extolling the
Vertues of her Hufband, and declare he was a
Man

Man of that Affable, Kind, and eafie Temper, and fo avers'd to Jealoufie, that fhe believ'd, were he to fee another Man in Bed with her he would be fo far from thinking her an ill Woman, that no-body fhould perfwade him they had been Naught together. A Third would be telling what a forward Baggage her Daughter *Nancy* was; for tho' fhe was but juft turn'd of her Seventh Year, yet the young Jade had the Confidence to afk her Father *Where Girls carry'd their Maidenheads that they were fo apt to loofe 'em?* A Fourth would be wifhing no Woman to Marry a Drunken Hufband, for her fake; for all the Satisfaction fhe found in Bed with him, was to creep as clofe to the Wall as fhe could to avoid his Tobacco Breath and unfavory Belches, Swearing that his Son *Roger* was juft like him, for that the Guzling Rogue would drink a pint of Strong-Ale at a Draught before he was Three Years Old, and would cry, *Mam, more Ale.* A Fifth would fit Sighing at her ill-Fortune, and wifhing her Hufband would follow the Steps of his Journyman; for that was as careful a young Fellow as ever came into a Family. A Sixth would exprefs himfelf forrowfully under the Character of a Widow; faying, *Alas, you have all Husbands, and ought to pray heartily that you never know the mifs of 'em, for tho' I had but a forry one, when I was in your Condition, yet, God help me, I have caufe enough to repent my Lofs; for I am fure, both Day and Night, I find the*

want

want of him. Thus every one, in his turn, would make a Scoff and a Banter of the little Effeminate Weaknesses which Women are subject to when Gossiping, o'er their Cups, on purpose to extinguish that Natural Affection which is due to the Fair Sex, and to turn their Juvenile Desires towards preternatural Polutions. No sooner had they ended their Feast, and run thro' all the Ceremonies of their Theatrical way of Gossiping, but, having wash'd away, with Wine, all fear of Shame, as well as the Checks of Modesty, then they began to enter upon their Beastly Obscenities, and to take those infamous Liberties with one another, that no Man, who is not sunk into a State of Devilism, can think on without Blushing, or mention without a Christian Abhorrence of all such Heathenish Brutalities. Thus, without detection, they continu'd their odious Society for some Years, till their Sodomitical Practices were happily discover'd by the cunning Management of some of the Under-Agents to the *Reforming-Society* ; so that several were brought to open shame and punishment; others flying from Justice to escape the Ignominy, that by this means the Diabolical Society were forc'd to put a period to their filthy scandalous Revels.

'Tis strange that in a Country where
Our Ladies are so Kind and Fair,

So Gay, and Lovely, to the Sight,
So full of Beauty and Delight;
That Men fhould on each other doat,
And quit the charming Petticoat.
Sure the curs'd Father of this Race,
That does both Sexes thus difgrace,
Muft be a Monfter, Mad, or Drunk,
Who, bedding fome prepoftrous Punk,
Miftook the downy Seat of Love,
And got them in the Sink above;
So that, at firft, a T——d and They
Were born the very felf fame Way,
From whence they draw this curfed Itch,
Not to the Belly, but the Breech;
Elfe who could Woman's Charms refufe,
To fuch a beaftly Practice ufe?
'Tis true, that Swine on Dunghills bred,
Nurs'd up in Filth, with Offel fed,
Have oft the Flow'ry Meads forfook,
To wallow Belly deep in Muck;
But Men who chufe this backward Way,
Are fifty Times worfe Swine than they:
For the lefs Savage four-leg'd Creature,
Lives but according to his Nature:

U   *But*

But the Bug'ranto *two leg'd Brute,*
Perfues his Luft contrary to't;
The brawny Boar will love his Sow;
The Horfe his Mare ; the Bull his Cow;
But Sodomites *their Wives forfake,*
Unmanly Liberties to take,
And fall in Love with one another,
As if no Woman was their Mother :
For he that is of Woman born,
Will to her Arms again return;
And furely never chufe to play
His Luftful Game, the backward Way.

But fince it has appear'd too plain,
There are fuch Brutes that pafs for Men;
May he that on the Rump fo doats,
Be Damn'd as deep as Doctor Oates,
That Scandal unto all black Coats.

CHAP.

CHAP. XXVI.

Of the BAWDS INITIATING Club.

IN one of the Streets Built out of *Clarendine*, alias, *Dunkirk-* House, there Lives a famous wither'd Lady, who, after a Univerfal Difpenfation of her youthful Favours, fo long as fhe had any remains of Beauty to oblige a Lover, was forc'd, in the *Autumn* of her Debauchery, to Commence Bawd for an Honeft, Comfortable Subfiftance; which commendable Imployment fhe had no fooner undertaken, but, for the better promotion of the good old Trade of Bafket-making, fhe got an Experienc'd Covy of Salacious Wagtails to fettle a Club at her *Cunicnlary Ware-Houfe*, upon *Mondays*, *Thurfdays*, and *Saturdays*, to fpend their Twelve-pence a piece in *Brandy*, *Ratefea*, and fuch fort of Liquors, which fhe Sold privately to Corret the coldnefs of Female Conftitutions: And when ever any She-Mem-

ber

ber could convert a Proſelite, and bring her
over from a vertuous Life to be willing to
Embrace that Earthly Tabernacle, Man, for
ſuch excellent Service done to the Church of
Venus, ſhe was to receive Ten Shillings of the
Mother of the Maids, provided the Conformiſt
was under Twenty Years of Age, had a tollerable ſhare of Beauty, and either was, or could
confidently put herſelf into the Hands of the
Old Matron, as a *Virgo intacta,* and would
ſubmit herſelf to be ſo diſpos'd on by her as
ſhould be moſt agreeable to their United
Intereſt; the Lady-Abbeſs of the *Brothel-Mo-
naſtry* never wanting, among the Salacious
Quality of her old Acquaintance; a Gouty
Courtier, or ſome Rich over-grown Officer, to
be Ready-money Chapmen for any of her
Punchable Nuns who had not, as yet, broken
the brittle Vow of Female Chaſtity. The
new Convert, after the firſt Surrender of her
undhandſel'd Pipkin, to be oblig'd, the next
Club-Night, to Treat the whole Tickle-Fool
Society with ſuch a plentiful Bowl of Punch
as ſhall be agreeable to her Ability, of which
herſelf is to drink the firſt Cup, toſs the empty
Vehicle over her unmaiden'd Head, and to
cry *Farwell Modeſty*; by which Ceremony ſhe
is firmly Initiated into the Edifying-Club,
where, without reſerve, ſhe is to be Candidly
Taught all Arts and Subtilties that properly
belong to the Buſineſs of Intrigue, and the
dark Miſteries of Harlotry; how to File a
                                         Drunken

Drunken Cully; Sweeten an Old Letcher;
Whedle a conftant Cuftomer; Deceive a Keeping Coxcomb; Humour a Town-Rake, Jilt a
Troublefome Bully; Bribe a Reforming-Con-
ftable, Soften the Sterrility of a Crabbed
Juftice; and how to pafs at once a Sham-Saint
and a Maidenhead upon a loofe Quaker, or an
Old Letherous *Non-Con :* Alfo how to manage
a Great-Belly to the beft advantage, to lay it
to Twenty Fathers, 'till fhe has feather'd her
Neft, and then to pafs it handfomely upon
the Parifh, without the danger of *Bridewell*;
to put off a Dun with as much Grace as a
Courtier; to make a Puritan Landlady wink
with both her Eyes, when fhe happens to carry Home a Cully for a Bedfellow; to be an
abfolute Miftrefs of all *Araton*'s Poftures; to
elevate her Coxendix according to the School
of *Venus*, to manage herfelf rightly in her
Approaches to, and Returns from a Students
Chamber in an *Inns-of-Court*, or *Chancery*;
and, amongft the reft, how to Swear like a
Bully; Domineer like a Tyrant; be as Coy as
a Mud; as Forward as a Widow; as Demure
as a Holy-Sifter upon a *Sunday* Morning, and
as Treacherous as a Wife who has a young
Gallant and an old Hufband: So that, let her
happen to fall into what Company foever, fhe
may be able to put on fuch a difguife, and to
act that part which may be moft agreeable to
her own Intereft, and the Temper and Character of every frefh Gallant that takes a liking

U 3   to

to her Perſon. And when thus qualify'd, it is highly preſum'd ſhe may riggle her Breech into ſuch taudry Silks as the Tally - man will Truſt her with, become a celebrated Punk in *Drury-Lane-Pit*, for the firſt Year or two; after that a Tatter'd Furbulo Cuſtomer for the Eighteen-Penny Gallery; from thence turn *Fleet-ſtreet* Stroler, in a Sarſnet-Hood and White-Apron, only a fit Miſtreſs for a *Water-Lane* Pick-Pocket; in which miſerable Station ſhe is likely to continue, till Pox and Poverty recommend her to an Hoſpital, where a thorough Salivation either ſends her to the Devil, or patches up her Rotten Carcaſe for ſome Foreign-Plantation.

To theſe Noble Ends and Purpoſes, this looſe Society of mercenary Wantons were procur'd to meet by the Old Diabolical Jezabel, that Young Girls out of Service; Forward Wenches without Parents, and ſuch who, thro' the ripeneſs of their Years, their natural propenſity to Lewdneſs, and the want of Vertuous Education, might be decoy'd by their own Sex to take thoſe vicious Liberties, which too many Young Creatures, in the Salacity of their Youth, are very apt to be inclin'd to: Nor has the wicked Project fail'd of the intended Iſſue; for there is ſcarce a Club-Night that the tempting Sirens meet, but there is ſome Innocent Wretch or other drawn in by Subtilty, or prompted by her own Luſt, who is raſhly reſolv'd to ſhift of her Modeſty, and

to

to refign her Maiden-Favours to fuch a Libertine as the Old Succubus fhall appoint; fo that fhe may be cultivated and qualified for that miferable Imployment, which, if the Devil himfelf fhould take upon him, tho' fo harden'd in his Wickednefs, would furely bring him to Repentance: For when the Hour of their Meeting draws nigh, in fhall bolt one airy *Phillis* with her taudry Silks half torn off her Back, juft Kick'd and Ruffl'd by fome mad Rake or Bully, whom Madam had feverely Clap'd the laft time he Lay with her. After her fair *Chloe*, without her Furbelo Scarf, which fhe had juft Pawn'd to free herfelf from the Clutches of a *Reforming-Conflable*. Next her, Mifs *Daphne*, Ratling in a Hackney to the Door, with torn Pinners, a black Eye, and her beautiful Phiz full of revengeful Scrathes, given by the angry Wife of one that keeps her Company: By and by Madam *Bibbington* in a Chair, as Drunk as the Devil, with her Garmants fo difoblig'd by Second-hand Claret, that fhe ftinks as bad as a Country Sheriffs Breath at the latter-end of the Sifes. After her, perhaps, poor Ghoftly *Althea*, with her Jaws as thin as lean Tripe out of the Belly of an Old Cow that Dy'd of the Blood-ftale; her Teeth as loofe, and as rotten, as a Set of old Park-Pails round the Seat of a decay'd Family, and her Countenance as heavy as a defponding *Puritans*, juft going to Hang himfelf, with all the other fevere Effects of a Vi-

tious

tious Life, and a late flabbering Salivation. Next, in comes *Chloris*, full of abundance of Joy, that her Spark had redeem'd her from the Hands of the Tally-Man, who had threaten'd to make Dice of her Bones, for the Non-Payment of what was due for her laft furbilow'd Petticoat. After her, Steps in the celebrated Madam *Pockly*, Curfing and Damning her Surgeon for refufing to fend her more Phyfick, till fhe had paid for the Cure of her laft Clap. Thus they are never free from fome Misfortune or other, yet, by that Time the Brandy, Ratefea, Punch, or what-ever Liquor they happen to be drinking, has gone twice or thrice about, they are as utterly Thoughtlefs of all their Sins and Calamities, as a Woman that vows future Continence in the Height of her Labour is at the Month's End after the paft Miferies of Child-Birth, but grow as merry over their Cups, amidft a Circle of Misfortunes, as if they had Infidelity enough to imagine there was no other Being hereafter: So that, quite carelefs of Heaven, and fearlefs of Hell, they fwear like *Scotch* Officers ; talk Bawdy like fo many Midwives ; boaft of their Bed-Adventures like Bullies of their Duels, and open all their loofe Intrigues with as much Pleafure, as they do their Arms to a vig'rous Gallant ; and fo far excell the lewdeft of Men in all Manner of Obfcenity, that it would make a Rake blufh, and the worft of Libertines abjure the Converfation of all Mercenary Harlots to

be

be Witneſſes of their Impudence. When they
are met together in one of their Brothel Sanc-
tuaries, where they lay aſide that Effeminacy
that ſhould be Part of their Nature, and without Diſguiſe, let looſe the very Devil that, to
their Shame, poſſeſſes them, till wrinkl'd Age,
a painful Decay, the Slights of the World,
and all the other miſerable Conſequences of a
wicked Life, either hurry them to Deſpair, or
bring them to Repentance; to the laſt of
which, before it be too late, I moſt heartily recommend them.

Would ſhe who can her Virgin Honour boaſt,
Conſider wiſely, e'er the Jewel is loſt,
That her own Happineſs, her Parents Joy,
Depends upon her proving Chaſte and Coy,
Unlawful Pleaſures ſhe would then deſpiſe,
Value her Beauty, guard her roving Eyes, }
And o'er her youthful Wiſhes tyrannize.
So he that is with too much Care oppreſt,
And hopes by one bold Stroak to purchaſe Reſt,
Let him but think before he gives the Blow,
And from his Breaſt he will the Dagger throw.

Woman, if once to Sinful Pleaſures won,
Can never ſtop till by her Ills undone;
One ſingle Folly does her Charms diveſt
Of all that Honour that ſhould keep her Chaſte,
Leaves

Leaves her ungarded, ready to comply,
When any Man she likes attempts the Joy;
So he that has a daring Robb'ry done,
Ne'er sticks at any, when he's flush'd with one.

Women should let their Virgin Thoughts aspire,
And learn themselves to prize what we ad-
                                    [*mire;*
When e'er they're told, that they're divinely
                                    [*Fair,*
Altho' they blush, they should believe they are,
And think it far beneath 'em to debase
The lovely Charms of such an Angel's Face:
Or that their Breasts with Beauty so adorn'd,
Should into Snakes, and Serpents Dens be turn'd:
For Woman of her Virtue dispossest,
Is but a Treach'rous Creature at the best;
When that's once lost, sh'as Nothing on her Side,
That can support a warrantable Pride;
Without which Champion to defend her Charms,
She lyes expos'd to e'ery Coxcombs Arms,
Who, has but Sence the yielding Dame to court,
And Courage to attack Love's feeble Fort;
For Lovers know 'tis easy to invade
Th' Hesperian Garden, when the Dragon's fled.
                                    Woman

Woman should be reserv'd both Maid, and
                                    [*Wife,*
An Hour misus'd condemns her for her Life ;
Nay all the Woes that can the Sex surprize,
From one unguarded Moment oft arise ;
Beauty's in Danger always, and must watch
To keep her Magazine from Cupid's Match ;
For if the Fire of Love be once mis-plac'd.
It blows up all that should preserve her Chaste,
And when the Walls of Virtue ruin'd are,
She's always Wretched, tho' she's ne'er so Fair ;
For none adore her Charms, to others free,
But further to compleat her Misery.

CHAP.

CHAP. XXVII.

Of SAM SCOTS

Smoaking Club.

MY Maggoty Man *Sam,* as his Mafter us'd to call him in the Time of his Apprenticefhip, when he fet up for himfelf, kept a Mufick-Shop at the *Temple-Gate,* where the Baftard of Sons of *Apollo* were accuftom'd to furnifh themfelves with Harps and Fidles, and the Tiptoe Mafters of the Mathematical Step, us'd to fupply their Occafions with new Minuets and Bories. *Sam Scot,* the better to ingratiate himfelf with his Cuftomers, affected fuch a fort of Life as he thought might be moft agreeable to thofe whimfical Performers, who, having their Heads ftuff'd with Grotchets, and their Heels full of Activity, could never reft in their Beds, till they had tam'd their Faculties, drown'd all Thoughts of their Airy Profeffions, and chain'd up their Qualificati-

ons,

ons, with an inebrious Excess. This, *Sam Scot* observing, was resolv'd to be as forward as any of 'em in all Bottle Adventures, and merry Midnight-Revellings, to which, he found the Brethren of the String, were not a little addicted, till at length, by Habitual Drinking and keeping late Hours, he became so great a Proficient in Drinking, Smoaking, and sitting up at Nights, that he found but few upon a Level with his Quality, that were able to cope with him, and those he selected to himself, as his dearest Bosom-Companions. One a Linnen-Draper, who, Marrying the Daughter of a Boarding-School without a Fortune, and being qualify'd in the Step, was forc'd to turn Dancing-Master. Another was a *Salisbury-Court* Barber, one of the City Musicians, who, us'd to act the Country-Man, upon My Lord Mayors Day, and play the Fool after Dinner, to please the Wise-Men of the City. A Third was a Graver, who us'd to dig new Songs upon Copper-Plates, for his Maggoty Musical Companion : And the Fourth a *Scotch* Writing-Master, who was famous for Graving the Lord's Prayer, which he seldom said, within the Compass of a Silver Penny. These had acquir'd such an expeditious Way of consuming a Pipe of Tobacco, that when they were met together, they would make no more of Smoaking a Pound in an Hour, than the Drinking Shoemaker does of a Gallon of Claret for his Mornings Draught, and were so extreamly proud of this singular

Qualification,

Qualification, that they took a Delight in smothering all the Houfes that ever they frequented; fo that, at the Requeft of the Victuallers, they were forc'd to adjourn from Place to Place; for tho' they fpent their Money freely, yet they were unwelcome Guefts, becaufe, where-ever they came, they poyfon'd the reft of the Cuftomers; for which Reafon, tho' they us'd no Houfe conftantly, they were call'd *Sam Soot*'s Smoaking Club. One unlucky Rogue of a Victualler on the Back-Side of St. *Clements*, having excellent Tipple, notwithftanding he had oftentimes defir'd they would find a new Meeting-Houfe, or to Smoak with more Moderation, yet the Goodnefs of the Liquor made them very unwilling to forfake their Quarters; fo that one Evening having juft tap'd a Pound of Tobacco, and the Mafter of the Houfe, who at that Time was Church-Warden, perceiving they were pufhing forward their old intollerable Cuftom, and that all his Rooms were to be fill'd with Smoak like a *Yarmouth* Herring-Houfe, ftep'd out to the Beadle, who liv'd near, and telling him the Story, order'd him to run prefently and bring the Parifh Engine, with two or three Buckets of Water in it, and to place it right againft his Door: The Mafter of the Houfe returning Home to acquaint all his other Guefts with his Project, that no-body might ftir but the Smoakers when the Alarm was given. No fooner was the Engine brought, but the Man

of

of the House, seconded by several that were
Drinking, roar'd out Fire as dreadfully as if
the House had been in Flames; upon which,
up started the Smoakers in a terrible Surprise,
throw'd down their Pipes, as if the Father of
everlasting Fire had been at the Heels of them,
in a hurry tumbled over one another down
Stairs, and just as they were in the middle of
the Entry, striving who should squeeze out first,
the Beadle, according to Direction, let fly the
Engine into the House, and made them as wet
as so many *Water-Lane* Divers, drag'd thro' a
Horse-Pond: However, the Cry of Fire, tho' they
met with Water, had so scurvily frighted 'em,
that the dread of Burning instead of Drowning,
never minding the Engine, made them fly the
House in as great a Consternation, as if a Gang of
drunken Bullies had been spurring their Arses
with the Points of their Weapons, till they
thought they were got far enough out of
Harms Way, and then assuming Courage, they
fac'd about to behold the distant Danger; but
seeing no Signs of the Fire, that had so lamen-
tably scar'd 'em, they ventur'd to return back by
slow Degrees, and with all necessary Caution,
to enquire further into the unknown Mischiefs,
they had so happily escap'd; but in all their
gentle Approaches, beholding no visible Signs
of any such Combustion as they had been thus
alarm'd with, they took Heart of Grace, and
re-enter'd the House, where they heard nothing but such a tumultous Laughture, as if
the

the Monstrous Outcry, according to the Fable, had ended only in a Mouse, upon which they sat themselves in a little Box, and knocking for Attendance, the Master, who was in the Kitchen making merry with his Guests at what had past, left his Company to wait upon 'em, crying, *Lord, Gentlemen, where have you all been, that you happen to return in such a dripping Pickle. Z——ds,* reply'd they, *did you not all cry out Fire as if the Devil was in you, and in Running down Stairs to discover where it was, some unlucky Rogue or other slap'd a Bucket of Water in our Faces.* Bless me Gentlemen, replies the Landlord, *some of my officious Neighbours, seeing such a terrible Smoak gush out of the Windows of your Club Room, ran, in a Consternation, and fetch'd the Parish Engine, and the Buckets, and here they have done me I know not what Damage, in playing into my House, believing 'twas on Fire.* Come, come, says Sam Scot, *it's well it is no worse, prithee bring us some Pipes, that we may fit and smoak-dry our selves a little.* By my Soul, Gentlemen, replies the Landlord,, *if you fall again to Smoaking, my Neighbours will run again for the Parish Engine, and the Buckets: Say you so,* replies he that was most wet, *then prithee let us Pay, that we may go dry our Jackets, and funk our Noses at another House ;* so they discharg'd their Reckoning, and the Victualler, by this Stratagem, got finally quit of their fumiferous Company. This Story spreading among their Ra-

kish

kiſh Acquaintance, they were all ſadly teaz'd,
and banter'd whereſoever they came; inſo-
much that, after this Affront, they never fix'd
themſelves at any particular Houſe, for fear
of meeting with ſome Jocular trick, or other, in
the like Nature, but made it their Buſineſs,
or rather their Diverſion, to haunt thoſe Coffee-
Houſes where they were unknown, that they
might ſlily puff out their Clouds inſtead of
Whiffs, among other Funkers in the publick Room till they had thin'd the Company,
without any bodys diſcovering who were the
div'liſh Smoakers that made ſuch a damnable
Smother; for where-ever they ſettl'd themſelves for that Evening, no Spectacle News-
Monger could continue the Reading of a *Poſt-
Man,* unleſs he was able to live in Soot and
Smoak, like a Brew-Houſe Stoker, or a Chim-
ny-Sweeper; for no ſooner were their Pipes
well lighted, but there would be ſuch a coughing Conſort among Nice Beaus, and Ptiſicky
Old Gentlemen, that a Man would be ready
to think he was got to Church in the Hundreds
of *Eſſex,* upon a *Sabbath-Day,* in an open Winter. When the Fog began to ſpread, up would
riſe an Old Shrivel'd Shop-Keeper, who had impair'd Life's Bellice by drinking Gills of *Canary,*
and ſtraining his Sides with a violent Fit of
Barking, would throw down a half-read *Ga-
zette,* in a mighty Paſſion, and before he could
recover Breath enough to tell what ail'd him,
ſhould be forc'd to fling down his Penny, leave

half

half his Liquor behind him, and run Head foremost out of the Coffee-Room, to suck in a little Street Air, to reconcile his Lungs to their accustomary Office; after him, perhaps, an Old Asthmatical Counseller, who had shorten'd his Breath by Sucking in *Thames* Fogs in boating it down to *Westminster*, would fall, of a sudden, into such a Fit of Wheezing, as if a Pauper Client was asking his Advice, without an answerable Fee, and that he had suddenly Counterfeited a Fit of the *Asthma*, to get rid of his Impertinence; crying out, *Ah, Smoak, Smoak; more Air for God sake*, till he had made a Shift to hobble slowly into it. Next him, may be, a Beau would start up in a mighty Passion, cursing, as he went out, all the Tobacco in the Kingdom, and swearing it was good for Nothing, but to spoil Gentlemens Wigs, or for a Saint to puff into the Devil's Nostrils. After this Manner, they would clear a Coffee-House in half an Hour, and all the Time make it their own Diversion by the by, that they had been so troublesome to others. This Sort of Trade the extravigant Fumigators drove for a few Years, till they had stupify'd their Sences, by the Narcottick Fumes of the Mundungus Weed; dry'd their Skins to Parchment; bak'd their Intrails to Cinders; exhausted all their radical Moisture, and made themselves such irrecoverable Sots, by excessive Smoaking and Drinking, the Want of regular Eating and seasonable Rest, that

that they all drop'd off, in the Prime of their Days, within a small Distance of Time of one another. Thus, as they led their Lives in a Cloud of Smoak, delighting to be always in a Tobacco Mist, so they all at last were lost in a Fog, and went out of the World as well dry'd as *Yarmouth* Herrings, *Yorkshire* Hung-Beef, or *West-Phalia* Bacon, as if they meant, whilst Living, to be their own Embalmers, and by the Power of Tobacco to preserve their Mortal Kexes after Death, from Vermiparous Putrifaction.

How far do such tenacious Sots exceed,
The Ratio of those Brutes which cannot
[*think?*
Who sacrifice their Lives to such a Weed;
Whose only Virtues are to Smoak and Stink.

Wine is a Cordial that revives the Soul,
Yet that's destructive, drank to an Extream,
But damn'd Tobacco makes the Fancy dull,
And surely was, long since, the Devil's Dream,

What wondrous Vertues must be first ascrib'd
To make the poys'nous fi'ry Leaf go down,
Or 'Man its stinking Fumes had ne'er
[*imbib'd,*
But the curs'd Plant had rotted still unknown.

Well might the Royal Scot *so much*
                              [*exclaim*
Against an Herb, that did such Mischief breed,
  Which in his happy Days had scarce a Name
Besides that odious Term of Indian *Weed.*

Nor would the nauseous Product e'er have
                              [*grown*
Within these Realms, so popular a Vice,
  Had it not brought large Incomes to the
                              [*Crown,*
And been a grand Promoter of Excise.

All Subjects may the Priviledge enjoy
Of turning Fools, to serve the awful Great,
  Or impious Knaves, if they can prove
                              [*thereby,*
They propagate the Int'rest of the State.

A Vice-Sick Nation soon might find a Cure
From those Wise Heads who do the Helm
                              [*Command,*
  Were not those Fipp'ries, made the Props
                              [*of Pow'r,*
Which spread the vile Corruption thro' the
                              [*Land.*

                                        If

If Wine or Weed are like to prove our
                                  [*Bane,*
Or other foreign Toys, our Sins encrease,
  Why do such Gluts in Triumph cross the
                                  [*Main?*
Keep out the Cause, and the Effect will cease.

  If the Temptation be allow'd to spread
By those who, by our Sins grow Rich and Great
  Why should they punish Fools? who are
                                [*Misled*
To gorg the Hook their very Rulers bait.

  So Town Rerformers full of Zeal and Grace,
Who only punish Whores that cannot pay,
  Protect those very Stews, they should sup-
                               [*press,*
As useful Traps to catch their heedless Prey.

  They punish not the Sin to spoil the Trade,
That would themselves as well as Whores un-
                                [*do,*
  By the same reigning Vice both get their
                                [*Bread;*
The wanton Harlot, and Reformer too.

            X 3   *Thus*

Thus ſhe that is moſt wicked in her Way,
To ſtaff Reformers is the ſureſt Friend,
   The more ſhe Sins the better ſhe can pay;
And thus in Gain, our pious Labours end.

   Juſt ſo, our ſober Zealots boaſt too late,
The Laws deſign'd our Vices to ſuppreſs,
   Since now 'tis made the Int'reſt of the
                         [State,
For Men to Drink and Smoak to an Exceſs.

CHAP.

CHAP. XXVIII.

Of the MARKET-WOMENS Club.

THERE are feveral of thefe Flat-Cap Societies of Female Tatlers, who, as foon as their Bufinefs is over, liquor their Weather-beaten Hides at the Taverns adjacent to the Markets which they ufe: But in a Defcription of one, you will have a View of the reft, for they are all fo alike, when merrily met over the briming Quart, that, without Injuftice, we may apply the old Proverb, *The Devil a Barrel the better Herring :* Therefore I fhall only give you a fketch of one of their principal Societies which, every Market-Day, is held at a certain Tavern in *Clare-Market*, where any Cuckold that will hold up his Head, e'er he enters the Houfe, may fee his own Picture. The Pocket-Apron Quality that commonly compofe this Tippling Sifterhood, are the Sun-burnt Dames who, from diftant Villages, come Riding into Town, like Kettle-Drummers, between their Gotch-bel-

X 4

ly'd

ly'd Panniers, well stuff'd with the Edible
Fruits of their own Rural Huslifry; and those
Gundy-Gut Matrons who deal in *Fee-Lane*
Tripes, and look, as they sit straddling o'er their
flabby Commodities that they bring to Market, as if Nature had shap'd them exactly for
their Imployments, and that the Skinny Provisions they expos'd to Sale, were no more than
the Pairings of their own invelop'd Sides, which
a Man must guess, by their abounding Udders,
hang in Folds and Wallops like the Hide of
a *Rhinoceros*: These, mix'd with two or three
Greasie Bacon-Cutters and Pot-belly'd Herb-
Women, make up the complement of the Club.
Their hour of meeting is about One a Clock, the
best of their Business being commonly over by
that time; so that they trust their Stalls, and
what is left of their Commodities, to the Care
of their Wenches; something that is Nice is
always sent In to be got ready against their
Coming; for tho' they Drink like Wine-
Coopers, they always Eat like Ladies. When
the Chickens and Sparagrass, or some such like
Dainty has suffic'd their Appetites, a Quart
of the best Claret is brought to the Table by
the handsomest Drawer in the House, who always takes care that it be brimming-full, because he knows they never part without remembring his Kindness. The Steeple Crown'd
Beldam, in respect to her Gravity, has the
honour to place herself at the Upper-end of
the Board, and when ever she Talks Bawdy,

is liſten'd to by the reſt, as the very Oracle of the Company.   The firſt Health that is begun in the Society, is, *To the beſt in Chri-ſtendom.*   The ſecond, *To their Cuckoldly Huſ-bands, wiſhing the two P's may never fail 'em.* And the third, *To all the jolly Jades that love the Bottle as well as a Bedfellow.*   By that time theſe good Wiſhes have gone chearfully round in flowing Glaſſes, one, tickled with the Diſcovery of her Neighbours Backſlidings, en-ters, perhaps, upon a Story how *John Jud,* the Bacon-Man, catch'd *Will Grub,* his Hog-ſticker, in Bed with his Miſtreſs, when the Cuckold came Home, from Buying Hogs at *Finchley;* and that the Hen-peck'd Booby had no more Wit than to run down Stairs into the open Street and proclaim his own Cuckoldom. *A pox of her Picture,* cries merry *Moll Bunch, this is ſhe that us'd to exclaim againſt Drinking; and cry, That a Drunken Furbilow kept no Porter : But I am glad ſhe has verify'd the old Proverb,* That the Still-Sow drinks up all the Draught.   Ano-ther, among the Accidents that had happen'd in her Neighbourhood, would report to the Company, how young *Beſs Dumbleton,* who was commended by every body for the mo-deſteſt Laſs in all *Hendon* Town, was got with Child by a Travelling-Tinker, who, be-ing call'd into the Houſe to mend the Old Brewing-Kettle, whilſt her Mother was ſtep'd to the bottom of the Orchard to look after her Frizzl'd Hen, ſtop'd a Hole too much; and

for

for a Cup of the beſt Beer made her Daughter's Modeſty Punchable, and that now the
Piſſſle-waſted Jade was grown as Pot-belly'd, as
if ſhe had not above a Month or two to reckon.
Marry, cries Goody *Runnet*, *they'll all do't, but*
my Daughter and I; and, as I live, we are forc'd
to watch one anothers Waters, when a Man comes
into the Houſe, for fear he ſhould run away
with one of us. A Third, more Baſhful than
the reſt, falling backward in her Chair, ſets
her Arms on Kimbo, with her Thumbs outward, to ſhew her Wedding-Ring; and when
ſhe has firſt Laugh'd a little till her Modeſty
bluſhes at the merry Conceit, begins a Story
of *Jeffery Gum*, a Neighbour of hers, who, being Preſs'd to Sea, was taken by the *French*,
and kept Priſoner ſo long, that when he return'd to *England*, his Countenance was ſo
alter'd with his hard Fare, a long Beard, and
the louſie Rags he came Home in, that his
poor Wife was puzzl'd to know her own Huſband; but as ſoon as he had convinc'd her by
ſome private Token, away goes the poor Woman and buys him a new Shirt, heats a Kettle of Water, pours it into her great Waſhing-
Tub, ſtrips him of all his Rags, and rubs him,
and ſcrubs him with her warm, comfortable,
Hand, to cleanſe him of his Vermin, before
ſhe ſhifted him; but as ſhe was thus ſtroaking
his dirty Hide, from Head to Heel, upſtarts a
third Perſon, in the middle of the Way, that
gave the good Woman ſuch a Bang upon the
Wriſt,

Wrift, that, dropping her Tears for Joy into the Tub of Water, she hug'd him about the Neck and cry'd, *Well, Jeff, I am now assur'd 'tis thee, for look, look, see the poor thing knows me too.* After they had laugh'd heartily at the lusheous Jest: *Efaith,* says *Sarah Stiff, there's nothing like a standing Evidence to convince a Woman of the Truth: I believe so too,* cries *Moll Blunt, that makes our Parson go so often to see the Malster's Wife.*

With such sort of Stories as these they make themselves merry, when they are met o'er their Claret, interposing, now and then, either extraordinary Commendations of their Husbands Manhood, or some witty Reflections on their slender Qualifications or their aged Impotence, that those who are half-Starv'd for want of a reasonable allowance between the Nuptial-Sheets, may be pitty'd by those who tantalize the rest, by boasting of their Plenty. They are such Jolly Jades that they scorn to fix their Expences to a certain Limitation, but Drink, as Women commonly do every thing else, more or loss, according as the Whim takes them. If they have any rule that gives bounds to their Extravagance, 'tis the Badness of their Market; but when they have a quick Sale, and a good Price for their Commodities, they will have a plentiful Dose, tho' they ride Home sleeping as sound between their Panniers, as if they were stretch'd upon a Feather-Bed, which Manner of Nod-

ding

ding they are so accuftom'd to, that they can take a refrefhing Nap, as heartily upon the Road, as they can at Church, when lull'd into a drowfy Fit by a dull Sermon. A Gallon a piece, after a good Market, is but an ordinary Allowance; for by habitual Drinking, they are moft of them arrived to fuch a wonderful Perfection in the Faculty of Wine Bibbing, that they look upon her to be but a weak Sifter, who cannot, upon Occafion, drink a Ters to her Share without fpewing, as fhall be made manifeft in the following Story.

A certain Vintner in *Cheapfide*, famous for curing the Tooth-Ach by wearing blue Pectacles, till he falivates his Gums by ftedfaftly ftaring thro' 'em, at the dazling Light of three or four great Candles: Happening fome Years fince to bid a Sum of Money for a parcel of Wines that he had a great Defire to be Mafter of, but the Merchant not complying with the Money he had bid, they digrefs'd from the Bufinefs, and among other Talk, chanc'd to touch upon the Subject of hard Drinking, which occafion'd the Merchant to pity the fair Sex, that Cuftom had deny'd them thofe happy Freedoms and Delights, which were only to be enjoy'd over the charming Bottle: In Anfwer to which, the Vintner urg'd, That Women no more exempted themfelves from the Pleafures of the Glafs, than Men; only

that

that they had the Modefty to Tipple with
more Privacy and Caution, for that he drew a
Quart of *Sack* a Day for a certain *Common-
Council* Woman, which was fetch'd privately
by her Chamber-Maid, and convey'd thro' the
Shop, under her white Apron, to keep the
comfortable Secret from the Knowledge of
the Apprentices, and that feveral jolly Dames,
Thanks to his good Neighbours, would cuddle
together in an Evening, and fip off their Half-
Crown Clubs, without wry Faces, whilft
their Hufbands were at the Coffee-Houfe;
Befides, fays he, *I'll engage to bring you three
Women that fhall drink a Hogfhead of Claret,
before they Sleep or Spew, provided you'll be at
the Charge, or I'll be bound to give you your
own Price for the Wines, and if they dispatch it fairly, you fhall then let me have them at
the Price I have offer'd you.* The Merchant,
pleas'd with the Conceit, and believing it
impoffible, readily agreed to the Propofal; fo
the Day was pitch'd upon, when the Bacchi-
nal was to be celebrated; and the Hogfhead of
Red was fent in, by the Merchant, in a potable
Condition within a few Days after. The Vintner having feveral Times had the Experience
of fome of the ftanch Members of the foregoing Club, thought the fureft Way to fit himfelf, was to have Recourfe to *Clare-Market,*
lay out fome Money at their Stalls, prefent
fome of thofe who had the beft Stowage,
with a liberal morning's Draught, and acquaint
them

them with the Bufinefs, which, upon the
firft Opportunity he perform'd accordingly:
But when he had them at the Tavern, after he had inform'd fuch as were fitteft
for his Turn of his notable Undertaking,
and finding one miffing, whom he had long
known to be an unquencheable Jade, *Now,* fays
he, *If* Nan Toply *was but here, there's* Befs
Gundy *and* Moll Bunch, *you three jolly Girls
would make Nothing of it;* Nan Toply, replies
Befs Gundy, turning up her Nofe with abundance of Scorn, *her laft Child has taken her
off her Speed: If I know,* Nan Toply, *I tell
you fhe'll be as drunk as a Witch, with fifteen Gallons; no, no, fhe is not fit to be a
third Woman; Leave it to* Moll *and I, we'll
bring you a merry Jade worth two of her;
an honeft Girl that will drink you a Kilderkin
before fhe piffes: Well thought of,* Befs, *this
will do,* replies the Vintner: So he treated
them handfomely, prefix'd the Day and Hour,
and fubmitted the Sequel to their difcreet
Management.

When the time came, the Hogfhead being
elevated up one pair of Stairs into a commodious Room, and two Thirty Gallon Tubs for
Chamber-Pots, placed behind a Curtain in a
convenient Corner, the Female Undertakers
of the Grand Exploit, very punctally at their
Hour, made their Perfonal Appeaiance, where
the Vintner and the Merchant, with a Difh
of Tongues before them, fat ready to receive
them.

them. After both Sides had pass'd their mutual Complements, down sat the Ladies in clean Home-spun Habits, who were to perform the Miracle, after they had relish'd their Mouths with two or three Slices of Tongue. *Prithee, Mr.* Flower, says *Bess Gundy* to the Vintner, *fill that* Monteth *there,* (which held about two Gallons) *that I may taste the Liquor; for we will not Poison our selves for e'er a Pimp in* England. Accordingly the Hogshead was broach'd with a larger Cane than Ordinary; the Crown taken off from the Rim of the *Monteth,* and her Commands fulfill'd with a capacious Bumper, which she presently dispatch'd at three or four Gulps, without breathing: *Good Tipple, Efaith, Girls,* cries the Dame to her Messmates: So the other two confiding in the Judgment of her Palate, pledg'd their Tunbelly'd Sister in the like Quantity, without winking all agreeing 'twas as good a Tub of Tipple as they would desire to make a Meal on. No sooner was this first Volley of *Monteths* discharg'd, but the same were repeated in Honour to the Founder's Health, which was chearfully swallow'd, and with as much facility, as if their Bellies had been Tuns, and their Mouths Bung-holes; now they call'd for Pipes and a Pound of Tobacco, which were presently brought 'em. *Come, dish about,* cries *Jenny Swank,* who supply'd the place of *Nan Topby, once before we Fill, and*

once

once before we Light, is a good old Maxim: Accordingly the third Six Gallons was very fairly defpenc'd with, without fo much as a Staring Eye, or the leaft fign of a Stomachical uneafinefs; and then they began to fill their Pipes with as much Gravity in their Countenances as if they had been fober Saints come from an Evening Lecture. When they had charg'd their Guns, *Come, Girls,* cries the Oldeft, *according to* Jenny's *Rule, once before we light, and then we may find time to Tittle Tattle.* No fooner was the Bowl replenifh'd but fhe advances its Mouth high between her Hands, crying, *Come, you merry Jades, here's our Old Health, To the beft in Chriftendom;* and off it went to a *fuper-naculum* Drop. *Well done, Girl,* cries *Moll Bunch, that's a Health no Woman ought to baulk, that knows the difference between a Good thing and a Bad one:* So round it went without any Heffitation, as currently as the former. *Nouns,* fays *Moll Swank, I think my Belly begins to fwell two or three Gallons before its time.* Prithee, Flower, *fend for a Quart or two of* Brandy; *we had as good take a Pint a Dram round, to make the Liquor pafs;* which was prefently fetch'd, and tip'd off accordingly.

Now the Merchant began to be under a defpondency of Winning, feeing them fo little concern'd at fo large a quantity, and thought it his Wifeft way to acknowledge he had loft, to fave the remainder of the Hogfhead; at
which

which Proposal the good Huffifs grew fo Angry, that they call'd him *Sneaking Cuckold,* and fwore, *That they came for a Bellifull, and a Bellifull they would have; and, That they would fee the laft of it, were it a Mile to the bottom:* So that the Vintner could not in Honour comply with the Merchant, but was forc'd to ftand to his firft Articles, and hazard what he had laid upon the final iffue of the matter. Now the Dames began to be pleafant Company o'er their Bowls: One telling a Story how her Grand-Mother Drank off a Butt of *March* Beer, at 'Squire *Crockum's,* in Four and Twenty Hours, and never Pifs'd but thrice till fhe came to the bottom. The Second afferting, That fhe Drank twenty Pitchers of Wort out of the Tun, when fhe was but Sixteen Years Old, and that it never gave her the wild-Squirt. The Third affirming, That the firft time that ever fhe try'd her Strength, before fhe was Marry'd, was at *Uxbridge*-Fair, and that fhe drank Nineteen Quarts of Sack and Sugar, to oblige young 'Squire *Cuddle,* and afterwards Rid Home a Straddle, three Miles, upon her Father's Mare without falling. In fuch fort of Stories they Tattl'd away their time; now and then, in their Turns, ftepping behind the Curtain to imitate the roaring of *London-Bridge,* which, according to Contract, the Men were to pafs by, without any immodeft Notice. Thus they Funk'd and Prattled, being continually mindful

Y
ful

ful of the Mainchance, till they had finifh'd
the Hogfhead, which was by Five in the Morning, and then each call'd for a Quart of mull'd
White-Wine to fettle their Stomachs, fip'd
it off with more Expedition, than a grave Citizen does a fober Difh of Coffee; thank'd the
Merchant for his kind Entertaiment, and away
they jog'd by fix in the Morning about as
merry as good Wives are, when they come
from a Goffiping, fo far from being Drunk, or
difabl'd from Bufinefs, that they match'd very
fteddily down to *Clare-Market*, to meet their
Horfes and their Drudges, who were to bring
in their Commodities, being dog'd by the
Merchant, who expected their Walking, together with the Air, would have put the Wine
upon a Firment, but he could not obferve
any Thing that look'd whimfical or frolickfome, till they came into *Lincolns-Inn-Fields*,
where they join'd Paws, took a fhort Dance
round, and fung, *Three merry Wives are we*;
then disjoining their Hands, Mother *Gundy*
advanc'd foremoft, crying, *Come, come, Girles,
Drunk or Sober, always mind your Bufinefs:*
Thus they all went off fairly without Stag-
gering or Spewing; fo that the Merchant was
forc'd to deliver the Wines according to Agree-
ment, and was thoroughly convinc'd from that
Time, that Women, as well as Men, under-
ftood the Pleafures of the Bottle.

Women

Women, who once from Virtues Paths recede,
And from the blushing Fear of Shame are freed;
Whatever darling Vice they chance to chuse,
Fanatick like, with too much Zeal they use;
Grow such fond Lovers of the sinful Toy,
That 'tis the only Idol of their Joy:
Nor can their Passions be content to taste
A mod'rate Sip of the delightful Feast,
But with unbounded Appetites fall too,
And always, to their Bane, their Lusts persue;
Ne'er check the Reins, if they the Chase approve,
But even worry what so well they love:
So the tame Cat, that's prone to play abroad,
If once she strays into some Neighbouring Wood,
Fond of her Freedom will the House refrain,
For Birds and Snakes, will Rats and Mice
*   [disdain,*
And grow too wild and pamper'd to return again.

If 'tis a Woman's Destiny to chuse
Those Stygean Spirits, so advanc'd in Stews;
Within the Reach of her extended Hand,
Both Day and Night the Fiery Juice must
*   [stand;*

Stop'd safely close 'twixt Glassy Walls im-
　　　　　　　　　　　　　　[*mur'd,*
Or she's too Sick to be without it cur'd :
Faints if deny'd it; hugs it when it's brought,
And soon revives, not with a Dram but Draught,
Till the Curs'd Fumes inflame her Giddy Brains,
Then of the Vapours she aloud complains;
Cries to her Maid, O feel my clamy Sweats,
Yet drinks it for that illness it creats :
Thus wedded to her Vice she wears away,
But finds new Causes for her swift decay :
On what she loves will no aspersion cast,
But hugs the Poyson till it proves her last.

Or if she doats upon a Tavern Treat,
And thinks the Charms of costly Wine most sweet,
From one to many Quarts she soon improves,
Till made a shameful Slave to what she loves :
No prudent bounds can her Desires inclose,
In what's her Vice she still Insatiate grows,
Will the vain Habit into Scandal wear,
And scoff the Friend that begs her to forbear.
Thus, if once enter'd, 'tis her foolish Pride,
To be undone before she's satisfy'd :

　　　　　　　　　　　　　　　　Just

Juſt ſo the Robber, who repents too late,
Ne'er quits his Roguries till he meets his Fate.
  Or if ſhe's laviſh of her Female Charms,
And too much Luſt her colder Nature warms,
That'tis her Vice to hunt the am'rous Game,
And Rival Crowds muſt fan her Reſtleſs Flame;
A Thouſand Ways to win you, ſhe'll deviſe,
Tempt you with Smiles, and Court you with her
                                    [*Eyes,*
And if ſhe finds your Modeſty too great
To uſe thoſe Freedoms ſhe would fain be at,
Or that your Want of Courage ſpoils her Sport,
And makes you fearful to attack the Fort,
Into your Soul her Eyes ſhall dart their Fire,
And your chaſt Thoughts, with Impudence inſpire,
Force you, in Spite of Grace, to prove unjuſt,
And hug you till you ſooth her craving Luſt;
Amidſt the Joy, will be ſo lewdly kind,
She'll charm you with thoſe ills you ne'er deſign'd;
Make you by Dint of Extaſie approve
Her Arts, and think her Impudence, her Love,
When all the while ſhe does her Powers exert,
'Tis but to eaſe her own laſcivious Heart,

Where

Where luftful Devils do in Legeons dwell,
Her melting Charms with double Forces fwell, }
And in her finful Pleafures help her to excell.

So practife modulates the Singer's Throat,
And makes it yield a more melodious Note.

If Gaming chance to be a Woman's Vice,
She's then a reftlefs Slave to Cards and Dice:
Hufband nor Children can the Shrew reclaim,
But all muft truckle to that Tyrant Pam:
Her kind allowance, tho' it's ne'er fo large,
Is all too little to fupport the Charge:
Fond of her Judgment, fhe conceits fhe knows
The Game fo truly well fhe cannot lofe,
Yet feldom Wins, but ftill perfues her Itch,
Till Beggar'd, thro' the hopes of growing Rich,
Except her prudent Spoufe fecures his Gold,
And gives her but the empty Bag to hold:
Which if he does, and wifely keeps her Poor,
If handfome then fhe in Revenge turns Whore:
Thus, let her Vice be what fo e'er it will,
Woman, without reftraint, will have her fill:
And if oppofed in what fhe moft approves,
Or by her Spoufe debar'd of what fhe loves,

In ſpite of all his Care ſhe'll Diſobey,
And plague her Nuptial Lord ſome other way.

For Woman, if provok'd ne'er wants the Sence
To out do Man in Craft or Impudence.

CHAP. XXIX.

Of the THIEVES Club.

HIS *Tyburn* look'd Society of audacious Defperadoes, who commonly had the Fortune to wear their Deftiny in their Faces, kept their daily Rendefvouz at the Sign of the Half-Moon in the *Old-Baily*, a little Hedg-Tavern, whofe Appearance was fufficient to give an honeft Man a Caution, how he fet his Foot into fuch a wicked Den of impious Thieves and Ruffains, who were not only content to fupport their Luxuries by Frauds, Robberies, and Murders, but us'd to meet in a Body at the aforemention'd *Rum-Droppers*, their cant for a *Vintner*, that they might drown all Thoughts of Shame, or Dread of Ppnifhment in their inebrious Exceffes, and glory in their Villanies, over their *Rum-Gutlers*. The pretious Mortal,

tal, who had the Happiness to Occupy this
Diabolical Mansion, was one *Whitwood* a Thief-
Taker, who, by his deep Insight into the Miste-
ries of Iniquity; his familiar Acquaintance
and daily Conversation with all Sorts of common Rogues, from the *High-Way*-Man to the
House-Breaker, had gain'd such an Ascendancy
over the whole Gang of *Newgate-Birds* that
infested the Town in his Time, that he could
help People to any Sort of stoln Goods, provided the Gratuity that the Loser offer'd, a-
mounted to about half the Value of what the
Rapparees had depriv'd him of; which is
commonly as much as the Rogues, with Safety, are able to make of their Booty, because
the Receivers, who either buy, or lend Money upon such Cargoes, always guess by their
Chapmen, how honestly they are come by,
and therefore will not Deal without unreasonable Advantages. *Whitwood*, at whose Mercy the precarious Lives of this down-look'd
Fraternity most commonly lay, always took
Care to keep a black List of their infamous
Names, and if he found any of them shy of
coming to his House, or unwilling to let
him have a profitable Fellow-feeling of
their sinful Earnnings, he would then
think it high Time to procure them the just
Reward of their hellish Labours, and use as
much Industry to Hang 'em out of the Way,
as he would to Protect and Save those who
were his better Customers. This occasion'd
the

the Nocturnal Miscreants to make his House
their Sanctuary, knowing the oftner they re-
forted thither, and the more Money they spent,
the less they were in Danger; and for this
Reason they settl'd a Daily Meeting at his
scandalous Tavern; which, indeed, was only
fit for the drunken Revels of such incorrigible
Wretches, as are always affected with those
sinful Pleasures, and obscure Places, that are
most obnoxious to honest Persons, who have
an Abhorrence of their Practices: So that Day
and Night, at this Tippling-Tenement, there
was a perpetual Society of the Devil's Operators, some returning from, and others going
to perpetrate some Villany, or other, that
they might not want Money to continue
themselves secure in the Friendship of their
Landlord, who was commonly made Privy
to all their Hellish Undertakings; for here,
over the Bottle, they us'd to project their
Rogueries, and hither return with the ill
got Fruits of their wicked Adventures; that
what they had gain'd over the Devil's Back,
they might spend under his Belly.   Here
the Gentlemen of the *Nig*, in their Cant,
but vulgarly call'd Clippers, us'd to wash
away the Profits of their treasonable Labours.
Gentlemen *Outers*, in plain *English*, *High-
Way*-Men, boast their dangerous Exploits
upon the open Road; *Water-lane* Divers,
alias *Pick-Pockets*, contrive new Stratagems
to amuse unwary Passengers, till they *File*
the

the Cly. Snaffle-Biters, as they call themselves Rogues, who make it their principal Business to steal Horses, talk what
rare Pads and Galloppers they had met
with in their Time, and what excellent
Pennyworths they had often fold to the
honest Horse-Coursers in *Smithfield*; and
where those infamous Villains who, as they
Cant it, *Go upon Fire and Faggot,* us'd to laugh
at the Rogueries they had committed, and
make themselves merry o'er their Cups, with
the past Success of their notorious Barbari-
ties, which they commonly effected by the
following Stratagem, *viz.* These Tremendi-
ous Furies cloth'd in Flesh and Blood, who us'd
to prepare their Way by Flames in this World
to those of everlasting, put their pollitick Villanies in Practice chiefly in the Country,
where Farmers often have their Barns built
at some Distance from their Houses, and
where-ever they met, in their Wanderings,
with such a Conveniency for their Purpose, their Way was to lye lurking about,
till the Evening, then to set Fire to a Parcel
of Straw near the Barn, and to allarm the
Family by an Outcry, that they might think
their Barn was on Fire; so that whilst the
Farmer and his Servants were run to save
what they could of their Corn or Hay, they
might have the better Opportunity of plun-
dering the House, and moving off with
their Booty.   Thus all Sorts of Villanies

were daily harbour'd under this unhallow'd
Roof, by him that knew their Practifes, till
they foolifhly had wafted what they had
glean'd wickedly, and then if any one grew
Idle, either thro' Cowardice, or Reluctancy,
and did not foon exercife their Talent for
a frefh Supply, their honeft Landlord, in a
little Time, would have a *Friday* Jeft, and
merrily fay that the Tree had robb'd him of
a good old Cuftomer: For *Whitwood*, who
before protected him for his own Profit,
would himfelf take him up if he found him
poor and lazy, bring Evidence againft him,
and hang him out of the Way for a worthlefs
Scoundrel, who was only a Dabbler in a Mie -
ry that he knew not how to live by,

Juft fo Reforming Conftables protect
The Harlot that can bribe as they expect;
But if fhe once grows Poor, thro' want of Trade,
In Triumph then, they flog the Needy Jade.

When thefe Sons of *Satan* were met over
the Bottle, and happen'd to be flufh of Money, by the Succefs of their Villanies, whilft
the *Smelts* lafted, nothing was too coftly for
their luxurious Appetites; then the fear of
Punifhment was kept at a diftance by their
Drunken Extravagance; and the chearfulnefs
of their Tempers would a little mend their
Saturnal Looks: So that an awkward Smile
                                    fhould

should hang upon their Beetle-Brows, and make their Faces refemble the unnatural plea-fantry of thofe Barbers Blocks, which, by a chance ftroke or two of the Chiffel, have, by meer accident, been Carv'd Laughing. Then, amidft their Jollity, when the power of *Bac-chus* had forc'd open Hell's Cabinet, One, to make a Jeft of his Villany, would merrily difcover that he once Robb'd an Old Lady of Three Hundred Pounds by the Confederacy of one of his Miftreffes who was got to be her Chamber-Maid, and would mimick how hear-tily the Old Granny Begg'd, at Fourfcore, that fhe might not be Ravifh'd: Another would up with a Story, how fix of them Robb'd an Old *Kentifh* Knight, who had newly Marry'd a young Beautiful Lady; and having bound and gag'd the Servants, and ty'd the Old Cuff to a Bed-Poft, whilft the reft were Rummidging, he took the Opportu-nity of obliging the Bride, that fhe might know the difference between a Fumbler and a Workman; the Old Knight crying, *Fie, my dear, what will you be a Whore?* The Lady replying, *L——d, my Dear, what would you have me do? Are you willing I fhould be Murder'd?* But, *Huffif,* crys the Old Cuckold, *if you was not as forward as he, you would not wag your Scut fo; there-fore keep your Rump ftill I fay, left the firft Child fhould happen to be a Baftard.* A Third, to fhew his Gallantry, would boaft how three of them ftop'd five Gentlemen upon the Road,

Robb'd

Robb'd four of them, and the other, being an Old Parfon, they had Compaffion upon him, and Difmounting the reft a little out of the Road, they made them tarry in the avenue of a Wood, till the Parfon fhould Preach to 'em: Upon which Condition, if the Sermon pleas'd 'em, they promis'd he fhould go unriffl'd. *I thank you,* reply'd the Parfon, *for your kind Propofal; but it is too fhort a warning for a good Sermon:* However, faid the Prieft, *I will endeavour to Entertain you with fuch an apt Difcourfe as may be equally acceptable:* So, to oblige his Comrades, the Rogue would give the following Repetition of the Parfon's Parrellel, *viz. Gentlemen you are the moft like the Old Apoftles of any Men in the World, for they were Wanderers upon the Earth, and fo are you; they had neither Lands or Tenements they could call their own; neither, as I prefume, have you; they were Defpis'd of all but thofe of their own Profeffion, and fo I believe are you; they were unalterably fix'd in the Principles they profefs'd, and fo I dare fwear are you; they were often hurry'd into Goals and Prifons; were Perfecuted by the People, and endur'd great Hardfhips, all which Sufferings, I prefume have been undergone by you; their Profeffion brought them all to untimely Deaths; if you continue your Courfe, fo will yours bring you: But in this Point, Beloved, you will differ mightily, for the Apoftles from the Tree afcended into Heaven, and thi-*
ther

*ther I fear you will never come : But as their
Deaths were recompenced with Eternal Glory,
yours will be rewarded with Eternal Shame
and Misery, without you mend your Manners.*

Thus, amidst their drunken Exceffes, they
us'd to pleafe one another with an Impudent
rehearfal of the Accidents they had met with
in the perpetration of their Villanies, and would
fhew themfelves as proud of all their Daring
Rogueries, as if they had the Infolence to fancy there was as much Honour in breaking into the Houfe of a High-Sheriff, or boldly
Robbing a Train-band Captain upon the
Road, as there was in wrefting a ftrong-Hold
from an Open Enemy, or taking a General Prifoner at the Head of his own Guards. At
length *Whitwood*, of ever pious Memory,
who was both the Encourager and Suppreffor,
the Protector and the Profecutor of this Infernal Gang, according as it beft fuited with
his immediate Intereft, happen'd, by a Natural Death, to efcape the Gallows, to which,
by all report, he had as good a Title as any
that ever made their Exit under that Trian-
gular Edifice; and the fcandalous Imployment,
as well as the infamous Tenement, which
Whitwood left behind him, were both jointly
Occupy'd afterwards by one *Jo. Hix*, who feem'd,
by his Bulk, to be one of the over-grown
Sons of the old Rebellious Gyants, who wa-
ging War with Heaven, tore up Rocks by the
Roots, and tofs'd them up againft the Gods,
to

to fhew their impious Audacity: But becaufe
he now keeps a Country Inn, and has re-
formed his Life, in a great meafure, from his
former Practifes, I fhall forbear to revive any
thing that may terminate in his Reproach, and
only heartily recommend him to a fincere
Repentance. The wicked Weeds I have been
here Treating of, have, of late Years, been
pritty well How'd up, and drawn out of our
Britifh Garden between the Wars and the
Gallows; and pray God fend, for the future,
that more ufeful Plants may fpring up in
their Places, that we may have no fuch Societies to fit and brafen Juftice betwixt *New-gate*
and the *Seffions-Houfe*, not only to the Shame
of the City, but the Scandal of the whole
Nation.

What difmal Tracts do wicked Mortals find,
If once to Luft and Infamy refign'd ?
What humane Laws can ftubborn Rogues re-
                                    [*claim,*
When paft the Fear of Punifhment, or Shame ?
Nor can the Threats of future Pains prevail,
Where Dread of Death, and prefent Tortures
                                    [*fail.*
For he that will no humane Laws Obey,
Will ne'er be aw'd by what the Priefts can fay ;
But harden'd in his Ills will ftill rebel,
And hazard Life and Heav'n, in Spite of Hell;
                                    So

So the fierce Bull-Dog, mischievously bold,
Disdaining, at his Sport, to be Controul'd,
Will Die by Peace-meal e'er he quits his hold. }

Some, when they're hurry'd to the brink of
                              [*Fate,*
Where forc'd Repentance shews its Tears too late,
Will on their Parents lay the sinful Blame,
And move our Pity, to Lament their Shame.
What Father then would let his Children want
Good Education, under due restraint?
Lest, if remiss in his Paternal Care,
His wither'd Age so sad a charge should bear.

Others, persuant to a Just decree,
Drawn to the brink of dark Eternity:
With trembling Nerves, and shaking Head declare
Their loose Companions Taught 'em first to Err:
Decoy'd them gently in, and by degrees,
Boldly Confirm'd them in their Villanies.
Let it, O Youth, be then thy early Care,
To truly know what thy Associates are;
That from the Bad thou may'st select the Good,
And shun the pois'nous Converse of the Lewd:
For he that rowles in Nettles must be Stung;
Nor can the Fool be clean that wades in Dung.

Z

Therefore

Therefore the only way to be secure,
And keep an honest Reputation pure,
Is to shew wisely 'tis your Care to be
Distinguish'd by your Vertuous Company.

CHAP.

CHAP. XXX.

Of the SMALL-COAL-MAN's

Mufick Club.

THIS Harmonious Society of Tickle-Fiddle Gentlemen, has been of long standing at the diminutive Habitation of an honeft Small-Cole-Man, who happens to be a near Neighbour to St. *John* of *Jerufalem*, who at prefent flourifhes his Banner before a noted old Tavern in *Jack-Adams* his Parifh, which ferves to fhew we have the Happinefs to live in fo reform'd an Age, that holds it no Scandal for a Saint to invade *Bacchus*'s Dominions; nor is the Painter blamable for depicting the Holy Champion in a naked Pofture, becaufe it ferves us as a double Emblem; *Firft*, to let us fee, that by frequenting the Tavern too often, we may bring our felves and our Families to the fame Nakednefs; and *Secondly*, it imports, that our modern Saints, in thefe Reforming Times, may

Z 2

march

march in bare-fac'd to a Bottle Engagement, without the Fear of being claw'd off by their Teachers at their next *Sunday's* Meeting; for the Shepherds, as well as their Flocks, have very wifely confider'd, that the good Things of this World were given to the Godly much rather than the Wicked; Excufe the Digreffion and now again to the Mufick-Club, which was at firft begun, or at leaft confirm'd by Sr. *Roger-le-Strange*, many Years before his Knighthood, who was a very Mufical Gentleman, and had a tollerable Perfection upon the Bafe-Viol, a very fafhionable Inftrument in thofe Days; tho' now hug'd only at Boarding-Schools, between the Knees of young Ladies, left their Virgin Modefty otherwife fhould caufe their Legs to grow fo clofe together, that whenever they marry, their Bridegrooms fhould be puzzl'd to perform the Nuptial Ceremony. The Reafons that induc'd Sr. *Roger*, and other ingenious Gentlemen, who were Lovers of the *Mufes*, to honour the little Manfion of the black and blue Philomat with their Weekly Company, were chiefly the unexpected Genious to Books and Mufick that they happen'd to find in their fmutty Acquaintance, and the profound Regard that he had in general to all Manner of Literature, beyond what-ever had been found before among the narrow Souls of thofe groveling Mortals, who are content to difguife Nature with

with fuch crocky colour'd Robes, and to hazard the Welfare of their Eyes in fuch a duf-
ty Profeffion; however, like a prudent Man,
tho' he might juftly boaft a great many Qualifications above any of his Level, yet he never fuffer'd the Flatteries of his Betters to
lift him up above the Care of his Employment; for tho' he always took Delight to
fpend his Leifure Houres in the Studies of
a Gentleman; yet he limited his Induftry
to the Trade he had been bred to; and
tho' he was Mafter enough of Mufick to
play his Part tollerably well, upon feveral Inftruments, yet he would not grow
too proud, for the profitable Tune of Small-
Coal, or lay afide his Sack till his Day's
Work was over, to dance after a Fiddle,
having Sence enough to confider, that fpare
Time and empty Sound were the moft a-
greeable Concomitants, and that Pleafure
always ought to be poftpon'd to Bufinefs:
This Sort of Diligence recommended him
the better to all prudent Gentlemen, who
lik'd his Company the more, when they
found themfelves out of Danger of incur-
ring the Curfes of his Family, becaufe he
would not be tempted into thofe Neglects
that might terminate in his Ruin: Thus the
Prudence of his Deportment, among thofe
who were his Betters, procur'd him great
Refpect from all that knew him, fo that his
Mufick-Meeting improv'd in a little Time to

be

be very confiderable, infomuch, that Men
of the beft Wit, as well as fome of the beft
Quality, very often honour'd his Mufical
Society with their good Company, that in a
few Years his harmonious Confort became
as publickly Noted as the Kit-Kat Club;
notwithftanding the former was begun by
a Small-Coal-Man, and the latter by a
Bookfeller. Sir *Roger* continu'd to be a conftant Meeter in the Zenith of his Glory,
and many other Gentlemen, who were fit
Companions for fo worthy a Perfon of his
Wit and Learning: So that *Briton*, when
equip'd in his blue Surplice, his Shoulder
laden with his Wooden Tinder, and his
Meafure twifted into the Mouth of his Sack,
was as much diftinguifh'd as he walk'd the
Streets, and refpected by the good Huffifs,
who were Cuftomers for his Commodity,
as if he had been a Noble Man in difguife,
who had only turn'd Small-Coal-Man, as
my Lord *Rochefter* did Quack, not out of
Neceffity, but to humour his Maggot; every one that knew him, pointing as he paf-
fed crying, *There goes the famous Small-Coal-*
Man, who is a Lover of Learning, a Per-
former in Mufick, and a Companion for a
Gentleman. The better to demonftrate his
Love of Ingenuity, he has made a very
good Collection, to his great Expence, of an-
tient and modern Mufick by the beft Mafters, had, fome Years fince, pick'd up in his
Walks

Walks a very handsome Library, which, not long since, was publickly dispos'd off to a confiderable Advantage, and has now by him a great many Curiofities, that, by Perfons of Judgment, are efteem'd valuable, yet the Hut wherein he dwells, which has long been honour'd with fuch good Company, looks without Side as if fome of his Anceftors had happen'd to be Executors to old fnarling *Diogenes*, and that they had carefully tranfplanted the *Athenian*-Tub into *Clerkenwell*; for his Houfe is not much higher than a *Canary* Pipe, and the Window of his State-Room but very little bigger than the Bunghole of a Cafk. Tho', fome Time fince, for the more commodious Entertainment of his *Thurfdays* Audience, he had taken a convenient Room out of the next Houfe that the Company might not ftew in Summer-Time like fweaty Dancers at a Buttock-Ball, or like Seamens Wives in a *Gravefend* Tilt-Boat, when the Fleet lies at *Chatham:* But a worfe ufe than he expected happening to be made of the additional Liberty he had given to the Company, occafion'd him, for fome Reafons beft known to himfelf, to reduce his Society to their primitive Station, who, tho' they have loft fomething of their primitive Glory, yet they conftantly continue their *Thurfday's* Meeting, where any Body that is willing to take a hearty Sweat may have the Pleafure of hearing many nota-

ble

ble Performances in the charming Science of Muſick, and amongſt the reſt, perhaps the following Song, very applicable to their harmonious Conſort, *viz.*

I.

Come all ye merry Beaus and Blades,
 Who love the charming Fiddle,
And airy Jades that paſs for Maids,
 Tho' kind below the Middle.

II.

Upon Thurſday's *Repair*
To my Palace, and there
Hobble up Stair by Stair;
But I pray ye take Care
That you break not your Shins by a Stumble,
 And without e'er a Souſe,
 Paid to me or my Spouſe,
 Sit as ſtill as a Mouſe
 At the Top of my Houſe,
And there you ſhall hear how we fumble.

III.

III.

For tho' I look black
When I carry my Sack
About Streets at my Back,
Crying, Maids do ye lack
Any Char-Coal, or Small-Coal, within;
Yet by Fits and by Starts
Do I study all Arts,
And can tickle your Hearts
With my sweet Tenor Parts
Upon Viol, or crack'd Violin.

CHORUS.

Altho' disguis'd with smutty Looks,
I'm skill'd in many Trades:
Come hear me Fiddle, read my Books,
Or buy my Small-Coal, Maids.

The

The Second Part.

I.

We thrum the fam'd Corella's *Aires;*
 Fine Solos and Sonettos,
New Riggadoons and Maidenfairs,
 Rare Jigs and Minuettos.

II.

We can run squeaking up
To the Finger-Board Top,
And from Ela *can drop*
Down to G with a Swop;
That would ravish ye were you but near us;
 And when cramp'd by hard Tugs
 At our Bottles and Mugs,
 Then we give ye such Fugs,
 That would startle your Lugs,
And amaze any Master to hear us.

III.

Sometimes we've a Song
Of an Hour or two long,

Very

Very nicely perform'd
By some Beau that's so warm'd
With the Charms of his Chloe's sweet Face,
That he chooes out his Love.
Like the Amorous Dove ;
Which the Ladies approve,
And would gladly remove
All the Cause of his sorrowful Case.

CHORUS.

Altho' disguis'd with Smutty Looks,
I'm skill'd in many Trades ;
Come hear my Fiddle, read my Books,
Or buy my Small-Cole, Maids.

The Third Part.

I.

Tho' our Reforming Pious Age
Does so in Grace abound,
And neither smiles upon the Stage,
Or Musick's Charming sound.

II.

II.

Yet a Fooll may Divine,
If his Thoughts are like mine,
That your Pious Defign,
Is to come at our Coin :
'Tis for that you Diffemble and Wheedle.
By your leave Mafter Cant,
Tho' as grave and as quaint,
As the Devil turn'd Saint,
It is Mufick I want ;
And we muft have a touch at the Fiddle.

III.

Lead away Mr. Prim ;
Sir do you follow him :
How the Parts fweetly Chime ?
Mr. Clod *mind your time ;*
'Tis a wonderful Tune tho' it's plain :
What a Cadence is there !
How it tickles the Ear !
You're too faft Sir, forbear ;
We are all out I fwear :
Since 'tis good, let's begin it again.

CHORUS.

CHORUS.

Altho' disguis'd with Smutty Looks,
I'm skill'd in many Trades:
Come bear my Fiddle, read my Books,
Or buy my Small-coal, Maids.

CHAP.

CHAP. XXXI.

Of the KIT-CAT Club.

THIS Ingenious Society of *Apollo's* Sons, who, for many Years, have been the Grand Monopolizers of those scandalous Commodities in this Fighting Age, *viz. Wit* and *Poetry*, had first the honour to be founded by an Amphibeous Mortal, Chief Merchant to the Muses; and in these Times of Piracy both Bookseller and Printer, who having, many Years since, conceived a wonderful Kindness for one of the greasie Fraternity, then Living at the end of *Bell-Court* in *Grays-Inn-Lane*, where, finding out the Knack of humouring his Neighbour *Bocai's* Pallat, had, by his Culinary Qualifications, so highly advanc'd himself in the Favour of his Good Friend, that, thro' his Advice and Assistance, he Remov'd out of *Grays-Inn-Lane* to keep a Pudding-Pye-Shop near the *Fountain*-Tavern in the *Strand*, encourag'd by an assurance
that

that *Bocai* and his Friends would come every Week to Storm the Crusty Walls of his
Mutton-Pies, and make a Consumption of his
Custards. About this time *Bocai,* who had
always a sharp Eye towards his own Interest,
having riggl'd himself into the Company of
a parcel of Poetical young Sprigs, who had
just Wean'd themselves of their Mother Uni-
versity, and by their prolifick Parts and promising Endowments, had made themselves the
Favourites of the late bountiful *Mecænas,* who
had generously promis'd to be an Indulging
Father to the Rhiming Brotherhood, who had
United themselves in Friendship, but were as
yet unprovided for; so that now, between
their Youth and the narrowness of their Fortunes, being just in the Zenith of their Poettick Fury, *Bocai* had a fair prospect of Feathering his Nest, by his new profitable Chaps,
who having more Wit than Experience, put
but a slender value, as yet, upon their Maiden
Performances. Besides, the happy Acquaintance of these Sons of *Parnassus* gave him a
lucky Opportunity of promoting the Interest
of his beloved Engineer, so skill'd in the For-
tification of *Cheese-Cakes, Pies,* and *Custards;*
so that *Bocai,* to Ingratiate himself with his
New Set of Authors, Invited them to a Colla-
tion of Oven-Trumpery at his Friend's House,
where they were nobly Entertain'd with as
curious a Batch of Pastry Delicacies as ever
were seen at the winding up of a Lord-
Mayor's

Mayor's Feaſt upon the Day of his Triumphs, that there was not a Mathematical Figure in all *Euclid*'s Elements, but what was preſented to the Table in Bak'd Wares, whoſe Cavities were fill'd with fine Eatable Varieties, fit for Gods or Poets. This procur'd the Cook ſuch a mighty Reputation among his new Rhiming Cuſtomers, that they thought it a ſcandal to the Muſes that ſo Heavenly a Banquet ſhould go untag'd with Poetry, where the Ornamental Folds of every luſhious *Cheeſe-Cake*, and the artful Walls of every Golden *Cuſtard*, deſerv'd to be Immortaliz'd; they could therefore ſcarce demoliſh the imbelliſh'd Covering of a *Pidgeon-Pie* without a Diſtick; or break thro' the ſundry Tunicks of a Puff-Paſte Apple-Tart, without a ſmart Epigram upon the glorious Occaſion. *Bocai* wiſely obſerving the good effects of this Paiſtry Entertainment; and finding that Pies to Poets were as agreeable Food, as *Ambroſia* to the Gods, very cunningly propos'd their Weekly Meeting at the ſame Place; and that himſelf would be oblig'd to continue the like Feaſt every Club-Day, provided they would do him the Honour to let him have the Refuſal of all their Juvenile Products, which generous Propoſal was very readily agreed to by the whole Poettick Clan: And the Cook's Name being *Chriſtopher*, for brevity call'd *Kit*, and his Sign being the Cat and Fiddle, they very merrily deriv'd

a

a quaint Denomination from Pufs and her Mafter, and from thence call'd themfelves *The Kit-Cat-Club:* And *Bocai*, in refpect that he was Donor of the Feaft, and promoter of this New Pudding-Pye Eftablifhment, had the Honour to be chofen Chair-Man of the Society; to which prefiding Authority, as moft believe, he owes the Statelinefs of his Brow, and the Haughtinefs of his Temper. When *Bocai* had thus far been Succefsful in his new molition, he had now nothing elfe to do but to lay frefh Foundations for his young Artificers to Build upon, and never to come empty without fome Project in his Head that might have a probable tendency to his own Profit. Now, every Week, the Liftening Town was Charm'd with fome wonderful Off-fpring of their Teeming-Noddles: And the Fame of *Kit-Cat* began to extend it felf to the utmoft Limits of our learned Metropolis: Not a Court Countefs could Compaffionate her Lover with the tendereft of her Favours: The Young Buxom Wife of an Old Impotent Alderman be beholden to a Courtier to make her fenfible of the difference between a ftrenuous Sportfman and a crazy Fumbler; a Gouty Lord felect a Jilting-Miftrefs from that Fruitful Nurfery the Theatre; or a Noted Beau be Cheated of a Hundred Guineas for a Second-Hand Maiden-head, but prefently the pleafing Adventure was moft notably handl'd by the *Kit-Cat* Bards, and Sung down

A a   to to Pofterity, nor indeed could a great Man dye whofe Memory was worth an Elegy, but they would find a Way to add ten Guineas to his Funeral Charges ; or a Man of Honour marry a celebrated Beauty, or a great Fortune, but they would draw him in with a charming *Epithalamium* to pay them Socket-Money.

Let them fend their Wits a Wool-gathering as themfelves thought fit *Bocai* having already tafted of the fweet Fruits of their early Labours, was refolv'd to venture at all, giving little elfe but Pies for Poetry, well confidering he had this Advantage, that what the Publifher return'd, his Friend the Paftry-Cook took off his Hands at a better Price than the Trunk-Maker; fo that the Poetical Fraternity had moft of their Pies bottom'd with their own Excrement, which prov'd fo confiderable an Advantage to all chance Cuftomers, that whoever came in for a Twopenny Tart, was affur'd to have a Penny-worth of Wit, or at leaft Poetry given into the Bargain, that when they had empty'd the Shell, they might have taught their Children to read upon the bottom Cruft, as well as a Horn-Book: Among the reft of the celebrated Pieces that ow'd their Original to this Witty Society, that moft accurate Banter upon the *Hind* and *Panther,* call'd the City-Moufe and the Country-Moufe, from thence ftole into the World, and knaw'd fuch an ugly Hole in Poet *Bays* his Jacket, that

It

it could never be mended without a Patch, as fcandalous as the Flaw the unlucky Mice had made in it. This fortunate Off-fpring, the Reverfe of the Fable Mountain, tho' it only promis'd a Moufe, it produc'd a Monfter, which was fo wonderfully admir'd by the whole Town, that a Man had no Title to open his Mouth in Company for the Space of fix Months after the Publication, if he could not demonftrate by fome fpecial Obfervation, that he had bleft his Eyes with a Sight of the Prodigy; Nothing but *Moufe, Moufe,* was crept into every Body's Mouth, and the Towring Monuments of Praife, which Mr. *Bays* thought he had fo firmly erected upon a lafting Foundation, were at once in Danger of being undermin'd by thefe diminutive Bacon eating Brethren, who were formidably fent forth in Battle Array to attack his *Hind* and *Panther.* This fuccefsful Flirt was fo well Tim'd, fo wittily Penn'd, and met with fo kind a Reception from all the Proteftant Readers, that the Fame of the *Kit-Cats* now fpread it felf univerfally, tho', thro' the Judgment of the Publick who are apt to be miftaken, he that had the leaft Share in the work, had the moft of the Reputation, and in a little time after by the Favour of their *Mecænas* was fingl'd out from the reft of the Herd, either as the beft quallify'd for fome peculiar Purpofes, or the moft deferving of his Lordfhip's Promotion, which of the two is fomething

thing difficult to determine: But so it
happen'd, that one Mouse run away with
all the Bacon, whilst the other got Nothing
but the empty Cubbard, upon which Occasion, the rest of the *Kit-Cat* Members, in a
merry Mood, scribbl'd the following *Epigrams,*
viz.

A London *Sheriffe kept so poor a House,*
His empty Cubboard starv'd a hungry Mouse;
But kind Mecænas *by two Mice addrest,*
Tho' he starv'd One, he did the Other feast.

Another upon the same.

Great Men like Fortune do their Gifts impart
To gratify themselves, not our Desert:
Why then, my Friend, art thou discountenanc'd,
To see less Merit for thy Wit advanc'd?
The Roman *Poet did the Lines devise,*
But he that stole the Fame, obtain'd the Prize.

A Third upon the same.

Since one industrious Mouse took all the Pains,
'Tis hard the other should ingross the Gains:
But smooth Tongu'd Confidence will still prevail,
When Wit, eclips'd with Modesty, shall fail.

A

A Fourth upon the fame.

'Tis hard that one Moufe fhould be made a Rat,
  Feed on whole Flitches, and on Cheefe of
                          [*Chefhire,*
Whilft t'other, who deferves to be as fat,
  Shall be deny'd the Comfort of a Rafher ;
But maftiff Poets oft are doom'd to Starve,
Whilft Lap-dog Wits are hug'd, who lefs
                          [*deferve.*

About the fame Time that one of the celebrated Mice was happily crept into the High-
Road of Preferment, here, at Home, another
of the witty Triumvirat, who had the Honour to be call'd my Lord *D——s* Boys, was
put in a fair Way to make his Fortune Abroad;
fo that the Third, who had given much better
Teftimonies of his Wit, than any of 'em, was
the only growing Genious of the Three that
was left unprovided for; however, the Club
being fam'd for the many fmart Poems, and
accurate Productions they had fent into the
World, and having ufurp'd the Bays from all
the Town, They had by this Time rais'd
themfelves to fuch a Pitch of Reputation, that
many of the Quality grew fond of fharing
the everlafting Honour that was likely to
crown the Poetical Society, infomuch that fe-
A a 3   veral

veral Great Perfons defir'd to be admitted
Members of the Rhiming Community, fome
in Hopes to be accounted Wits ; and others to
avoid the very oppofite Imputation ; So that,
by the Majority of the Members, it was now
thought high Time to move out of the Scent
of the Oven in hot Weather, and to adjourn
their Club to the Fountain Tavern, it being
wifely agreed by the whole Board, that à noble Cellar of Wine was a better Foundation
for a Society of Wits to erect their *Pyramids*
of Fame upon, than the Arch of an Oven,
whofe voracious Mouth had fwallow'd fo many Reams of their inchanting Labours. But
notwithftanding they had thus determin'd to
withdraw the Mufes from the purring Mufician, and her dancing Mice, from whence it is
prefum'd the Poetical Partners had borrow'd
the lucky Title of that celebrated Piece that
had fo redown'd to their Credit, yet, in Honour to *Bocai*, they were ftill refolv'd to thankfully accept of his Weekly Banquet, and to
continue him in the Poft, which they had
obferv'd he was fo proud of, fo that tho' they
chang'd their Refidence, they preferv'd their
Cuftoms, and being now ftrengthen'd by the
aweful Prefence of Right Honourable Wits,
and other wealthy Pretenders, who, tho' not
quallify'd to be Poets, they were rich enough
to be Patrons, and ready with an open Hand
to befpeak the Honour of the next flattering
Dedication, they began to fet themfelves up

for *Apollo's* Court of Judicature, where every Authors Performance from the Stage-Poet to Garret- Drudg, was to be read, try'd, applauded, or condemn'd according to the new Siftem of Revolution Principles, of which, like Zealous Subjects, they have been always violent Afferters. Upon the additional Improvement of this High-Conrt of Wit, compos'd of Patrons, Critticks, Great Lords and Poets, *Bocai*, who had ftill the Honour of the Chair, thought it now high Time to look about him, and to charge his Blunderbufs with that neceffary Confidence, that might propagate his Intereft among great Men, and make him a fit Affociate for thofe honourable Dons, who had favour'd the Club with their magnificent Appearances; fo that tho' he had no Title to fet himfelf up for a Wit, yet he had found by others, that if he did but varnifh o'er his natural Endowments with a little fawning Conformity, and anoint the Tip of his Tongue with a due Quantity of *Irifh Pomatum*, he might ingratiate himfelf as well in the Favour of the high and ftately, as thofe Wits who had the Knack of blinding their Betters with the Afhes of the old Poets, and topping Falfe Quotations out of defunct Authors, to juftify their own Errors. By this Sort of Conduct *Bocai* made a very good Shift to get more by his Bookfelling, than his Authors did by their Wit, and what was wanting to make his Company delight-

ful

ful, he was careful to fupply with Cringe,
Confidence and Cunning, fo that he daily
gain'd Ground in Refpect to his Intereft,
and was Taught, in a little time, by the great
Example of his honourable Cuftomers, to exact as much Refpect from his own Shop
Fraternity, as he was forc'd to pay to his
Betters: That tho' he look'd but like a
Bookfeller feated among Lords, yet, *vice verfa*
he behav'd himfelf like a Lord when he
came among Bookfellers. When their Pye
Feaft was over, and they had done commending of the Rofe-Water Codlin-Tarts for their
Helliconian Flavour, it was the Drawers
next Bufinefs to clear the Board, bring
every Man his Bottle and a clean Glafs,
and then the Wits, according to Cuftom,
for the Divertion of the reft, would be fo
liberal of their Talents, that not a *Roman*
Author, or a mouldy Worthy, could reft
in their Graves for two Hours, but muft
be box'd about the Board, till every one
had run over his whole Catalogue of Dead
Bards and Emperours, to fhew his Learning in remote Antiquities, neglecting all fore-
fight to talk of Things paft, as if, like Crabs,
they had got a Faculty of running backwards.
The Duke of *M——h* could not be nam'd
without a *Scipio* to confront him, nor Prince
Eugene mention'd without a *Hannibal* to op-
pofe his Character, *Ben Johnfon, Shackfpear* or
Dryden remember'd without fuch a contemp-
tible

tible Pifh, as if they were only fit to write
Stage Speeches for a Mountebanks Orators, or
Ballads for Pye-Corner, yet their own Works
fometimes fhould be blufhingly repeated, that
they might have a friendly Opportunity of
tickling each other with reciprocal Flattery,
and put that Policy in Practife; fo much
in Vogue among fcabby Friends, *viz. I'll
fcratch you, do you fcratch me.* In thefe
Sort of learned Recreations that exercife the
Mind inftead of the Body, the *Kit-Cat* Wits
us'd to wafte their Hours, whilft the reft of the
Members, who, perhaps, were not bleft with
fo prolifick a Genious, would manifeft by their
Liberality, when the Reckoning came to be
paid, the Satisfaction they had found in the
witty Difcourfes of their wifer Brethren.
Thus honeft *Bocai*, and his fruitful Semenary
of tranfcendant Wits, eftablifh'd and continu'd
their *Kit-Cat* Club for a Succeffion of Years,
till at laft burnt out of their dear *Parnaffus*,
where they had long been fettl'd, and fince they
happen'd to be dethron'd by this furprifiing
Miffortune: Whether their Joint-Wifdoms
have thought it confiftent with their infallible
Prudence to remove nearer to, or farther from
the old *Kit-Cat* Oven, I cannot as yet determine, but inftead of a further Account, fhall,
according to the Method I have hitherto obferv'd, conclude the Chapter with a Poem.

Bright

Bright Phœbus, *Parent of the tuneful Quire,*
To whose kind Rays the Muses owe their Fire,
Shall now no more in mournful Lays complain,
That British Dullness clouds the Monarchs Reign,
Since Kit-Cat *Wits thy ancient Title own,*
Support thy Glory and assert thy Throne;
Great as Apollo's *Court, the Brethren sit,*
Claiming a Pow'r from thee, to judge of Wit;
Nor will their Juncto let unpolish'd Swains,
Prophane thy Altars with their croaking Strains;
But damn the Dross, will let no Counters pass,
That are not of their own Corinthian *Brass;*
So Princes, who the Right of Coinage claim,
Punish the Slave that dares to do the same,
Drag the poor Traytor to his farewell Pray'rs,
And hang him, tho' his Coin's as good as theirs.

Supreme in Fancy, Tow'ring in Conceit,
The learn'd Cabal o'er Shoals of Custards meet,
Mix'd here and there with Gellies and with
                                    [*Tarts,*
Set off with all Kits *Culinary Arts.*

In lusheous Piles the charming Dainties stand
As if compos'd by some nice Ladies Hand;
                                    One

One on his Plate does half a Cheese-Cake lay,
O'er which he Sings the Praise of Curds and
[*Whey.*
Like a great School-Boy reds the Childish Food,
And stroaking of his Belly, swears 'tis good.

The next, to satiate his Luxuriant Gust,
Attacks a Pidgeon fortify'd with Crust,
Breaks down the Walls, and does most proudly
[*say,*
Thus did the *British* Heroes take *Tournay.*

A Third, to sweetly sooth his craving Youth,
Ladles down Custard to delight his Tooth;
By Kit's Ambrosia does his Fancy Tune,
And hopes to grow more Wise by dint of Spoon.

On a Minc'd-Pie a Fourth with fury falls,
Compares it to that fam'd Escurial Pauls :
That Nook, *says he,* which does this way ex-
[tend,
Resembles very much the Western-End ;
This the North Porch, and that the side that's
[South,
Then claps at once the Chancel in his Mouth;

Grinds

Grinds down the Walls, does in a Paſſion cry,
Thus ſhall the Low-Church Triumph o'er the
                                    [High.

A Fifth with Gelly ſwells his Youthful Veins;
Pleaſes his Palat, and recruits his Reins:
Then fir'd with Luſt he ſtretches on his Chair,
Crys, My dear *Cloe,* O ye Charming Fair:
What Mortal can thy powerful Darts with-
                                    [ſtand?
My *Cloe* ſhall have all at ſecond Hand.

A Sixth upon the Pile a ſally makes,
And on his Plate a Curran-Tart he takes.
In pow'rful Words that do the ſubjeƈt ſute,
Admires the Flavour, and extolls the Fruit:
To ſhew his Zeal affirms the grateful Juice,
Excels the Wine that Gallia's *Grapes produce:*
With a much richer Colour tempts the Eye,
And ſtains the Palat with a nobler Die, ⎫
Altho' his Conſcience tells him 'tis a L——. ⎭

Bocai, *the gen'rous Maſter of the Treat,*
Not fix'd to one, picks here and there Bit:
But leſt the Female Food, ſo ſweet and fine,
Should Rob him of the flavour of his Wine,

                                            A

A Mutton-Pye, well season'd, is the last
Bak'd Toy he chuses to restore his Taste.
For kind Bocai, tho' now he's past his Prime,
Has been an Old Sheep-biter in his time;
Not only in the Gainful Skins a Dealer,
But of the Flesh has been a Fellow-Feeler.

Thus once a Week the great divan of Wits
Inspire their Fancies with their dainty Bits:
Why not, since we in sacred Story find
That one fair Apple first inform'd Mankind:
Why then mayn't Modern Poets grow more Wise
By the Rich Taste of Kit-Cat's Apple-Pies?
One Cup of Hellicon the Bards allow,
Tho' Drank by Corridon that hands the Plow,
Will breed Poetick Maggots in his Head,
And make the new Rins'd Booby Write like Mad:
Therefore, since such strange Vertues have been
[found,
In Springs that rise in such Lean Baren Ground,
Who knows but Kit-Cat's Helliconian Tarts,
In time, may make a Dunce a Man of Parts.

Feed on Luxurious Heroes of the Pen;
Poets, tho' next to Gods, may Eat like Men:

Some

Some think the Race Divine, so Wise and Good,
Owe all their Knowledge to their Heav'nly Food,
And that if we, who move beneath the Skies,
Could once to Nectar and Ambrosia rise:
One Meal, from Death our fading Limbs would
                                    [*free,*

And give us Mortals Immortality.

Who knows but Kit-Cat Pies may do as well,
By them already you in Wit excell;
Triumph like Monarchs o'er the Riming Crowd,
Who tug like Slaves to Sing your Fame aloud,
Attend your Levies, dread your awful Pow'r,
Scribble beneath, whilst you have leave to tow'r,
And proudly have Usurp'd from all the Town
The very Right of Scandal and Lampoon:
So Tyrants, when they're too Puissant made,
Are not alone content to be Obey'd,
But will their Subjects Properties Invade.

Go on great Wits, since from the Kit-Cat
                                    [*board,*
A Poet has been made a mighty Lord,
An honour to the Pregnant Sons of Rhime,
Scarce known before in any Age of time:

                                    Who

Who knows but by the dint of Kit-Cat's *Pies,*
You may, e'er long, to Gods or Monarchs rise;
Then shall your Fame thro' all the World dif-
                                    [perse,
Your own learn'd Pens your mighty Deeds re-
                                    [hearse,
And we your Subjects glory in your Verse.

C H A P.

CHAP XXXII.

Of the BEEF-STAKE Club.

AS the refin'd Wits of the *Kit-Cat* Club us'd to feed their Fancies with female Dainties in Respect to the *Muses*, who are always said to be of the Feminine Gender, so the Masculine Worthies of the Beef-Stake Club having more regard to the Strength of Body than the Activity of the Mind, chose a more substantial Food that might coroborate their Limbs, and recommend them the better to another Sort of Ladies, who prefer *Mars's* Truncheon to *Apollo*'s Harp, and would rather have their Charms commended by the convincing Hugs of a strenuous Lover, than by the fullsome Praises of the best Poet in Christendom. As the gen'rous Master of a plentious Table would rather see his Friends give a real Ap-

probation

probation of the Food he has provided by their
eating heartily, then for a puny Gueſt to extoll in Words what his Pidling ſhews he has
but little Fancy for. This new Society of
griliado'd Beef-Eaters firſt ſettl'd their Meeting at the Sign of the Imperial Phiz, juſt oppoſite to a famous Conventicle in the *Old-Ju-
ry*, a Publick-Houſe, that has been long eminent for the true britiſh Quinteſſence of Malt
and Hops, and a broil'd Sliver off the juicy
Rump of a fat well-fed Bullock, where brawny Wine-Porters, and ſturdy Carmen, us'd to
ſtrengthen their Backs with full *Whincheſters*
of powerful Two-Threds, and delicious Slices
of the beſt Trainband Food, ſwimming in its
own Gravy. This noted Boozing-Ken, above
all others in the City, was choſen out by the
Rump-Stake Admirers, as the fitteſt Manſion
to entertain the Society, and to gratify their
Appetites with that particular Dainty they
deſir'd to be diſtinguiſh'd by. No ſooner
had they fix'd the Preliminaries of their Club,
but the Aſſembly met at the Place appointed,
that, according to the Cuſtom of ſuch worthy
Societies, thay might chuſe their Chair-Man,
and eſtabliſh their new Project upon a laſting
Foundation, accordingly, for a Prolocutor; they
choſe an *Iriſh* Comedian, moſt wiſely conſidering that *Bog-Land* Bulls over Beef-Stakes
were the moſt agreeable Jeſts to add a Reliſh
to their Food; and that the Wit of a Bull,
when they were Knuckle deep in the Gravy

B b   of

of a Bullock's Rump, might prove such fine, thin, airy Sauce to their gross Banquet, as might help Digestion, and propagate Laughter, like a Midwife's Tale at a Gossiping.

No sooner had they confirm'd their *Hibernian* Mimick in his Honourable Post, but to distinguish him from the Rest, they made him a Knight of St. *Lawrence,* and hung a Silver Gridiron about his Neck, as a badge of the Dignity they had confer'd upon him, that when he Sung *Pritty Parrot,* he might Thrum upon the Bars of his new Instrument, and mimick a haughty *Spaniard* Seranading his *Donna* with Gittar and Madrigal.   The Zany, as Proud of his new Fangle, as a *German* Mountebank of a Princes Medal: When he was thus dignifi'd and distinguish'd with his Culinary Symbol hanging before his Breast, took the highest Post of Honour, as his Place at the Board, where, as soon as seated, there was not a Bar in the Silver Kitchin-stuff that the Society had presented him with, but was presently hansel'd with a Theatrical Pun, or an *Irish* Witticism: Nor could a Jack-a-napes play so many Tricks with his Chain, as the merry President of the new Divan did with his Honorary Bauble, and by the dextrous use of his Screwtore-Key upon the silver Strings of his new Fashion'd Theorbo, would tinkle forth such Harmony, that far exceeded the Musick of a *Black-bird,* when he Whets his Bill along the Wires of his Cage.   Now the Worshippers
of

of the Rump having fix'd their Club in a regular Decorum, according to the Scheme their Leaders had projected, Orders were difpatch'd to the Superintendant of the Kitchen, to provide feveral nice Specimens of their Beef-Steak Cookery, fome with the Flavour of a *Shallot* or *Onion*; fome Broil'd, fome Fry'd, fome Stew'd, fome Toafted, and others Roafted, that every judicious Member of the new erected Club, might appeal to his Palat, and from thence determine, whether the Houfe they had chofen for their Rendefvouz truly deferv'd that publick Fame for their inimitable Management of a Bovinary-Sliver, which the World had given them. No fooner were their true *Englifh* Delicacies, fo pleafingly diverfify'd by the feveral ways of Dreffing, brought up to the Table, but every ones brown Mefs was tofs'd up fo favourly, done fo exactly, and according to Direction, fo carefully feafon'd to every Bodies Tooth, that, when their Charm'd Appetites gave their Tongues a little Leifure, there was nothing heard for an Hour together, but fuch Pathetick Speeches upon the glorious Occafion, as if they were Practifiing o'er their Rump-Steaks that they might know the better how to Prattle in a Rump Senate, in Cafe fome unexpected change fhould give them the Opportunity. When they had moderately fupply'd their Beef Stomachs, they were all highly fatisfy'd with the Choice they had made, and from that time refolv'd to repeat their Meeting

once in a Week at the same Place, and to set
themselves up in direct Opposition to the Kit-
Cat Club, that the Members thereof might
learn to know that Substantial Beef, was as
prolifick Food for a true *English* Wit, as Pies
and Custards for a Kit-Cat Beau, or Bonni-
clabber and Potatoes for an *Irish* Poet.

Being thus settl'd to their Minds, the next
Time of their Meeting, they began to mend
their Constitution, and to add several By-Laws
for the better Regulation of their new Little
Common-Wealth, and for the further Encouragement of Wit and Pleasantry throughout
the whole Society: As for Instance, their
Chairman they now honour'd with the Title
of Secretary, and order'd him, by a Committee
of the whole Assembly, to provide a very volu-
minous Paper-Book, about as thick as a Bail
of *Dutch* Linnen, into which was to be ente-
red every witty Saying that should be spoke
in the Society, the name of the Member to
whom the Honour was due, the Day of the
Month, and the Date of the Lord, that any
of the Society, by a future Retrospection,
might presently inform themselves what time
of the Moon, or Season of the Year, they us'd
to be most Witty in, and for every such Entry a certain Fee was to be paid to the Secretary, that the Perquesites of his Place might
keep his Grid-Iron bright, make his Honour
amends for the Loss of his Time, and defray
the growing Charge of Pen, Ink, and Paper,
which

which were always ready upon a Side-Board
Table, that if any mufing Member fhould
want to unburthen his Brains of a fudden
Flight, he might prefently ftep up and com-
municate the darling Prodigy to the Board, by
Pen and Paper. But notwithftanding their
fincere Defign of prefenting the World with a
new Cabinet of choice Bulls, Puns, and Witti-
cifms, as foon as they had fill'd their vo-
lumnous Regifter with Minutes and Memo-
randums of their pregnant Ingenuity, yet it
has fo fallen out, notwithftanding the Affiftance
of Rump-Gravy, that they have not as yet
fill'd up the firft Page; but however, if the
Publick will have Patience till their Volume
is compleated, they will certainly be enrich'd
with the immittable Treafury: For the
Grays-Inn ingroffer of all modern Wit, has fet
up a Printing-Houfe on Purpofe to carry on
the great Work, in which the Club are fo very
careful, that Nothing will be introduc'd, but
what fhall be truly worthy of Pofterity's Adimi-
ration, fo that every notable Flirt, Flight, Diftick,
or Epigram that is offer'd to the Board by its
fond Father, muft be firft put to the Vote, and
carry'd by the Majority as an unexceptionable
Piece of Wit, before it is permitted to be ente-
red by the Secretary, and that the Reader may
have a Tafte of their moft exquifite Performances, I fhall recite fome of them that have
been ftol'n out of their Journal, by a falfe
Brother, *viz*,

On

On an Ox.

Most noble Creature of the Horned Race,
Who labours at the Plow to earn thy Grafs,
And yielding to the Yoak ſhews Man the way
To bear his Servile Chains, and to Obey
Thoſe haughty Tyrants, who uſurp the Sway.
Thy ſturdy Sinews Till the Farmers Grounds,
To thee, the Grazier owes his hoarded Pounds:
'Tis by thy Labour we abound in Malt,
Whoſe pow'rful Juice the meaner Slaves exalt;
And when grown fat, and fit to be devour'd
The Pole-Ax frees thee from the teaſing Goard:
Thus cruel Man, to recompence thy Pains,
Firſt works thee hard, and then beats out thy
                                        [Brains.

In Praiſe of Beef.

Of all Proviſion, Beef's the beſt
  To pleaſe an Engliſh *Palat,*
Eſpecially a Steak well dreſt,
  And ſeaſon'd right with Shallot.

Beef

Beef swells our Muscles, fills our Veins,
 Does e'ery Way improve us,
Strengthens our Sinews, and our Reins,
 And makes the Ladies love us.

Stand off ye Veal-Fed puny Beaus,
 The brawny Dutches crys,
The Beef-Fed Mortal I espouse,
 That yields me large Supplies ; .
Give me the Spark that hems and thumps,
 And digs like Slave with Mattock ;
The Man that feeds on Bullocks Rumps,
 Ne'er fails a Female Buttock.

On a Rump Steak.

Of all the Parts of noble Beef,
Giv'n by the God's, for Man's Relief,
The juicy Rump is still the best
Betwixt the Tail, and Horned Crest ;
A Steak from thence with whetted Knife,
Cut off by D——y, or his Wife,
Salted and Pepper'd to the Tooth
Of him that dares to venture both ;

Then

Then broil'd and crusty'd o'er the Fire,
What Prince can richer Food desire?
If hungry, no delicious Dainty
On Earth, will half so well content ye:
A Venson Pasty's but a Fool to't,
Wild Fowl to th' Pallat is but dull to't:
O Cavaliers! *What Foolish Fellows*
Were you, to shew your selves so Zealous,
In madly Burning and Disguising
The Rump, which only wanted Broiling;
As if to prove the Proverb true,
When Cock-a-hoop, you meant to shew
That a Rump Steak, in which we glory,
Was always Poyson to a Tory.

Beef-Steak Rapsody.

Why should the Gods to Slaves allow
    Such Food that's fit for Courtiers,
Tho' Lords, we ne'er were blest, till now
    We feed like brawny Porters.

By Vertue of this noble Steak,
    How I could hug my Phillis;
For by my Life, I find my Back
    As strenuous as my Will is.

In

In such Sort of Performances, they us'd to exercise their Wits to the Honour of themselves, and the Advantage of their Secretary, who always has the Sence to give his Vote in the Affirmative, becaufe, when any Thing is allow'd to be Wit by the Majority of the Affembly, there is a certain Fee belonging to their Scribe, for entering it in their Journal, for the Sake of which Perquefit he is the more willing to play all the Tricks of a Dancing-Bear for the Diverfion of the Society; nor, indeed, can any Man of His Faculty boaft a greater Variety of Qualifications than himfelf, for the Promotion of Mirth among good Company, for he is fo great a Mafter of Humour and Gefticulation, that, *Proteus* like, he can change his Shape and Mein, and put on any Man's Gefture and Deportment with fuch wonderful Exactnefs, that he can give ye the true Refemblance of a whimfical Lord, an affected Critick, a formal Blockhead, a talkative Argumentator, a fantaftical Beau, or, indeed, Mimick any Man's Gate, manner of Talking, and all his habitual Vanities and Singularities with fo much Art and Pleafantry, that he can fhew any Sort of Coxcomb his ridiculous Likenefs, as truly as a Looking-Glafs: So that by this Means he always preferves a full Community, for what-ever Member neglects to appear upon the Club Night, is affur'd in his Abfence to be fo comically reprefented by their officious Buffoon, that they are made the Jeft and

Laughing-

Laughing-ftock, of the whole Company: The
Fear of which, makes them all fo very punctual,
that they feldom fail of having a full Club, where
every Thing is perform'd with fo much Rule
and Order, that a Man can neither eafe his
Brains of their frothy Excrement, but it muft
be put to the Vote, or ftep into the Vault to
empty his Guts without an Order of the Board.
The fame Spirit of Ambition to be thought
witty that poffeffes the Kit-Cat Members, is e-
qually diffufive thro' this Society alfo, for the
Man of Title and Authority is not here con-
tented to be only reverenc'd for his Wealth
and Dignity, but defires to perpetuate his Memory in their bulky Regifter, and to be complemented more for his Wit than for his Riches,
from whence it may be reafonably conjectur'd, that fome of the difgufted Members of
the foregoing Club, were the firft Formers of
the Beef-Steak Society, or rather new Rump
Parliament, who, perhaps, being Offended that
others fhould be allow'd before themfelves to
be *Apollo's* Darlings, turn'd factious Diffenters
from the Kit-Cat Community, and fo fix'd an
oppofite Affembly of revolted Wits, in hopes
thereby to eclipfe the Glory of their Competi-
tors; and, like True bred *Britons*, to fhew their
Refentment in Contempt of Kit-Cat Pies, very
juftly gave the Preference to a Rump Steak,
moft wifely agreeing that the venerable Word,
Beef, gave a more Mafculine Grace, and founded better in the Title of a true *Englifh* Club,
than

than either *Pies* or *Kit-Cat*, and that a Grid-
Iron, which has the Honour to be made the
Badg of a Saints Martyrdom, was a nobler
Symbol of their Chriſtian Integrity, than two
or three Stars or Garters; alſo learnedly re-
collecting how great an Affinity the Word
Bull has to *Beef*; they thought it very con-
ſiſtent with the Conſtitution of their Society,
inſtead of a *Welſh* to have a *Hibernian* Secretary. Being thus fix'd to the great Honour of
a little Ale-Houſe, next Door to the Church,
and oppoſite to the Meeting, they continu'd
their Community for ſome Time, under much
Order and Regularity; till their Fame ſprea-
ding over all the Town, and deſcending ſo
low as to reach the Ears of the great Boys,
and the little Boys, who were ſo highly plea-
ſed with the pretty Diſtinction, that the Club
had choſen, that as they came in the Evening
from *Merchant-Taylors* School, they could not
forbear hollowing as they paſt the Door
to expreſs their Joy that the City ſhould be
honour'd with the Rhiming Preſence of ſuch
a Witty Society, Thus, when once the forward
Youths had made themſelves acquainted with
the Nights of their Meeting, they ſeldom
fail'd, when the Divan were ſitting, of comple-
menting their Ears with a Huzza, Beef-Steak,
that they might know from thence, how much
they were reverenc'd for Men of Learning by
the very School Boys. But the modeſt Club
not affecting Popularity, and chuſing rather to
bo

be deaf to all publick Flatteries, thought it an Act of Prudence to adjourn from thence into a Place of Obscurity, where they might Feast Knuckle deep in lusheous Gravy, and enjoy themselves free from the noisy Addresses of the young Scholastrick Rabble; so that now, whether they have heal'd the Breach, and are again return'd into the Kit-Cat Community, from whence it is believ'd, upon some Disgust they at first separated, or whether, like the Calvs-Head Club, they remove from Place to Place to prevent Discovery, I shan't presume to determine; but at present, like *Oats*'s Army of Pilgrims, in the Time of the Plot, tho' they are much talk'd on, they are difficult to be found.

Where e'er your pow'rful Muses sing the Praise
Of good fat Rumps, in your immortal Lays,
There only must Apollo fix the Bays.

Such strenuous Lines so charming, soft, and sweet,
That daily flow from your Conjunctive Wit,
Proclaim the Pow'r of Beef, that noble Meat.

Your tuneful Songs such deep Impression make,
And of such aweful, beauteous Strength partake,
Each Stanza seems an Ox, each Line a Steak.

As

As if the Rump in Slices, broil'd or stew'd
In its own Gravy, till Divinely good,
Turn'd all to pow'rful Wit, as soon as chew'd,

O gallant Beef thou mak'st the Soldier Fight,
The Rump-Stake Poet, like an Angel Write,
And the kind Husband vigorous at Night.

Thy Juice does not alone our Lives sustain,
And stuff our Bellies, when our Guts complain,
But fructifies as well the teeming Brain.

Or sure Apollo's *Sons, those charming few,*
Who Tune their Lyres, their heavn'ly Art to shew,
Would ne'er adore thy Rump, as now they do.

To grind thy Gravy out, their Jaws employ,
O'er Heaps of reaking Steaks express their Joy,
And sing of Beef, *as* Homer *did of* Troy.

In a right Choice, we shew that we are wise,
Who then can blame such Worthies, who despise
For noble Beef, *that Childish Diet* Pies.

Wits

Wits us'd with Study to be pale and lean,
Cow'rdly and Sneaking, over run with Spleen,
But now they feed on Beef, they look like Men.

And will, in length of Time, not only write
Like Greeks *or* Romans, *but like Heroes fight,*
And like ſtrong Gyants, give the Fair Delight.

You need no longer then, your Fancies tire ;
Some Muſe at Court, inflam'd with hot Deſire,
Will teach ſuch Bards to tune a diff'rent Lyre.

Thus, by Degrees, may you to Honour riſe,
From Steaks of Beef, as ſome from Kit-Cat Pies,
Since a ſtrong Back, the Want of Wit ſupplies.

Thus, of all Diets, you have choſe the chief,
And Ladies know a Woman's beſt Relief
Is found in him, that feeds on noble Beef.

F I N I S.

9 781170 441572